Celluloid Indians

Native Americans and Film

Jacquelyn Kilpatrick

University of Nebraska Press
Lincoln and London

Publication of this book
was assisted by a grant from
The Andrew W. Mellon Foundation.

Library of Congress
Cataloging-in-Publication Data
Kilpatrick, Jacquelyn.
Celluloid Indians : Native Americans
and film / Jacquelyn Kilpatrick.
　　p.　cm.
Filmography: p.
Includes bibliographical references and index.
ISBN 0-8032-7790-3 (pbk. : alk. paper)
1. Indians in motion pictures.　I. Title.
PN1995.9.I48K56　1999
791.43′6520397—dc21　　　99-17814
CIP

For Grandpa Jack, who loved picture shows

In a display case off the main corridor there is a musty little book, the work of an English missionary who ministered to a Massachusetts tribe in the 1600s. For years he labored to translate the gospel into their language. By the time the manuscript was printed and bound, however, most of the people it was meant for had either been killed or had died of disease. The book is a strange emblem for Christians, a Bible that nobody was left to read. What would the Indians have thought if they'd had the chance to read it through? I guess we'll have to wait for the movie. – Aims McGuinness, *The New Republic*

Contents

Photographs

Acknowledgments

I would like to thank Louis Owens and Julianne Burton-Carvajal for their encouragement and insight, without which I could not have begun this book. George Burdeau allowed me to view *Witness* before it was finished, which is beyond the call of duty and very much appreciated. I also appreciate Tom King, Gerald Vizenor, and A. A. Carr for their gracious contributions of photos from their own files. And to all the people who gave so generously of their time and knowledge in personal interviews—thank you.

Introduction

In undertaking an exploration of Native American representation in film, it is tempting to get caught up in questions of "correctness"—political and otherwise—"authenticity," and "historical accuracy." These are appropriate questions because the history and the cultures of Native Americans have been miscommunicated in films, and the distortions have been accepted as truth, with sometimes disastrous results. Most of the studies of Native Americans in film have therefore focused on an analysis of stereotypes, in terms of their characterological, sociological, and historical plausibility. Given the misuses to which Native American images have been put, these studies tend to have an irritated if not genuinely angry tone. They also have an understandable preoccupation with realism in the interest of correcting errors and distortions. This desire to set the record straight is true for publications from a hundred years ago and for current articles and reviews on films such as Disney's *Pocahontas* (1995) and Michael Mann's *Last of the Mohicans* (1993), where the focus is generally a heated defense of a particular version of reality.

This book also deals extensively with questions of historical and sociological "reality" in the depiction of Native Americans in film; it must do so because the distortions have been both incredibly blatant and generally unquestioned by reviewers of the day as well as viewing audiences. However, this study places those pseudo-realities in the historical and social context within which they were devised and consumed.

Film is more than the instrument of a representation; it is also the object of representation. It is not a reflection or a refraction of the "real"; instead, it is like a photograph of the mirrored reflection of a painted image. The image perceived by a film's audience has passed through layers of interpretation and representation. To understand the "Hollywood Indian," it is necessary to peel back these layers and place them in perspective. This requires a delicate balancing act when evaluating depictions of Native Americans in over a hundred years of film history. The films must be viewed as art, and art is a social, historical, cultural artifact—a socially situated utterance, a reflection of the film's time of birth and the social and political milieu into which it was born.[1] At the same time, Native Americans were and *are* living human beings, not evanescent avatars of alterity, and therefore questions of appropriate depiction must be addressed.

Film, like texts of all sorts, must enter what Mikhail Bakhtin called a "dialogically agitated and tension-filled environment."[2] Like all forms of utterance, films engage in a political struggle for supremacy, and for those cultures defined and represented in film, it would seem that the struggle is one with a medium that strives, intentionally or unintentionally, for the status of authoritative discourse, for the final word on what one can expect from, in this case, Native cultures.

For a dialogue to truly exist, the represented subject must be able to talk back. An important question considered here is, do Native Americans have a space within mainstream Hollywood films to utter a response? The final section of this book will discuss an important attempt to "talk back" found in recent films and documentaries written, directed, and/or acted *by* Native Americans.

So What Exactly Are the Stereotypes?

This book examines the layers of social, ideological, and political construction that have resulted in seemingly simple stereotypes of Native Americans. It is important that the idea of the stereotype not be limited by such uncluttered definers as simple, erroneous, secondhand, or unchanging. Therefore, the descriptions of the term *stereotype* below are meant to be thumbnail sketches of complex representations of Native Americans that will become more fully developed later.

Sociologist Theresa Perkins states that "[s]tereotypes are evaluative concepts about status and role and as such are central to interpreting and evaluating social groups, including one's own."[3] In the building of a new American national mythology, we see this self-identification by a dominant (Euro-American) group emerge as primary in importance, largely because American identity, like all national identities, is determined by its relationships to other cultures. For an immigrant nation where the Euro-American is anything but homogenous, the Native became a clearly definable Other.

One way to see how a group defines itself—to itself as well as to Others—is to look at those it makes its heroes. The self-definition at stake in most films with a Native American presence has been that of a Euro-American westering male. When we look at the writing of James Fenimore Cooper or the films of John Ford, we see this American self-definition repeatedly reinforced by its juxtaposition to the image of Native Americans. In that way, the challenge presented by the "savages" can be interpreted as a confirmation of the dominant value structure.

The stereotypes of Native Americans in film can be divided into three categories: mental, sexual, and spiritual, the most meaningful of which is probably the mental.

Although the actual words *stupid* or *dumb* are seldom seen in descriptions of Natives—perhaps because fighting a stupid enemy or having a dumb sidekick is not especially flattering—Native peoples have been firmly placed in the lower echelons of intelligence by many Euro-Americans since first contact was made. Benevolent terms such as "innocent," "primitive," or "unsaved" indicate a lesser intelligence, and the more antagonistic descriptors certainly point to comparative dimness. For instance, while the word *stupid* does not imply lack of cleanliness, the word *dirty* does imply stupidity, and we are all familiar with the terms *dirty redskin, filthy heathen,* and so forth. This follows the pattern of stereotype development Perkins notes: "The most important and the *common* feature of the stereotypes of the major structural groups relates to their mental abilities. In each case the oppressed group is characterized as innately less intelligent."[4] As we will see, these ideas about Native intelligence took visible form in film—mental acuity has not generally been the celluloid Indian's strong suit.

The presumed lack of mental prowess may have something to do with the image of the Native American as intensely sexual—more creature than human, more bestial than celestial. Sexuality has historically constituted an important dimension of Hollywood Indians, both male and female, producing a very scary character. We repeatedly see the lustful savage attacking the white woman, requiring that he be killed immediately. And we have the lovely "Indian princess" who is enormously attractive but must die before any real damage is done to the purity of the gene pool. Miscegenation has historically been a taboo for the Hollywood Indian.

The "spirituality" of Native Americans is brushed off as primitive or heathen in many run-of-the-mill westerns. Paradoxically, the perception of an inherent native closeness to the earth has led some to endow Native peoples with a certain nature-based nobility and spirituality—the Noble Savage, the alter ego of the Bloodthirsty Savage, on and off the screen. This presumed spirituality and closeness to the earth has spurred in recent years the creation of a related stereotype, the Natural Ecologist.

It would be impossible to discuss, even marginally, all the films made during the last hundred years that have in one way or another made use of Indians, real or imagined. This study includes only a small percentage of them, and they are presented in roughly chronological order. A complete analysis of each film is not the purpose of this book; the films have been chosen because they are examples of stereotype development, or use, or because they show deconstructions of the stereotype, or because they markedly reflect mainstream American society's perception at a specific point in history. Plot lines have been included only as far as is necessary to ensure understanding for viewers who may not have seen the film lately or at all. Some films are dealt with in depth; others have been mentioned only for a particular element that explicates the depiction of American Indians in film.

1

Genesis of the Stereotypes

I like to read these books because they're always making up stories, and that's how they make the world the way they want it. . . . You see, we got to be aware of the stories they're making about us, and the way they change the stories we already know. – Luther McCurtain, in Louis Owens, *The Sharpest Sight*

To begin a discussion of the cinematic portrayal of Native Americans, it is necessary to touch briefly on the roots of Euro-American perceptions that led to the images developed and/or used by Hollywood. Films have been around for only a century, but the stereotypes within them have their origins in over five centuries of perceptions—and misperceptions.

In the Beginning Was the Word
To get to the genesis of Native American stereotypes requires investigating the artistic language that has propagated them. Human consciousness and art, including the arts of literature and by extension cinema, do not result from or even come into direct contact with the real world but rather represent its languages and discourses.[1] Authors cannot help but invest in their work their own preconceptions and attitudes. This is undeniably true in the literary depictions of the inhabitants of the "New World" sent back to Europe by early explorers. They took back stories of wild savages that fit neatly into the preconceived notions the Europeans had of what a savage would be. This was the beginning of the "Indian" invention. Even the more accurate reports about individual communities were often generalized and made to stand for the whole of the inhabitants of the Americas, for the over two thousand cultures and societies that existed at the time. Although Europeans were unlikely to confuse the French with the English or a Norwegian with an Italian, they were generally unable or unwilling to draw distinctions between the peoples of the Americas. The term *savage* or *sauvage* was most often used to describe the native populations

the English and French settlers initially met. Infidel, heathen, and barbarian were also used, but "Indian" did not achieve common popularity until the seventeenth century.

Stories of Indian savagery were quite popular in the sixteenth and seventeenth centuries, and captivity stories were particularly well received. The basic elements in these tales were those of the adventure story, with plenty of blood, sorrow, perseverance, and danger. They were also written for didactic purposes, to show the grace of God in providing for the captives' deliverance. The authors of these "memoirs" would probably be astounded to hear that most modern critics see a sexual motif lying just beneath the surface of the action. Many critics have, in fact, referred to captivity tales in general as violence pornography, a connection not lost on the makers of decades of Hollywood films.[2]

The Native Americans in these stories could occasionally be noble; for instance, in the story written by Mrs. Rowlandson, an Indian woman brought the captive's child to see her, establishing a brief but touching cross-cultural connection between mothers.[3] But the noble savage usually existed in the singular. As literary critic Gretchen Bataille has pointed out, "[i]ndividual Indians could be 'good,' but the group had to be depicted as 'bad' in order to justify the existing philosophies of government and religion."[4] The capture of a white woman by the vicious Indian man would later become a mainstay for screenwriters from the very early silent movies to the 1996 film, *Follow the River*, in which dangerous Indians steal the white woman and her children, the husband/father/brother searches for her, and she returns with her purity still intact because she would have died before submitting to loss of virtue.

Mr. Cooper's Contributions

When James Fenimore Cooper wrote *The Leatherstocking Tales* in the first decades of the nineteenth century, he had a wealth of literature— mostly "non-fiction" filled with these good and bad Indians—to draw upon. But it was Cooper himself who most thoroughly established in the realm of fiction the stereotypical extremes of the Indian—the noble savage and the bloodthirsty savage—and introduced a depiction of Native American behavior that book and film audiences would come to expect. Cooper's most famous novel, *The Last of the Mohicans*, has been made into a Hollywood film five times, the latest in 1993, a time of supposedly heightened sensitivity and new sensibilities.

Cooper's work has often been purported to be sympathetic to the Indian,[5] but in reality its orchestration of discourse and the choices he made in character development and placement dramatically polarized and simplified Indian experiences. This was perhaps necessary for the use he made of those experiences, to depict metaphorically the workings of a changing America, the discarding of aristocracy for the idea of natural leaders. In a move away from the aristocratic ideals of the British, Cooper looked for the most American and least British element he could find and settled upon the image of a backwoodsman with an indigenous sidekick.

In effect, Cooper was building an American nationalist mythology through identification with the natural landscape and its original inhabitants. If we think of Cooper as a settler colonist striving to separate the American from the British while simultaneously occupying a position as an imperialist in the new land, his work becomes a type of imperialist discourse that draws the differences from the Native Other with a heavy line, while at the same time maintaining a connection or even identifying with that Other, thereby gaining (from the settler's point of view, at least) psychic as well as physical control.

Even when it uses historical events or characters such as the siege at Fort Henry or Delaware Chief Tamenund, Cooper's work is an elaborate fabrication of myth. In developing this new American mythology, Cooper effectively threw into the same melting pot a number of tribes and cultures and then separated them into two groups—the good and the bad—in a Manichean binarism that effectively nullifies the "positive" aspects of his depictions. His "history" reduces the complex societies of the Indians of the northeastern United States into a simple background for a colonial story.

If his Indians were to contribute to the representation of a quintessential American experience, then some of them, especially those in league with the hero, must be positively portrayed. Chingachgook and Uncas are positively regal characters, but it is important to note that they are the *last* of their breed. These proto-American allegories were conveniently vanishing, leaving the land open for Euro-Americans to take their "rightful" place.

Cooper's conflicted representations of Native peoples were quite in line with the very dichotomized thinking of his day. On the one hand, Natives were considered valuable enough as human beings to make a Civilization Fund Act necessary. This act, initiated in 1813, provided education for Native peoples and allotted ten thousand dollars annually for that purpose. On the other hand, the Supreme Court ruled, in the 1823 case of *Johnson and Graham's Lessee v. William McIntosh*, that "the Indian inhabitants are to be considered merely as occupants, to be protected, indeed, while in peace, in the possession of their lands, but to be deemed incapable of transferring the absolute title to others."[6] The ruling established the supremacy of the government's title to the land. The Natives were not only vanishing, they were being evicted.

Although Cooper was later criticized for romanticizing the Indian, and as Robert Montgomery Bird noted in his preface to *Nick of the Woods* (1837),[7] providing the ideas that motivated the "sentimentalists, she-males, Quakers and other philanthropists," Cooper probably placed himself among the ranks of the "manly realists."[8] Although Chingachgook is a far more attractive and equal companion than Defoe's man Friday or Kimo Sabe's Tonto, Cooper's self-description bodes ill for truly equal partnership. Unpopular in Cooper's own time but very popular by the 1870s and 1880s, the manly realist view held that the apparent differences between the American Indian and the American colonist were inherent; today we would say genetic. This view of inherent inequality, a precursor to the proposition of "scientific racism," is one of the underlying themes in *The Last of the Mohicans*, not the natural goodness or nobleness of the American Indian.

Cooper's creation of the "manly" and Indianized white intermediary and hero of the new American mythology would later become a buttress of the film industry, with stars like Gary Cooper, John Wayne, and even Paul Newman playing savvy woodsmen or plainsmen who were raised by Indians. They were, in fact, generally better at being Indian than the Indians, just as Natty Bumpo always managed to be a better Indian than either Chingachgook or Uncas.

Cooper's depiction of Indians is generally humane, and his mythologizing of the noble savage is sufficiently attractive to have convinced many critics that he was a friend to the Native American, but that is a misreading of his probable intent and of the actual result. It is likely that at least some of Cooper's readers felt they were getting a glimpse of the real American Indian, that his noble and ignoble savages represented the cultural reality of Native peoples. However, the fictional characters in his books represented a constructed ethnographic encounter—albeit one based on Heckelder's *History, Manners, and Customs of the Indian Nations*—fictional characters that suited the new American mythology he was developing.[9] Cooper *created* his Indians in the guise of relating the Native story.

Cooper's loquacious Indians never existed, but in the twentieth century they have been construed and misconstrued in five feature films, three television series, and two television movies, all according to the prevailing attitudes of their day. Cooper's Natty Bumpo, Chingachgook, Uncas, and Magua had actual existence only in the mind of James Fenimore Cooper, but their very malleable presence has shadowed and foreshadowed the image of the American Indian for over a century and a half.

A New Nationalism

Nationalism is perhaps the most successful political ideology in the history of humanity. As Wexman notes, "[T]his relatively new concept—developed in the nineteenth century—has as its main function the ratification of the "claims of the state to impose its will on individuals within its sphere. A nationalist movement seeks to bind together people in a particular territory as an endeavor to gain and use state power."[10] The major powers of Europe and North America have invented an impressive assortment of "ancient traditions" that lend credence to the nationalism they promote. The main product of nationalism is a body of people who are loyal to the imagined community established by nationalist discourse.

Modern mass media, including cinema, have played a major part in the production of national symbols. As these symbols become part of each individual through the media, they effectively break down the separation between public and private, local and national. This produces a nationalist discourse, a primary function of which is to develop a national mythology of historical origin. In America, it is the myth of How the West Was Won. As film critic Peter Wollen noted,

> Nationalism depends crucially on the creation of an invented national history, with its monumental heroes, dramatic climaxes, narrative goals. The myth of the West—the ever-expanding frontier, the manifest destiny that underlay America's westward dynamic, the civilizing mission of the settlers, the taming of the wilderness, the appropriation of the land in order for it to be cultivated—stands alongside other national myths that justified the unification of Germany, or the expansion of Tsarist Russia to the Pacific, or the scramble for Africa, or the imposition of the British raj in India.[11]

The West made a perfect crucible for the development of a mythology intrinsically American. The "frontier" provided a challenge against which Euro-Americans, particularly white males, could pit themselves. The natural environment supplied its own challenges, but it was the cultural frontier that established the identity of the American West and the settlers and cowboys who pushed that frontier ever westward.

In the early 1800s, Euro-Americans were increasing in power and number, and those numbers needed more land, Indian land. Acquiring that land was one of the most problematic issues of the early nineteenth century. The conflicting emotions and ideas engendered by that issue are clearly seen in the debate surrounding the Indian Removal Act of 1830. This act provided for the removal of the eastern tribes to an area west of the Mississippi and was brought to a head by the efforts of the Cherokees to remain outside the control (and confiscation of land by) the state of Georgia. President Andrew Jackson came down heavily on Georgia's side and promoted the removal of the Cherokees and other tribes. Others, such as Senator Frelinghuysen, expressed embarrassment that the government would disregard what he regarded as natural, human law. In an impassioned speech to the Senate, he made the case that "Indians are men, endowed with kindred faculties and powers with ourselves . . . and, with this conceded, I ask in what code of law of nations, or by what process of abstract deduction, their rights have been extinguished?" However, he also expressed the opinion that the tribes were in "childlike" need, an assumption shared by most Euro-Americans of the time who considered themselves friends of the Indians. He quoted from a treaty made in 1809: "[W]e shall consider them as our children, and always hold them firmly by the hand."[12]

The debate in Congress and in the public press was heated on both sides, but on 28 May 1830, Congress passed the Indian Removal Act, empowering President Jackson to proceed with the removal of the southern tribes. In a last ditch effort, the Cherokees took their case to the Supreme Court, claiming status as a foreign nation. Chief Justice John Marshall delivered the court's opinion that the Cherokees were not a foreign nation but rather a "domestic dependent nation . . . in a state of pupilage. Their relation to the United States resembles that of a ward to his guardian." And although he said, "If Courts were permitted to indulge their sympathies, a case better calculated to excite them can scarcely be imagined,"[13] the die was cast, and the Cherokee people were herded to the plains of Oklahoma, with many thousands dead of exhaustion, exposure, and hunger along the way. They and other tribes were pushed west into lands already occupied by other nations of

American Indian peoples. The same basic story can be told of tribes across the continent.

During the time of westward expansion, the removal of American Indian tribes was regarded by the majority of Euro-Americans as the painful but proper course of action. They were certain of the rightness of expansion and progress which the American Indian could only hinder. Expansion was Euro-America's manifest destiny. Arnold Krupat describes the concept of manifest destiny as a tale America told itself in order to create the self-image Euro-Americans needed. Manifest destiny was God's will, and the colonizers' role was that of the tool of God's will in the "inexorable advance of civilization."[14]

The rich fertility of the continent was perceived by many as unused and therefore open for the taking. The Indians who happened to be on that land, even land "given" in treaty agreements, could most easily be dismissed or, if necessary, physically exterminated if they were thought of as bloodthirsty beasts set on inhibiting the God-given right of hardworking Euro-Americans to till the soil. This thinking was seemingly verified when the "savages" actually fought back and Euro-American people were killed.

The rather titillating horror of frontier warfare is reflected in the popular reading material of the time. In the 1800s, Robert Montgomery Bird's *Nick of the Woods* (1837) was second in popularity only to Cooper's *Leatherstocking Tales*. Bird had little sympathy for Indians and provided his hero, Nathan Slaughter, with his own solution to the Indian problem. This self-appointed, one-man genocide squad made his way through twenty-four American editions, echoing the creed that the Indian race was made up of brutal beasts who were beneath contempt and beyond redemption. The preface to the revised edition of *Nick of the Woods* includes a note from Bird that "[t]he Indian is doubtless a gentleman, but he is a gentleman who wears a very dirty shirt, and lives a very miserable life, having nothing to keep him alive except the pleasures of the chase and the scalp-hunt—which we dignify with the name of war."[15]

Bird found a ready audience in a Euro-American public already saturated with stereotyped, generally fictional American Indian history, sensationalized newspaper reports of very real, current Indian uprisings, and their own preconceptions. He also reinforced the sense that the genocide actually taking place was necessary and justifiable. He made it "okay" the way Rambo would later make it okay to slaughter Asians or James Bond the "evil" Soviets. Unfortunately, even respected scholars of the mid–twentieth century have been persuaded by Bird's depiction of the American Indian. In his 1963 book, *Robert Montgomery Bird*, Curtis Dahl wrote,

> But the most striking aspect of realism in the book [*Nick of the Woods*] is the treatment of the Indians. . . . He had seen "the proud warriors" in the Muscogee groves—but, alas, "they always came to sell green strawberries, and beg tobacco." Among the Creeks he had seen one noble, proud, and lofty brave, fierce and Apollo-like (the usual comparison of the time), but that one seems to have been unique. . . . But by the time he wrote *Nick of the Woods* Bird, perhaps from his travels through the frontier, had assimilated the feelings of the frontiersman toward the savages. Thus in the novel they are "red niggurs," dirty and drunken, with an unquenchable bloodlust. The frontiersmen, who are nearly as savage (they, too, delight in taking scalps), slaughter them like rattlesnakes. Though Bird does not express approval of the extremes to which the whites go, he certainly makes the reader sympathize with Nathan's wish for bloody vengeance, and he pictures the Indians as a brutish race which must inevitably be destroyed by the advance of white civilization. He will stand for no romanticizing or sentimentalizing of the Indians.[16]

Aside from bloodthirstiness, Bird's Indians seemed only slightly more intelligent than the rocks they hid behind. One very effective method for transmitting their stupidity to the reader was linguistically through the use of pidgin speech, recognizable now as Tonto-talk.

Bird must be acknowledged for his ability to differentiate his characters by their dialects, real and created, so it is no surprise that he would create a language for his savages.[17] Cooper's Indians were not only articulate but downright loquacious, and Bird made it very clear to his readers that the "real" Indians were nothing like the obviously intelligent Chingachgook and Uncas. Bird's Indians were among the first to discover that they were pronoun-challenged. In *Nick of the Woods*, Nathan Slaughter meets Wenonga, a villainous Shawnee. "'Me Injun-man!' said the chief, addressing the prisoner, and therefore in the prisoner's language, 'Me kill all white-man! Me Wenonga: me drink white-man's blood: me no heart!'"[18] He may have been heartless, but he was at least bilingual, more or less. Unfortunately, the pronoun fault and the addition of "um" to every other word became the all-purpose Indian speech for authors who came after Bird, so it is he we can "thank-um" for the only recently diminishing dialect of the all-purpose Hollywood Indian.

The Dime Novels

The opening of the Oregon Trail and the gold strikes in California spurred a swarm of white men, women, and children moving across Indian lands. Clashes were frequent, and the government assigned thousands of military men to protect the Euro-American citizens from the non-citizen Indians. It was the stuff of which legends are made, and the excitement of real and imagined dangers created a reading public that was well prepared for the heroic Indian-fighter of the dime novels, first published by Irwin P. Beadle & Company in 1860.

Authors of these short, fast stories took the ingredients in Cooper's works about woodland and plains Indians, Bird's attitudes about all American Indians, and the romance and danger of the frontier and made them into a mix-and-match recipe for western fiction that has survived well over a hundred years of use in novels and provided the basis for the model Indian in Hollywood's movie making.

In looking back at these dime novels and the old movies based on them, the so-called thrilling scenes seem rather adolescent. The Indians come into the stories to slaughter a few people before swiftly and dramatically dying at the hands of the hero. It makes one yearn even for Cooper's Indians—at least they were well spoken. The "pesky redskins" of the dime novels were almost completely silent, except for blood-curdling war whoops and occasional slaughter of the English language after Bird's fashion; generally, they were reduced to the ubiquitous "ugh." "Ugh" was about as much conversation one could expect from Indians constructed for consumption, and even their yells were primitive: "'On, on, my good steed, for you have a brave duty to perform, and the bright eyes of beauty are upon you,' cried Deadly-Eye [Buffalo Bill], as he turned in his saddle, and glanced back toward the camp. Seeing the action the pioneers gave him three hearty cheers, which the Indians answered with their discordant yells."[19]

For white Americans portrayed in the dime novels and early films the language of choice was that of common people. The comparatively inarticulate nature of the American Indian in these stories solidifies the ranking of the Native Other as well below that of even the most scurrilous or backward but still semi-articulate white person.

The overwhelming success of these novels was in part due to the

government's accelerating removal of the Indians to reservations farther and farther west. By the last quarter of the nineteenth century, un-
acculturated Indians had become a rare commodity in the East. All that
most eastern Americans knew about them was gleaned between the
bright yellow covers of the novels, mostly written by men like Ned
Buntline (Edward Z. C. Judson) who didn't actually meet an American
Indian until late in his life. The noble savages had all but disappeared,
according to the prevailing "serious" authors of the day, and a vanishing people seemed to have no place in any type of literature except the
pulp fictions, where Indians were rendered as one-dimensional and ultimately extinguishable targets.

The setting for the western dime novel and later the western film is
necessarily at the point of contact between the civilizing white presence
and the savages of the West, providing the conflict central to the genre.
The stories bore little resemblance to the historical facts of those encounters. The Board of Indian Commissioners appointed by President
Grant offered in their report of 23 November 1869 an alternative view of
Native-white relations on the frontier:

> The history of the border white man's connection with the Indians is
> a sickening record of murder, outrage, robbery, and wrongs com-
> mitted by the former as the rule, and occasional savage outbreaks and
> unspeakably barbarous deeds of retaliation by the latter as the excep-
> tion. . . . The testimony of some of the highest military officers of
> the United States is on record to the effect that, in our Indian wars,
> almost without exception, the first aggressions have been made by
> the white man, and the assertion is supported by every civilian of rep-
> utation who has studied the subject.

The reasons for the public's misperceptions of western Native peoples
are numerous, but Grant's Board of Indian Commissioners pointed to
at least one source of the problem:

> In addition to the class of robbers and outlaws who find impunity in
> their nefarious pursuits upon the frontiers, there is a large class of
> professedly reputable men who use every means in their power to
> bring on Indian wars, for the sake of the profit to be realized from the
> presence of troops and the expenditure of government funds in their
> midst. They proclaim death to the Indians at all times, in words and
> publications, making no distinction between the innocent and the
> guilty. They incite the lowest class of men to the perpetration of the

darkest deeds against their victims, and, as judges and jurymen, shield them from the justice of their crimes. Every crime committed by a white man against an Indian is concealed or palliated; every offense committed by an Indian against a white man is borne on the wings of the post or the telegraph to the remotest corner of the land, clothed with all the horrors which the reality or imagination can throw around it. . . . In his most savage vices the worst Indian is but the imitator of bad white men on the border.[20]

The publications to which the Board referred were newspapers, of course, and one could also point to the dime novels that found their way into the hands of countless Euro-American readers.

The frontier formula developed in those novels requires that the "savage" presence must give way to the dominant white presence, but not before offering a challenge to the heroes, the point men of "civilization." Although the actual moment of this interaction was of relatively short duration, the western saga gave it a broad field in time and space, allowing plenty of room for heroics.

The woodsman of Cooper's work was usually transformed in these stories into the six-gun-toting cowboy whose role was to eliminate the opponents of civilization, either outlaws or Indians. An Indian man was a particularly useful character, since he could fill either description. As outlaw-Indian, he was usually a bloodthirsty savage intent on wreaking havoc among peace-loving white settlers. There was little or no motivation given for his actions, aside from a nasty nature. This image still lives on in novels and films such as Larry McMurtry's popular *Lonesome Dove*, whose character Blue Duck is an amoral killing machine.

The very popular dime novels thrilled readers with outrageous feats of gun-slinging, riding, and bravery, all of which quickly became part of the definition of what an American was/is, a definitive part of the "imagined community," as Benedict Andersen has named it, and a bulwark of American national identity.[21] They also reached a frenzied level of sensational violence that spoke loudly about the perceptions of Indians held by the common reader. As Russel Nye points out, the emphasis was strictly on action.

There was a wild, fierce yell, such as only Sioux throats could utter, as they leaped to their feet and made a dash toward him. Quick as was their movement, Bill had gained his feet ere the red devils gained the thicket. There was no time to use his Winchester, but the two six-shooters leaped from his belt, and the scout was soon surrounded by a flame as his deadly revolvers vomited leaden hail into the scarlet foe. The fight was short, sharp, and decisive, and was soon at an end, with seven scarlet bodies weltering in their blood under the midnight sky.[22]

Occasionally, the dime novel Indian could assume the noble savage guise and function as a trusty sidekick to the white hero, assisting in the demise of the white—or Indian—outlaw. The Native Other as sidekick has always been comforting to that part of the audience that desired a painless solution to racial harmony, and one could be certain that Tonto would be true to Kimo Sabe, no matter who might be wearing the black hat that week. Eventually, the perceived disappearance of actual, threatening Indians made it even easier to romanticize them as part of the past, and the sidekick provided a direct link between the natural nobility of the vanished American Indian and the Euro-American hero.

Buffalo Bill and the Wild West Shows

By the late nineteenth century, the bloodthirsty savage and the western hero were firmly entrenched in the new American mythology, and one of the American heroes in perpetual confrontation with the savages was Buffalo Bill Cody. A prolific self-promoter, Buffalo Bill was one of the most popular of the dime novel heroes and a seminal figure in the rise of the modern cinematic western. A natural showman, he used his popularity as a dime novel hero to launch his Wild West Show, which ran for most of the last quarter of the nineteenth century.

The Wild West Show was an American original, and it was Buffalo Bill Cody's creation. Cody had been an army scout and Pony Express rider, and he had already become a star of stage melodramas when, in 1882, the promoters of the Fourth of July rodeo at North Platte, Nebraska, asked him to direct the "cowboy" events for them. It was an absolute success. The show drew thousands of people and convinced Cody that folks in the East would flock to a similar show if it were brought to them. He created a spectacle that combined elements of theater and circus with rodeo and hit the road with the Wild West Show, featuring steer riding, rodeo contests, shooting exhibitions, an attack on a mail coach, and a dramatization of the Pony Express.

Aside from Cody's obvious flair for the dramatic, what made the show such a smashing success was that it included *real* cowboys and *real* Indians as well as a Congressional Medal of Honor winner—Cody himself, but his show reinforced and reified the simplified and largely erroneous conceptions of what an Indian "is" for American and European audiences of his time and for film audiences around the world since that time. His imaginative, staged encounters have provided grist for the Hollywood mill for over a hundred years.[23]

It is largely due to the Wild West Show that cowboys and Indians became so closely intertwined. For a nation infatuated with the heroic deeds of Indian-fighters but who had never seen either an American Indian or a cowboy, Cody's show provided a dip into a life of adventure and danger that was rapidly passing out of existence by the 1880s. It was a combination of circus and melodrama, with plenty of shooting and whooping to keep things interesting. The eastern United States in the last half of the nineteenth century was becoming industrial, and the shows were enormously popular with factory workers and immigrants, but everyone, including presidents of the United States, came to see them. When the shows toured Europe, kings and queens got a taste of the "real" American West. In fact, during one stellar afternoon performance in England, while the Indians were once again attacking the stagecoach as it sped across the arena, the Deadwood Coach carried four kings as passengers. The kings of Denmark, Greece, Belgium, and Saxony rode within, while Buffalo Bill drove and the Prince of Wales rode shotgun.[24]

The Battle of the Little Big Horn (1876) was still recent history, and Cody enlisted Indian leaders such as Sitting Bull and Crazy Horse to add authenticity to the performances. Later, Chief Joseph and Geronimo would join the show. White audiences flocked to the performances to cheer their heroes and gape and sneer at the defeated enemy.

Why, one wonders, did these important Indian leaders take part in an entertainment organized by a white man, much less one that depicted the Indian so negatively and so crassly? For one thing, the American Indians may have felt they could seize the opportunity to show the white world what they were really like. Or it may have been that because the shows were clearly play-acting, they assumed that the viewing public would see that the Euro-Americans and Native Americans were *both* acting. If either of these was the case, the Indian actors may have underestimated the power of "show business" and overestimated the sophistication of their audiences.

Another powerful reason was surely the fact of confinement made worse by hunger. For example, after the Battle of the Little Big Horn, Sitting Bull and his people lived in exile in Canada until forced by hunger to surrender to U.S. government authorities, who confined them on the Standing Rock Reservation. In June 1865, he agreed to join the Wild West Show for fifty dollars per month for four months and the ability to travel off the reservation. Audiences initially jeered Sitting Bull because they held him responsible for the death of Custer, an American hero of mythic proportion. However, newspapers soon found that Sitting Bull made for great stories, and he was increasingly depicted as noble and dignified.

A third reason for joining the Wild West Show was to borrow and learn from the dominant culture. When Buffalo Bill toured Europe with the show, he took along an impressive contingent of American Indians, including the warriors Red Shirt, Rocky Bear, Flat Iron, Cut Meat, Red Dog, American Bear, Kills Plenty, Poor Dog, and Tall Horse. Also in this group was the great Sioux medicine man, Black Elk. In early 1931, Black Elk revealed to John G. Neihardt (Flaming Rainbow), his personal reason for joining the show. "They told us this show would go across the big water to strange lands, and I thought I ought to go, because I might learn some secret of the Wasichu [white people] that would help my people."[25]

When the show returned to the United States for the winter in 1890, the homesick Black Elk and the other American Indians in the show got to go home. The press had begun criticizing the Wild West Shows for mistreatment of the Natives, so Buffalo Bill took Rocky Bear and Red Dog to Washington to testify about the good treatment they had received. While the treatment might have been much worse than they described, it was presumably much better than reservation life during that time. Prolonged death due to hunger, disease, and boredom reigned on the western reservations, which were filled with disillusioned people who had tried farming without proper instruction or equipment, tried ranching until the cattle died of disease, and tried to eat the rotten food provided for them.

Not surprisingly, a number of Native peoples gravitated toward the revival of the Ghost Dance in 1890. By focusing on their traditional lives and denying all that the white world had provided or denied them, by putting their faith in a Native man with a vision, and by praying and dancing, they hoped to return to a world without white people, the world of their ancestors. Although a dance of peace, the Ghost Dance was perceived by many in the military and the American government as a threat. This misunderstanding precipitated the Seventh Cavalry's massacre of three hundred men, women, and children at Wounded Knee on 29 December 1890.[26] One of the men who showed up during the last days of the "campaign" was Buffalo Bill. He asked General Miles to allow him to take some of the prisoners, including Kicking Bear and Short Bull, to become part of his Wild West Show, which was about to depart for Europe again. Miles saw it as an opportunity to get the troublemakers out of the country for a while, but the commissioner of Indian affairs, Thomas Morgan, felt that circus life was demoralizing and refused to allow the Indians to leave. The Nebraska congressional delegation disagreed, however, and Buffalo Bill took his Indians across the water one more time. The tragedy of the "Battle" of Wounded Knee became just another part of the show.[27]

The Wild West Show had lost its glamour and sparkle before it faded away in the early 1900s. It had been replaced by a new invention, the moving picture. But in many ways, the dime novel and the Wild West Show lived on in those movies, a large percentage of which were westerns, and most westerns included at least an Indian or two. Unfortunately, Native peoples would remain largely unseen, displaced now by the Hollywood Indian, a cinematic creation springing directly from the ubiquitous images of the old bloodthirsty savage and his alter ego, the noble savage.

2

The Silent Scrim

But the distance I felt came not from country or people; it came from within me. I was as distant from myself as a hawk from the moon. – The Protagonist in James Welch, *Winter in the Blood*

In the year 1894, Thomas Edison presented to the world the first Kinetoscope—the penny arcade "peep shows." It had been four years since the massacre at Wounded Knee. The previous twenty years had seen the development of much sympathy, some helpful but most not, for Native Americans, of which the most powerful sympathizers were a group of influential and well-intentioned reformers that met at Lake Mohonk each year from 1883 to 1916. There they discussed the plight of Native peoples and made recommendations that ultimately had a tremendous impact on federal policy.

In order to civilize the Native American, they recommended that tribal organizations be disintegrated, that land allotments be made to individuals instead of the tribe as a whole, and that adult males be given citizenship. They also suggested that Indian youths be taken "from the reservations to be trained in industrial schools placed among communities of white citizens . . . [and the] placing of the pupils of these schools in the families of farmers or artisans where they may learn the trades and home habits of their employers."[1] These suggestions ultimately led to the General Allotment Act (Dawes Severalty Act) of 1887, which broke reservations into individual allotments and eventually led to ninety million acres of land moving from American Indian hands to Euro-American control.[2] Schools were set up to train Native American youths in the "trades," and the "employers" mentioned above gained free labor during the summers, when the students were sent to individual homes to learn how civilized families lived by performing domestic chores and other manual labor. In *The White Man's Indian*, Robert F. Berkhofer Jr. described the off-reservation schools: "The most famous of the off-reservation manual-labor boarding schools was the Carlisle (Pennsylvania) Indian Industrial School, founded in 1879 by Captain Richard H. Pratt. In its distance from its pupils' homes, its close, prisonlike supervision of the students, and its outing system, in which students spent summer months or a year living in the home of a good Christian White family, Pratt hoped to destroy the 'Indian' in the 'race' in favor of the 'man,' as he was fond of saying."[3]

Commissioner of Indian Affairs J. D. C. Atkins also took the advice of the conference and forbade Native students in these schools to speak their own languages, frequently with very stiff punishment attached to transgressions. In his annual report, he stated that "Nothing so surely and perfectly stamps upon an individual a national characteristic as language. . . . This language, which is good enough for a white man and a black man, ought to be good enough for a red man. . . . If we expect to infuse into the rising generation the leaven of American citizenship, we must remove the stumbling blocks of hereditary customs and manners, and of these language is one of the most important elements."[4] The intention was simply to cleanse Indians of their Indianness so that assimilation could be seamless.

To many Euro-Americans at the turn of the century, it must have seemed that the remaining American Indians were being assimilated successfully into mainstream America at a reasonable rate. With the transformation of tribal governments, the acquisition of citizenship for some, and the forced schooling of children away from the influence of their families, American Indians appeared well on the way to becoming just plain Americans. Indians were no longer perceived as an overt threat, and a nostalgic image of the historical noble savage, the vanishing "first" Americans, became increasingly popular.

It was therefore understandable that Edison's first film vignettes would include titles such as *Sioux Ghost Dance* (1894)—although there is no evidence that the dance filmed was in fact the Ghost Dance—*Parade of Buffalo Bill's Wild West* (1898), *Procession of Mounted Indians and Cowboys* (1898), *Buck Dance* (1898), and *Eagle Dance* (1898). Even such embarrassments as *Serving Rations to the Indians* (1898) made for novel entertainment. In 1896 the peep shows were first projected onto a screen at Koster and Bial's Music Hall in New York City, and the new medium for representing American Indians began in earnest. The peep shows were followed by moving pictures of the American West, which included flickering ghosts of invented as well as real Native people.

Most audiences of the turn of the century did not have the historical or personal experience to question the reality of the screen images; seeing for oneself had always before been the litmus test for reality. Immigrants, the poor, and rural dwellers were going to the movies for escape and to experience places and situations that were far beyond their economic, social, or cultural grasp; they were going to learn about the world. Moving pictures were persuasive. They were seen on the same screen as the newsreels that told of world events, and while most viewers presumably understood the made-up stories to be fiction, they trusted the images. The particular Indian on the screen, whether noble or savage, might have been a screenwriter's fleeting invention, but the viewer was repeatedly exposed to the same general *ideas* about Indianness represented in the characters.

Besides being a product for consumption and an art form, movies were—and are—very powerful social agents. As the newest and most widely disseminated form of communication, films possessed far-reaching power. They were and are intensely effective as a means of communication, and, as Judith Mayne states, "formidable agents of social control."[5] The film images of American Indians presented in those early years, images based on literature, dime novels, and wild west shows, helped shape the way America thought about Indians then, and the stereotypes crystalized on the early screens are those with which we still live. The audiences of the first films might have believed they were seeing the "real" American Indian, but what they were actually witnessing was the first of the new tribe of Hollywood Indians.

That tribe has changed very little in the last century, although recent filmmakers have sometimes tried to reinvent the Indian in positive ways. As noted by film scholar Angela Aleiss, "[f]inally, studios say, Indians will be portrayed as accurately as possible; they will now play themselves in major roles and their non-Indian antagonists will be seen in a less than positive light."[6] While an applaudable notion, this is not really new.

Much more effectively than most mainstream films of the 1990s, *some* of the films of the early years managed to sidestep the more invasive clichés. Since many during that time believed that America's Native peoples were being quickly assimilated into mainstream society, it was presumably not surprising that they would also enter the film industry. Natives had participated in wild west shows; they continued their involvement in public entertainment by being brought in by busloads for the silent films. Thomas Ince even had a Sioux settlement of "Ince Indians" on the California coast. A Winnebago woman called Princess Redwing (Lillian St. Cyr), Yakima Chief Yowlache, and many other Native Americans played major cinematic roles. In some films, the evil presence was white, not Indian, and a few mixed couples actually lived happily ever after. Some films were even made *by* American Indians, such as *White Fawn's Devotion* (1910), which was directed by a Winnebago man named James Young Deer.

Perhaps the most interesting point about the silent movies was not that there were negative portrayals or positive portrayals but that the negative portrayals were the ones that continued. D. W. Griffith made films with positive images of Indians, such as *The Redman and the Child* (1908), the Huckleberry Finn story of a white boy and his Indian companion, protector, and avenging angel. However, it was his films on the order of *The Battle of Elderbush Gulch* (1914), with its savage Sioux warriors, that achieved lasting fame.

By the second decade of filmmaking, America was involved in or preparing for World War I. Audiences increasingly responded to the all-American hero on the screen, a hero nicely captured by the image of the frontier tamer. As during the Indian Wars of the previous century, negative depictions of Natives best fit the story Americans were telling themselves about themselves, and those images became the cinematic norm by the middle of the century.

Buffalo Bill Rides Again

Not one to be left behind, after the demise of his traveling Wild West Show Buffalo Bill started his own film company, the Col. Wm. F. Cody (Buffalo Bill) Historical Picture Co. The subject of his films would be, naturally, himself. Cody described himself as a cowboy, and more than any other single source, Cody made cowboys and Indians a unit as a result of the exaggerated emphasis he placed on the pairing in his Wild West Show and later films. They were rapidly becoming, as Donald Kaufmann observed, the world's "longest surviving siamese twins."[7]

The Indian Wars (1914)

The making of *The Indian Wars*, a film about the battles Cody fought against the Indians, gained support from some surprising sources. The secretary of state sent troops and equipment for the filming, General

Miles himself agreed to appear in the film, and the war department put the Pine Ridge Sioux at Cody's disposal. The film was presumably given such overwhelming support because it was to be used for war department records and to enlist recruits. As the United States prepared to enter the First World War, it was important to bolster morale and present the military as a force with a noble history, invincible, and quintessentially American. The film was also designed to show the "excellent" treatment contemporary Indians received from the U.S. government.[8]

The impact of *The Indian Wars* is difficult to overestimate. This was a film that affected the leaders of the country as well as the children one reviewer suggested see the film. (A *Motion Picture World* reviewer recommended taking a young person to *The Indian Wars* "for an afternoon with the great leaders of our army, with the great chiefs of our Indian tribes and two hours in the open world that has been made sacred by heroic blood of the nation's fighting heroes," 12 Sept. 1914). Directed by Theodore Wharton, the film was first shown to cabinet members, congressmen, and other dignitaries in Washington, and it became an "official" government record—a frightening fact, considering the absolute dedication of its primary producers to presenting the battles, particularly the massacre at Wounded Knee, as unquestionably justifiable and heroic.

Although most films have used non-Indian actors to play Indians, *The Indian Wars* did, as stated above, use Sioux Indians. The *Motion Picture News* of 22 November 1913 described their role in the film's depiction of the massacre at Wounded Knee:

> [A] permanent record has been made of a bit of history which very nearly eradicated a mighty nation, the Sioux Indian. . . . Chiefs, bucks, and squaws, generals, officers and soldiers who held arms against each other in the battles of '90 and '91 again opposed each other on the very field they did some twenty odd years ago. . . . For several days previous to the taking of the first battle scene the air seemed to be charged with danger; both Indians and soldiers were loath to commence operation. It was during this battle many years ago that so many on both sides were lost, not only soldiers, but women and children.

It should be noted that many soldiers died in other clashes with the Sioux, but in the reenactment of the incident at Wounded Knee very few soldiers were killed, while hundreds of Sioux, mostly elderly men and women and children, did die. It is no wonder that, according to *Motion Picture News*, Native women sang the death song throughout the filming of the scene.

The Indians had reason for complaint about the making of the film. As Henry Blackman Sell and Victor Weybright described it in *Buffalo Bill and the Wild West,*

> [t]he plan called for the battle to take place right over the Indian graves, which seemed to the Sioux a horrible desecration. General Miles could see nothing wrong with the idea, however, for that would make everything historically accurate. . . . Iron Tail came to Buffalo Bill and warned him there would be trouble. Colonel Cody told him to call together the old men of the tribe. Short Bull and No Neck came to the council. Buffalo Bill told them how hopeless it would be to turn this movie battle into a real one, to shoot real bullets at the white men, for the Indians would be pursued and caught, and probably tried for murder. The Sioux warriors finally saw his point, and the following day the sham battle went before the cameras.[9]

The mood was somewhat lighter in the 4 March 1914 review in *The Moving Picture World,* in which the reviewer reported that the Indians had at times "refused to remain 'dead' after being 'killed' unless they were completely out of ammunition, and then they would roll over that they might get a better view of the antics of their brothers." This provided comic relief in the filming, which broke up the "otherwise very serious affair." He goes on to report that "[t]he effect of the pictures on an audience was evidenced by the alternate handclapping, cheers and hisses which greeted individual action."

The battles in *The Indian Wars* are followed by bucolic scenes of American Indian boys and girls in the uniforms of the government schools saluting the American flag, scenes that must have been debilitating for parents whose children had been forcibly taken away from them and placed in those schools (assuming the parents were in a position to see the film at all). Only smartly dressed Indian children are shown, behaving in a very "civilized" manner. Indian farmers and the modern buildings that housed the schools and agencies are also depicted, and one scene features Indians in a seven-passenger touring car.

As a propaganda piece, the film was probably a great success. It tied up "the Indian problem" in a neat package to be purchased for the price of a ticket. It validated and valorized the cavalry troops who fought the Indians, and it showed the generosity and humanity of the U.S. government toward a defeated enemy. It is an excellent example of the rewriting of the history of Indian–white relations, with the cinematic version becoming a hyper-reality.

D. W. Griffith

Indians were popular fare in silent films. Over one hundred movies about Indians were made each year between 1910 and 1913, and almost that many in each of the remaining years of the silent screen. Although the long-standing stereotypes of noble and bloody savage were always present, in the very early films the noble image prevailed, whereas the bloodthirsty image became more popular toward the end of the silent film era.

A Pueblo Legend (1912)

It was in the mode of the primitive but noble stereotype that D. W. Griffith cast the characters of *A Pueblo Legend*. The film is set in "the mystical and primeval setting of Isleta Pueblo, 'before the coming of the Spaniards.' "[10] The plot is about idealized Indians performing "mystical" acts in an idealized world. As Richard Schickel pointed out in his lengthy biography of D. W. Griffith,

> [n]o doubt he was influenced toward these subjects by the romanticizing of the savage and of the natural environment which coincided, in this period, with the nation's first awareness that the frontier had finally closed, that it had just lost something it had always taken for granted—*untamed, untouched lands to the west* [emphasis mine]. . . . It should be observed, of course, that Griffith's interest in the prehistory surely represented an extension backward in time of the mystique of the Noble Savage, which so intrigued American middle-class culture at this time.[11]

And so, Griffith set about to make a love story that touched chords of nostalgia and longing for the lost frontier.

At the Spring Dance of the Green Boughs at Isleta Pueblo, a young, visiting Hopi girl (played by Mary Pickford) falls immediately and madly in love with the handsome war captain, Great Brother. Things are going well until the Sky Priest emerges from the Kiva and tells Great Brother he must go on a quest to find the Turquoise Sky Stone, which will bring peace and prosperity to the pueblo. While on the quest, Great Brother and his friend are attacked by the enemy, the Apaches. Only the fact that the girl, too lovesick to stay behind, has followed him, sees the attack, and returns for help allows the Isletas to survive. At the victory celebration later on, the girl offers Great Brother the wedding blanket, but he refuses it. He cannot accept happiness until he rescues his friend who was captured by the Apaches. He gathers some warriors and they ride off to find the friend.

The girl talks to the Sun Priest, who gives her what is condescendingly subtitled a "toy image of the Sky God," and she prays to the god for Great Brother's return by spreading honey on a corn husk in front of the kachina (the "toy doll"), sprinkling it with corn meal, wrapping it up, placing a feather on top, and holding it up to the sun. In the meantime, Great Brother finds the Apaches, frees his friend, and flees back toward the pueblo, angry Apaches right behind. The girl prays with the kachina again, the renewed battle ends with a peace talk between the "hereditary enemies," and Great Brother begins his quest once more. This calls for another prayer, but this time the girl miraculously finds the Turquoise Sky Stone under her altar. When Great Brother returns, empty handed and dejected, she shows him the stone, and he wraps both of them inside the wedding blanket.

The plot and the moral of *A Pueblo Legend* are likely to bring a smile to modern audiences in much the same way that the mustache-twirling villain of the early films evokes a grin instead of the fright he originally intended. As Enrique Lamadrid points out, "D. W. Griffith's portrayal of the Indian as the 'Mystical Other' is so overt as to become immediately ludicrous . . . a sense that must have been shared at least in part by the 1912 audience. The residents of Isleta Pueblo in 1912 became offended soon after filming began because they sensed that the film might be a parody of their culture."[12] And, of course, they were right, but Griffith's portrayals of the "exotic" Indians and their "primitive" beliefs, as deleterious as they were, had their foundations in the long-standing tradition of attitudes and assumptions about the Native Other. His depiction of the Isleta religious beliefs as distinctively innocent and primitive helped perpetuate the belief of many that mainstream American society had a responsibility to care for, feed, and save the souls of the noble, primitive, native "children" of America.

During the same year, Griffith perpetuated the other popular stereotype of Native peoples through *Massacre* (Biograph, 1912), a film about Custer and his last stand in which the Indians were definitely not portrayed as the primitive children of *A Pueblo Legend* but surfaced once more as bloodthirsty savages standing in the way of civilization. In an essay on D. W. Griffith, Nicholas Vardac called *Massacre* "a romanticized historical subject . . . reproduced with realism." The realism to which he refers is one of visual realism, a comment on Griffith's brilliant directing, particularly his innovative use of intercut shots to relate simultaneous story lines and his framing of shots to achieve psychological effects.[13]

Of *A Pueblo Legend*, Vardac says that it was "authentically spectacular and filmed on location in [the] old pueblo of Isleta, New Mexico. Costume plates and shields, weapons and accessories were loaned by the Museum of Indian Antiquities at Albuquerque." Like most reviewers and film scholars, Vardac seems to have given little attention to the Indian reaction to these "realistic" films. The Native accessories that had been borrowed for *A Pueblo Legend* from the Museum of Indian Antiquities included garments reserved for sacred ceremonies, the use of which prompted the Isleta Pueblos to insist that Griffith cease filming. He managed to complete the last few scenes in the pueblo by engaging the Indian leaders in discussion about the filming while his crew shot the scenes.

Griffith knew the impact his films had on their audiences. In an article he wrote for *The Independent* in 1916, he referred to his films as "influential" and noted that "in twelve months one of many copies of a single film in Illinois and the South played to more people and to more money than all the traveling companies that put out from New York play to in fourteen months."[14]

Due to the sheer numbers of viewers as well as the persuasive nature of film, Griffith's work was immensely important in perpetuating the noble savage and bloodthirsty savage stereotypes to new generations of Euro-Americans.

The Progressive Era

The one-dimensional stereotyping of Indians in Griffith's work was to a large extent due to the melodramatic nature of silent films, where characters were exaggerated caricatures of their everyday equivalents. The dependable happy ending, where the villains get what's coming to them, was also a typical popularization of the ideals and attitudes of the Progressive Era. According to Alan Casty, "[m]ore than a political movement, Progressivism seemed to capture a national tone: an innocent optimistic faith in progress and human potential, in the efficacy of

1. From D. W. Griffith's *The Battle at Elderbrush Gulch* (1914). Photo Museum of Modern Art Film Stills Archives; courtesy Biograph.

change; a moralistic seriousness, a no-nonsense soberness; a mixture of sentimental idealism and gruff, athletic confidence."[15]

Louis Reeves Harrison, a very influential reviewer for *Moving Picture World*, was a major proponent of the Progressive attitude in filmmaking. Harrison believed in the power of film to provoke social change. Films could hasten the "dawn of enlightenment" and promote "cultivation of the social muscle" with their ability to "affect the manners and habits of the people, to cultivate their taste for the beautiful, to soften harsh temperament by awakening tender sympathy, to correct primitive egotism and avarice, to glimpse history and travel, to nourish and support the best there is in us."[16]

An understanding of American Indians evidently did not fall within the parameters Harrison set for the best there is in us, for in his article, "The 'Bison 101' Headliners," in the 27 April 1912 issue of *The Moving Picture World*, he stated that

> [t]here were probably less than a million indians scattered over that part of the continent now known as the united states, subject to the ravages of relentless killing and torture—(among themselves)— cruel, crafty, and predatory with no universal language, no marks of gradual enlightenment and incapable of contributing anything of value to human evolution when european races began to fight their way from ocean to ocean under all sorts of difficulties, including methods of warfare disastrous to the invaders. The natives were so well protected by natural advantages and their methods of fighting that it was a difficult matter to kill a redskin, whereas the whites were constantly exposed by their peaceful occupations to indiscriminate slaughter.

Harrison wrote for the average American reader, and his ideas about the history of white/Indian relations were fairly typical of his day. Indian land had become more desirable with the discovery of oil and mineral deposits, and many white Americans resented the "free ride" the Indians were receiving at the taxpayers' expense, particularly since increasingly they believed American Indians were now just like everyone else. It was Harrison's view that in the Bison 101 Headliners

> [c]onditions alone are presented, especially those which existed after the government attempted to regulate and control the various tribes, according them privileges still unenjoyed by white citizens, and punishing with severity acts of oppression by responsible whites. Race hatred was unavoidable and it is only modified to-day. The average descendent of colonial families has little use for the red man, regards him with distrust and, with poetic exceptions, considers him hopelessly beyond the pale of social contact.

Harrison may have been one of those descendants who had little use for the "red man," but he did agree with the many directors and producers of silent films that the Indian made an interesting museum piece, if nothing else. He stated,

> [T]he Indian, however, remains one of the most interesting and picturesque elements of our national history. He is almost typical of the

fighting male, a restless, dominating, ever-struggling human creature, principally engaged in works of destruction, but representative
of the ancestral strain that conquered all the other creatures delivered
from the fertile womb of Mother Earth. He was essentially a man of
physical action, using only that part of his brain which enabled him
to be crafty in the hunt for food, though he had vague poetic ideals
and nebulous dreams of barbaric splendor. Mentally he was far below the Egyptian of 6,000 years ago, but he was the physical superior
of any man on earth except the strong-armed European who culti-
vated brain along with brawn.

Savage but crafty and endowed with physical prowess, the Indian
was a perfect foil for the heroic white man in the silent films. And it was
perhaps those "vague poetic ideals and nebulous dreams of barbaric
splendor" he was suspected of harboring that made him noble, especially in the past tense.

America's "Vanishing" Race

By the early twenties, some Americans had become frustrated with the
government's inability to solve the "Indian problem," and there was increasing disagreement about and dissatisfaction with the treatment of
Native Americans. Those interested in reforming the reservation system were at odds with the traditionalists and bureaucrats who defended
the administration's and the missionaries' efforts to civilize and Christianize the American Indian. Some still thought the best thing to do
with the American Indians was assimilate them into mainstream America, and some saw value in Native Americans retaining their cultural
identity. Among the latter were John Collier, who helped organize and
became general secretary of the American Indian Defense Association
in 1923, and celebrities like D. H. Lawrence, who was living in Taos,
New Mexico, at the time.

In 1924 Lawrence wrote an article for the *New York Times* in which he
clearly defined what he saw as the reasons behind the contradictory and
extreme Euro-American attitudes toward American Indians.

> It is almost impossible for the white people to approach the Indian
> without either sentimentality or dislike. . . . Both reactions are due
> to the same feeling in the white man. The Indian is not in line with us.
> He is not coming our way. His whole being is going a different way
> from ours. And the minute you set eyes on him you know it.
>
> And then, there's only two things you can do. You can detest the

insidious devil for having an utterly different way from our own great way. Or you can perform the mental trick and fool yourself and others into believing that the befeathered and bedaubed darling is nearer to the true ideal gods than we are.[17]

Lawrence and Collier were reacting to the latest Indian Problem. As usual, at the heart of the matter was land ownership, this time with an emphasis on mineral and petroleum rights.

In the early 1920s, Secretary of the Interior Albert B. Fall ruled that executive-order reservations were available to developers and opened twenty-two million acres of reservation land to drillers. In 1922 he supported the Bursum Pueblo Land Bill, which confirmed squatter's rights to Pueblo land and required the Pueblo Indians to produce proof of title, which was, of course, difficult if not impossible. This bill passed in the Senate but was ultimately killed by intense rebuttal by American Indians and their popular and vocal supporters.[18]

In addition, the public was becoming aware of the deplorable conditions on many reservations and the injustices committed on them by the people ostensibly there to assist the Indians. This was not news; as early as 1869, the Board of Indian Commissioners reported that "[t]he agent, appointed to be their friend and counselor, business manager and the almoner of the government bounties, frequently went among them only to enrich himself in the shortest possible time, at the cost of the Indians, and spend the largest available sum of the government money with the least ostensible beneficial result."[19] In the 1920s articles appeared in major magazines and newspapers exposing some of these problems and engendering public indignation. People like John Collier, then executive secretary of the newly formed American Indian Defense Association, referred to the Administration of Indian Affairs as a national disgrace dedicated to policies of land theft and cultural destruction with the ultimate goal of eliminating the American Indian entirely.[20]

On the other side of the argument were those who wanted the Indian land, particular bureaucrats whose jobs might be endangered by changes in federal Indian policy, and moralists who attacked Indian religion, charging that their cultural traditions, especially traditional dancing, were lewd and morally destructive. The lines between the forces were blurred by others who, like the National Indian Association, attacked the handling of the reservations but defended the missionary effort to Christianize the Indian.[21]

The Vanishing American (1925)

Another outspoken critic of the government's treatment of American Indians was Zane Grey. Grey's novels often depicted Native Americans as victims of greed, betrayal, and neglect, but the first of his novels to specifically focus on Natives was *The Vanishing American*. Grey wanted to use not only the text but the cinema to convey his message, and he invited Jesse Lasky, vice president of production at Paramount Pictures, to visit with him in the desert around Navajo Mountain and Rainbow Bridge in Northern Arizona. After two months there, Lasky was sold on the area as the setting for a motion picture.[22] Grey began writing what he intended as a cinematic tribute to the American Indian, *The Vanishing American*.

Grey may have in part been reacting to the many stories about the Pueblo Indians in the news at the time. One such article that took the side of the Pueblos in the Bursum Land Bill controversy was a *New York Times* editorial on 25 January 1923. "In losing these picturesque people . . . we should be losing a great national asset of beauty and strangeness, as expressed in their sacred observances. Still another [reason for saving the Pueblos] is their value as an archaeological asset. But the chief reason, after all, is that it would be neither decent nor civilized to let these people die." With editorials such as this one reaching the public, it must have seemed the perfect time for Grey, who had firsthand knowledge of the American Indians of the Southwest and thought of them as something more than artifacts, to tell an American Indian story through the newest media, motion pictures.

Grey's story first ran as a serial in *Ladies Home Journal*, and the novel was supposed to be released simultaneously with the film. However, Grey's depiction of the missionaries was not what the magazine's readership wanted to see, and when the editors at Harper responded to the pressure by requesting changes, Grey considered withdrawing his manuscript altogether. In a letter to William H. Briggs on 23 May 1924, Grey wrote, "I have studied the Navajo Indians for twelve years. I know their wrongs. The missionaries sent out there are almost everyone mean, vicious, immoral useless men [*sic*] . . . and some of them are crooks. They cheat and rob the Indian and more heinously they seduce every Indian girl they can get hold of."[23]

Although Grey was not disposed to change his story of reservation reality by purifying the missionaries' image, the film studio, like the magazine, definitely was. What troubled Paramount most was the fact that the villains were the victors. In an era of melodrama and Manichean divisions of good and evil, it seemed unthinkable that good would not in some way triumph, no matter how much a film wanted to depict the reality of the distressing conditions of reservation life. In his "Story Synopsis and Comment," April 1923, M. C. Lathrop wrote that "the story is one of heart-rending distress, in which injustice, greed, and the baser passions are invariably triumphant and *remain unpunished*. . . . Every character (without exception) that earns the sympathy of the reader is either dead or left in a pitiable plight at the end of the story; and the miscreants who are the authors of this misery and death, are amusingly hale, hearty, and prosperous."[24] The depiction may have been accurate, but it certainly wouldn't sell tickets, so significant script changes were made and George Sietz was hired to direct.

The Vanishing American illustrates the noble but doomed Native stereotype, the brave warrior who loses the Darwinian struggle for survival. The film retains elements of the book's Social Darwinism, which in fact Paramount accentuated by removing all references to the main Native character's East Coast education. By gaining a mainstream American education, he would have appeared as an assimilated Indian who was just like other residents of the continent, not the distinctive, romantic, noble savage the filmmakers wanted.

The filmmakers also added an interesting prologue that depicts human evolutionary history, starting with the cavemen. Native Americans were set firmly in this line of cultural development—further along than cavemen but not as evolved as white men.

The film features a brave Native hero named Nophaie (Richard Dix) who reappears in each segment and finally becomes the main character in the central plot. In the prologue, he leads the people who overtake the cliff dwellers of the Southwest, but one of the cliff dwellers prophesies that a "stronger race" will come to overtake the Indians, with an obvious nod to the survival of the fittest, the fittest being, of course, Europeans and Euro-Americans. Nophaie is ultimately killed by a single shot from a Spanish rifle as he rides his white horse back and forth on a bluff. His people bow in homage to the Spanish and sway drunkenly. Although this scene is presented to engender sympathy for the Indians, the reality is that the warrior dies (vanishes) and the rest of his people are made infantile by fire-water and the knowledge that a "superior race" has indeed come to their land.

The second time Nophaie appears in the film, three hundred years have passed, and he is confronted by Kit Carson and the U.S. Cavalry.

He again rides his white horse, highlighted against the sky on a high bluff, and again he is killed. This time, the "superior race" knocks him off with a cannon. Kit Carson then makes promises to the Indians, but those promises are not kept, and Nophaie appears one last time on a reservation dominated by malevolent Indian agents in the film's present, the period surrounding the First World War.

The main segment of the film presents the struggle for survival of the Nopah, a fictitious name for what is obviously the Navajo people. The white agent, Amos Halliday, is a bureaucrat who cares about his paperwork but pays little attention to his charges. His assistant is the ultravillainous Booker (Noah Beery), an example of Grey's idea of white agents in general. He is a thoroughly despicable human being who starves the Indians, shuttles them off to desolate lands, strikes Indian elders, cheats on a regular basis, and even abuses children. Had there been a puppy in the movie, he would surely have kicked it. He is, of course, promoted to head agent upon Halliday's departure.

In sharp contrast to Grey's story, in which the missionaries share the negative portrayal, the film's Booker embodies all that is evil on the reservation. The filmmakers of the twenties were apparently reluctant to anger the Christian majority of their audience by presenting the missionaries as Grey saw them, so they were simply omitted. However, Booker's treatment of the Nopah is sufficiently harsh to engender sympathy for them. In one particularly effective scene, a veteran returning from the war imagines a warm and wonderful homecoming but instead finds his young wife dead and his home abandoned.

The film is decisively sympathetic to the Indians, but the changes made between Grey's script and Paramount's film clearly define what was acceptable to the American public at the time. The elimination of the missionaries' malevolence is a major change, but others are just as telling. For instance, whereas Grey's Nophaie was educated in the East, the filmic Nophaie first encounters Euro-American "civilization" in the form of Indian agents and Marion (Lois Wilson), the white schoolteacher, who teaches him to read the Bible.

In Grey's story, Nophaie dies of influenza, and he is carefully described as having become white. "Nophaie! His eyes were those of an Indian, but his face seemed that of a white man. . . ." His eastern education, his term of service in the army, his adoption of Christianity, and his romance with Marion seem to have turned the Nopah warrior away from his own people. His dying words indicate that white and Indian can never intermix—"White woman . . . go back to your people." In an unpublished version of the story, the romance between Marion and Nophaie results in an interracial marriage. Although at first this may seem to be an even more sympathetic approach, underlying it is Grey's idea, and that of other assimilationists, that the races should be united so that their strengths would be combined, a result that would not only symbolically but literally bring about the very real "vanishing" of the Native Americans.

Paramount, however, changed Grey's script for two reasons. First, it was terribly undramatic to have a hero die of the flu, so instead, Nophaie is shot during a confrontation between the Indians and Booker. He is actually shot by one of his own people when he tries to put a halt to the violence. Before filming started, the story went a little differently. As Lucien Hubbard's synopsis shows, it was planned that Booker shoot Nophaie, and that the Indians "perceive the wounded Nophaie to be his spirit, and in their fear of death, they give up the attack. As Nophaie lies dying, he tells Marion that they can never marry, and he places her hand in that of a white man's. The Indians carry Nophaie's body over the ridge until the last rider gradually fades into the West. . . . Nophaie thus becomes a martyr of White injustice."[25] He also dies an Indian in this version, as he states his conviction that the two races must live unmixed.

In the conclusion of the final film version, Marion reads from the Bible, while Nophaie nods in agreement. He "finally understands," and what he understands is that assimilation, especially the adoption of Christianity, is the solution for the Nopahs' situation. As Aleiss states, "The film tries to invest Indians with a tragic stature, yet its appeal to Christianity emerges as a conciliatory resolution to racial reform."[26] Bullets and cannons have killed the warrior in the prologue, but he keeps returning until he is converted to Christianity by the lovely white woman and is killed by one of his own people while trying to bring peace between the whites and the Indians, thus becoming a Christian martyr and killing, finally, the warrior spirit.

In the final film version, Nophaie and his people represent a noble but doomed race. It allows the viewer to "tolerate" the Native Other, even feel deep sympathy, but without responsibility since the Indians are soon to be no more. Nophaie and his people are presented as noble creatures who simply succumb to the old law of survival of the fittest. *The Vanishing American*'s first viewers could leave the theater feeling sad about the demise of so exotic a people but also feeling good that evil was punished (Booker is finally killed) and peace restored. It fit the melodramatic formula many American movie-goers at the time expected.

Melodrama and the Indian

The melodramatic formula of silent films deserves some discussion. Just what is the typically melodramatic fashion of silent film, and how did that formula affect the depiction of the American Indian?

In *The Melodramatic Imagination*, Peter Brooks makes the point that melodrama, whether literary or cinematic, deals with the world in Manichean terms of good and evil, with no mediating middle ground—a type of binarism. The good and evil in the melodramatic form are, according to Brooks, highly personalized. "[T]hey are assigned to, they inhabit persons who indeed have no psychological complexity but who are strongly characterized."[27] In the case of the American Indian, that characterization could be evil, as in the bloodthirsty savage stereotype, or good, as in the noble savage. Indians who were multidimensional human beings with faults and virtues were not to be found in the silent films that first introduced them to the American film audience. There was no middle ground between good and evil and no middle ground between nobility and a thirst for blood. It is the formula of melodrama to present without ambiguity two characters in conflict, with one coming out entirely victorious. There is no compromise, no reconciliation, just the presentation of a social order to be cleansed of evil, a set of cultural ethics to be clearly established.

Although films like *A Pueblo Legend* and *The Vanishing American* presented the American Indian sympathetically and to a small extent realistically, a nation caught in the frontier mythos could hardly have failed to understand which social order was to be cleansed and whose cultural ethics were to be made clear, even if the Indians were interesting archaeological artifacts.

Carving a Hollywooden Indian

The early persona of the celluloid Indian was developed visually with camera angle and body language and aurally with nondiegetic sound (off the screen) produced mostly by theater pianists. (Westerns were rarely shown in the elegant theaters, where artistically arranged scores were played by orchestras.) The sights and "sounds" of silent-film Indians became an ingrained part of popular mythology about Native peoples, refining the preconceptions of the viewing audience or providing instant images for those who had never experienced an Indian presence. The tom-tom beat, even when played on a Steinway, still means to most Americans that the Indians are on the warpath and trouble is brewing.

The look of the all-purpose, generic Indian was developed in the silent era, most obviously in body language. Although many Native Americans worked in silent films, Hollywood producers evidently felt that anyone could play an Indian. If the important characters were Indians, the roles were almost always taken by white people using darker makeup and wigs. Most male Hollywood Indians of the silent screen and the following era stood flat-footed with their arms folded high on their chests, said very little but could be seen grunting, and had an almost perpetual scowl on their faces. Females were soft, meek, and lovely, wore long buckskin dresses with much fringe and beading, and looked longingly at the white hero. When striking a pose, both sexes generally placed a flat hand above their eyes as though looking far into the distance.

This inarticulate caricature was presented to the American public in whatever combination of tribal dress suited the taste of the director, with little if any attention to accuracy; most of the public would not, after all, know the difference. In 1914 Alanson Skinner, assistant curator of the Department of Anthropology at the American Museum of Natural History, wrote the *New York Times* to complain about the inaccuracies in costuming:

> From the standpoint of the student, most of the picture plays shown are ethnologically grotesque farces. Delawares are dressed as Sioux, and the Indians of Manhattan Island are shown dwelling in skin tipis of the type used only by the tribes beyond the Mississippi. If the Indian should stage a white man's play, and dress the characters in Rumanian, Swiss, Turkish, English, Norwegian and Russian costumes, and place the setting in Ireland, would their plea that they thought all Europeans looked alike, and that they had to portray the white man's life through standards of their own save them from arousing our ridicule?[28]

Unfortunately, very few films, even those made in the 1990s, have corrected the ethnological distortions that so upset Skinner.

So How Can They Be Wrong?

Thus was the identity of the Indian first written cinematically in the American mind. From adventure stories, reports of first contact, and captivity narratives, to the Indians of Cooper's woods, the fabrications of Ned Buntline and other dime novelists, and finally the wild west shows and the first two decades of filmmaking, the public was presented with and consumed a distorted, shifting, polarized set of images that gave them a way to categorize and redefine the first residents of the continent. The early films were based on Buffalo Bill's Wild West Show, and those performances had included Indians of historical fact and fame, so how could they be "wrong"? Those shows were based on dime novels, but there were also references to historical Indian uprisings, so how could they be "wrong"? The dime novels were based on literature by well-known authors like Cooper and Bird, so how could they be "wrong"? This regression could be taken all the way back through John Smith to Columbus, each representation building the myth a piece at a time, constructing reality as it best suited the purpose at hand. The resulting invention is an imaginary Indian—not a group of widely diverse peoples—that could be easily digested by the consumer.

3

The Cowboy Talkies of the 1930s, 1940s, and 1950s

I tell the bus driver
but he doesn't hear,
"Keep to the hills
and avoid America
if you can.
I'm a fugitive
from bad, futureless dreams
in Southern California."
– Simon J. Ortiz, "East of San Diego"

The most important development in the film industry after the invention of the first camera and projector was sound. Careers took immediate turns as audiences first began to hear their idols' voices, and a new set of considerations developed for the directors. Not only were the words of more importance—so was the diegetic noise (coming from within the scene) and nondiegetic noise (such as a voice-over). With sound, the nuances of story lines became more accessible, and the melodramatic form of the silents appeared unsophisticated by comparison.

Cinematic Language
As previously noted, in the early sound films stereotypes of Native Americans were conveyed to a large degree by language or, perhaps more importantly, the lack of language. The signs that accompanied the Indians of the silent film, the scowling face and rigid body, were carried over to the sound western as the "natural" pose of a Native American. Rarely were Indians heard, and when they were, they were depressingly devoid of humor, although humor was often directed at them. Most had little to say beyond the ubiquitous grunt, which could

mean anything from "I'm pleased" to "Scalp him, kill him, and then tie him over an anthill."

Aside from the obvious boundaries of language difference—the differences between English and Navajo for instance—there exists a stratification within languages. Differences between generations, professions, races, genders, politics, time, space, and innumerable other classifications produce differences in speech. The human voice holds within it a "code" that humans read almost instinctively, and when language is missing, the instinct is generally to place the voiceless into the margins, which is exactly where most filmic minorities have historically resided.[1]

But it was not much better when directors and script writers gave their Indians voices in the early westerns. Since all voices in film come equipped with an accent and an intonation, a voice can make a comment that is very different from the words spoken. For instance, if an Indian says, "White man speaks with forked tongue," he is doing more than simply dropping the articles. A command of English has been written out of the script already; in addition, the delivery of such a line was usually either ponderously slow or angry, a translation into voice of the stoic, stone-faced "bloodthirsty redskin" in silent movies, which effectively perpetuated the stereotypes of Native Americans as dim-witted or violent, or possibly both.

Use of an alien-sounding language that was rarely a genuine native language also contributed to the distancing and Othering of Native Americans for mainstream audiences. Hollywood had its own ideas of what an Indian sounded like, and the industry went to fairly extreme lengths to get the "authentic" sound. In *Scouts to the Rescue* (1939), for instance, the Indians were given a Hollywood Indian dialect by running their normal English dialogue backwards. By printing the picture in reverse, a perfect lip sync was maintained, and a new "Indian" language was born.[2]

As in silent films, body language continued to be an important form of communication. Audiences were already accustomed to the "classic" poses of cinematic Indians and the melodramatic sweep of gestures. But the talkies, as an audiovisual medium, were able to combine words with gestures, facial expressions with body movements to create more complex meanings. This discursive sum allowed for greater character development, since one message (I love you) could be rendered in body language while a contradictory message (I hate you) was delivered orally. Many romantic comedies depended on this push-me/pull-you communication, but the same idea worked in slightly more subtle but extremely effective ways in the early westerns. "Me friend to white-eyes," could be delivered by a very dignified and obviously powerful chief, but his language was a clue that he was a part of the past, not a part of the audience's world. Since a number of lawmakers, educators, and even Hollywood producers placed as the test of cultural survival the ability to assimilate, many in the audience presumed that the chief was an anachronism at best, linguistically and perhaps mentally deficient, and bound to lose/die/vanish.

A form of language in film that is rarely addressed is the written word. Whether a newspaper headline, a signpost, or a subtitle, written language can play an important part in a film. Subtitles were not often used in the earlier Hollywood westerns, partly because they would have looked old-fashioned to audiences who remembered the silent era. But more importantly, subtitles were generally unnecessary because the words and thoughts of Indians were not particularly important to most scripts. Genuine Native languages were rarely used, and when a white hero learned to speak an Indian language, the script conveniently reproduced it in English, as in *Broken Arrow* (1950) and hundreds of other films. There have, of course, been a few exceptions; a fairly recent one is *Dances With Wolves* (1990), in which the Lakota language was spoken with a fair degree of accuracy, and subtitles were used. The effect was one of privileging a Native language, and therefore culture, in a manner that Hollywood movies have rarely attempted.

Music and noise also function as languages in film. The lyrics on soundtracks can often transfer information and emotion even more effectively than dialogue. They communicate with an audience on a level that adds to the visceral impact of melody and tone. But even without words, music can generate lyrics within the consciousness of the viewer. (Robert Stam cites as an example Kubrick's use of the melody without words to "Try a Little Tenderness" during a visual image of nuclear bombs dropping in *Dr. Strangelove* [1963].)[3]

As noted before, the "tom-tom" beat of drums signal to an American audience that Indians are about to appear. Actual Native forms of music are rarely heard, probably because they are so different from what mainstream audiences would expect. In the rare instances in which Indian music and dance are presented, as in the later film, *A Man Called Horse* (1970), they are generally portrayed as simultaneously primitive and exotic. The wild drumming, movements, and costumes, in addition to the hero's near-delirium, produce a chaotic image closely resembling a Dionysian orgy. Purpose and beauty are absent from the scene.

Noises are not without purpose either. Whether an obvious sound such as that of a knife being sharpened or one "lost" in the background like crickets in a forest, noise communicates place, time, and circumstance in definite though generally subconscious ways. When a character in a western appears and the noise in the background is a low rattle, the audience makes an obvious association between the character and a rattlesnake and identifies him as the dangerous and sneaky villain.

There is also the language of the camera itself. For instance, a director can position a camera to "look up to" a character—John Wayne was most often filmed from a low angle, giving him a superior position appropriate to his role as hero. It can also "overlook" a person or place, such as the positioning of camera angles to "look down on" Indian camps or women of any race.

The "Frontier"

The most common motifs in the western genre owe their genesis to the ideas articulated by Fredrick Jackson Turner in 1893. In a paper delivered to the American Historical Association, he presented his "Frontier Thesis." It was based on prevalent ideas of the late nineteenth century regarding social progress and evolution in which the Native American was presented as an obstacle to the civilizing of the continent, a stage in the evolution of human society that preceded agrarian development, which in turn would lead to full-fledged urban civilization.[4]

Turner described the settling of the West as the experience that, more than any other, formed American identity. It was the proving ground where civilization met the wilderness and overcame it with courage, ingenuity, and self-reliance. This idea of what the frontier represented was so pervasive that it found itself naturally at home in history textbooks across the nation for much of the twentieth century. For most Americans, the frontier was cherished as a locus of ultimate challenge, a right of passage through which the civilized white American male earned his superior position on the continent and in the world. This is at least part of the reason westerns have historically been most popular when poverty and unemployment were at their worst.[5] During the Depression, for example, the landless, moneyless, and hopeless could lose themselves in a fantasy of a time when all it took to "make it" was hard work and courage.

Turner's thesis represents a set of values that did not take into consideration the very real and fundamental differences in the American—white and Indian—experience and landscape. The Turneresque nature of the western genre in novels and film clearly positions the American Indian as the savage (bloodthirsty or otherwise) who is part of the wilderness that civilization must overcome in order to bring order to a wild continent.

Social historians have begun to rethink this view and to define the term *frontier* not as the last outpost of civilization but rather as the shifting point of contact between cultures. As Alfonso Ortiz notes, "we must remind each new generation that one culture's frontier may be another culture's backwater or backyard."[6]

Given the pervasiveness of the frontier mythos, it is likely that the western films of the first half of the twentieth century would lack accuracy and subtlety in their portrayal of Native peoples. The fundamental importance of that misportrayal is that it is tied to the formulation of the American myth and the development of the all-American hero.

National Policy in the Early Twentieth Century

While Hollywood was inventing and reinventing the celluloid Indian, Native peoples were experiencing the effects of a series of changes in U.S. federal policy. In 1924 the Indian Citizenship Act gave U.S. citizenship to every Native American born on U.S. property. In 1928 the Institute for Government Research (Brookings Institution) published the Meriam Report, which for over twenty years was regarded by lawmakers as a trustworthy description of the Indian situation. One of the major tenets of the report was that American Indians "wish to remain Indians, to preserve what they have inherited from their fathers. . . . In this desire they are supported by intelligent, liberal whites who find real merit in their art, music, religion, form of government, and other things which may be covered by the broad term *culture*."[7]

During the Roosevelt administration, Collier became Commissioner of the Bureau of Indian Affairs, and he promoted his own views of what the American Indian needed. He battled Congress, the bureaucrats, the missionaries, and even the Native Americans who disagreed with his liberal though paternalistic ideas. He and his supporters developed one of the most important pieces of legislation to pass in Congress during the first four decades of the twentieth century, the Wheeler-Howard Act of 1934, also known as the Indian Reorganization Act. The result of a long fight, this act reversed the policy of allotment and encouraged tribal organization. In his *Annual Report of the Commissioner of Indian Affairs* in 1934, Collier referred to the act as "repair work" and pointed out that "Congress and the President recognized that the cumulative loss of land brought about by the allotment system, a loss reaching ninety million acres—two-thirds of the land heritage of the Indian race in 1887—had robbed the Indians in large part of the necessary basis for self-support."[8] The Wheeler-Howard Act provided the mechanisms for tribal governments to organize and interact with state and federal governments and was a significant step forward in Native American self-rule.

That the Wheeler-Howard Act made its way into law, given the conflicted attitudes about American Indians during the 1920s, can be partially explained by the Depression. Great numbers of Euro-Americans found themselves in an economic no-man's-land or worse, and this engendered more sympathy for the disenfranchised Native Americans. In addition, it seemed that the American ideals of individualism and the power of civilized, industrial society had failed, and the preconceptions held of the noble savage began to make a kind of sense.

Still, the 1934 Indian Congress (called by Collier to explain the Wheeler-Howard Act) met with biased news reporting that must have had an impact on public attitudes. Journalism historian Mary Ann Weston noted that when the three-day meeting was distilled into a short report in *Time*, for example, "the delegates became relics of the past who 'shuffled' into Rapid City, made camp 'not in clay-painted buffalo hide wikiups, but in closed government school buildings' and met 'not crouched around council fires but seated in armchairs in an oak-paneled room.'" That article goes on to report that "'[t]hree hundred years of suspicion stared from his copper-skinned listeners' eyes' as Collier urged the Indians to support the New Deal. Collier was quoted at length, but the Indians were not."[9]

It would appear that in the 1930s, views of Native Americans continued to be distorted and mutable, ranging from sympathetic or empathetic to hostile. If articles like the one in *Time* are any indication, the general public still thought of Native Americans as shuffling, red-skinned primitives more at home in a tent than a house. At best they were looked on nostalgically, as relics of the past. In 1933 *Parents Magazine* printed an article advising parents to let their children "play Indian" because the values of Indian life were good ones, but the entire article was written referring to the American Indian in the past tense. The same year *Scientific American* ran an article entitled "The Disappearance of the Red Man's Culture" which sadly reported that "the Indian is now a creature of the past, who can be studied mostly in books and museums."[10]

A Question of Real Estate

In *The Legacy of Conquest*, Patricia Limerick wrote, "If Hollywood wanted to capture the emotional center of Western history, its movies would be about real estate. John Wayne would have been neither a gunfighter nor a sheriff, but a surveyor, speculator, or claims lawyer." She makes the point that the intersection of races and the allocation of property unified Western history, since that history has been an "ongoing competition for legitimacy—for the right to claim for oneself and sometimes for one's group the status of legitimate beneficiary of Western resources."[11]

The quest for land was from the first a primary motivation for immigration to the continent, and it is the idea that everyone can own a piece of America that has made the American national identity so unique. In the western movie, the necessary obstacle against which the hero struggles in the acquisition of his "rightful" place is the American Indian, who happened to have been keeping the seat warm for twenty thousand years or so. The western movie accurately if unintentionally displays the mental gymnastics the settlers and pioneers had to perform in order to declare the land their own.

The first requirement for validation of land seizure is that the land be empty. That was no problem, since a large portion of the western United States was inhabited by nomadic tribes that followed the buffalo in portable housing. That Indians in the Southwest had been successful agrarians for thousands of years was perhaps the most difficult fact to rationalize, but the tribes in the East and Southeast had also been settled farmers, so there was precedence at least. Native groups had complex cultural traditions, but they were oral-based, so Natives were perceived by many as effectively having no history at all. The land they lived on was thus a historyless land, and therefore the white settlers could give the land not only purpose but also historical ties—in short, civilization.

Allegheny Uprising (1939)

Though impressive, the land depicted in westerns is often arid or wild and therefore of little value as "raw" land. The value, then, lies in the sacrifice and hard work poured into the land by the settlers. In films such as William Seiter's *Allegheny Uprising*, starring John Wayne, the appropriation of the land is justified by the labor invested by the settler who has made the uncharted wilderness his home and assumed his position as the "natural" proprietor. The land becomes the fruit of his labor, and his physical and emotional investments give him a moral right to it.

In Seiter's film, the uprising in the Allegheny Mountains at first appears to be an Indian uprising. The hero and his sidekick have been captured by Indians and been living with them as "blood brothers" for three years while the English and French battle each other for the new land. On the hero's return, we find that he is the finest Indian *fighter* of them all, that he refers to his "blood brothers" as painted devils, and that he echoes the disdain of his friend, who says the only trustworthy Indian is a dead Indian. When the local Indians make their only appearance in the film—after we hear they have killed a whole settlement and scalped a schoolroom full of children—the hero leads the chase. The white pursuers paint their faces and chests with bear grease and charcoal, smear some ridiculous looking war paint over that, and don some scarves to cover their heads. Looking more like pirates than Indians, off they go to rescue two captive children. The Indians in this film are not very intelligent, and as they wade along knee deep in the river, the hero and his band jump them from trees in what looks like a parody of Cooper's Stupid Indian Tricks. That is the last we see of the Indians.

Again, the white hero is able to "out-Indian" the Indians, becoming a superior form of native fighter and supplanting the "vanishing" Indian. In *Allegheny Uprising*, the Indians serve to present a real danger, are firmly placed as inferior, savage beings undeserving of the land, and then conveniently disappear while the community fights its own allies, the British, for control of the land.

Allegheny Uprising is an interesting display of colonialism at work. The heroic settlers are colonists and imperialists, but they are fighting the representatives of the mother country, which also presents them as the colonized. The historical layers of colonialism are transparent, as are the early to mid–twentieth century attitudes, prejudices, and stereotypes woven through the film.

The Euro-American Hero and "American" Land

John Wayne is one of America's favorite heroes, well recognized as the quintessential American male during the whole of his long career. His

2. From William Seiter's *Allegheny Uprising* (1939). Photo Museum of Modern Art Film Stills Archive; courtesy of RKO Radio Pictures, Inc.

on-screen persona made him a hero, and that persona was initially developed in the western. As Louis Owens has commented, "[t]he essential truth about the great American hero, however, is its falseness. And that falseness is illuminated brilliantly in the shape-shifting that allowed a young Iowan named Marion Morrison [John Wayne] to journey into the mythical American West and become something grand and new and strangely pure."[12]

This new American hero was idolized, suggesting he embodied the values mainstream America held most dear, and his attitudes, including those regarding American Indians, were generally indicative of the attitudes of the majority of white citizens. His attitude toward American Indians can be summed up in his own words during a *Playboy* interview: "I don't feel we did wrong in taking this great country away from them. There were great numbers of people who needed new land, and the Indians were selfishly trying to keep it for themselves."[13] This is an interesting attitude for a man, or a nation, that feels not only a right but a duty to protect *his/its* ownership of the land.

For many Euro-Americans, land that was not in some way used was wasted. To use land properly, one should invest oneself in that land, make something of it, as did the settlers in *Allegheny Uprising*. Here, the mainstream idealization of the private family farm is presented as obviously superior to the Indian attitude toward land, where all was held communally. The general assumption was that the Indian was not using the land properly and therefore dispossession was not only inevitable but also righteous.

The concept of land as property is one of the fundamental ideas upon which the American ideal of freedom is based. If one *owns* the land one lives upon, security is nearly absolute. Since American Indians had not generally adhered to the principles of individual ownership, their claims were easily ignored and the settling of the West became a heroic enterprise. As Virginia Wexman points out,

> [T]he Western understands possession of the land as an integral part of its theme of dynastic progression, for land is seen both as a place that binds the family together as a physical unit and a source of wealth that binds them together as an economic unit. Significantly, the production of Westerns languished during the 1930s, when the ideal of the family on the land was seriously endangered by the economic hardship to farmers brought about by the Depression. By contrast, the heyday of the sound Western occurred during the 1950s, when the development of suburbia was fed by the nostalgic fantasy of the family on the land that the Western promoted.[14]

Since land was imperative to the settlers, and since that land was not actually empty but occupied by hundreds of different peoples, it was necessary, not only in the actual westward movement but also in the depiction of that movement in the western film, to provide some way of exculpating the ambitions of those settlers. From the nineteenth to the mid-twentieth century, a theory that helped support that exculpation was "scientific racism."

Scientific Racism

This view divided the people of the world into three separate and distinct "races" according to those phenotypical appearances observable to the naked eye. The three races were dubbed Caucasian (white), Negroid (black), and Mongoloid (red, yellow, and brown), and use of these divisions replaced the cumbersome and often vexing problems associated with differences—Otherness—due to religion, culture, and environment. Differences that appeared biological and natural were much easier to distinguish and manipulate.[15]

The "scientific" basis of this approach downplayed the historical role of ambition and greed as motivating factors and provided a seemingly empirical foundation to the nostalgic views of many Americans. Instead of approaching the American Indian relativistically as another ethnicity or culture, the more "scientific" term, *race*, explained differences and helped vindicate Darwinistic ranking. According to Social Darwinism, the fittest survive, and those who do not survive become extinct because they are incapable of evolving, and even Francis Parkman once believed the Indian unchangeable. He said,

> [S]ome races of men seem molded in wax, soft and melting, at once plastic and feeble. Some races, like some metals, combine the greatest flexibility with the greatest strength. But the Indian is hewn of rock. You cannot change the form without destruction of the substance. Such, at least, has too often proved the case. Races of inferior energy have possessed a power of expansion and assimilation to which he is a stranger; and it is this fixed and rigid quality which has proved his ruin. He will not learn the arts of civilization, and he and his forest must perish together."[16]

Almost one hundred years after Parkman's lament many Americans, if they weren't convinced that Natives had indeed perished, saw them as immutable, forever stuck in the nineteenth century.

A vast majority of the Mexican population is *mestizo*, of mixed Spanish and Indian blood,[17] and therefore they, too, were classified as Mongoloid. Attitudes toward Mexicans and Indians were often similar, as exemplified in the testimony of a Los Angeles Sheriff's deputy during a 1943 murder trial, recounted by Wexman: "The Sheriff's deputy identified the Mexican defendants as Indian and went on to state that 'the Indian, from Alaska to Patagonia, is evidently oriental in background. At least he shows many of the oriental characteristics, especially so in his utter disregard for the value of life.' He concluded that such qualities were 'biological—one cannot change the spots of a leopard.'"[18]

One could make a good case for this attitude resulting as much from exposure to western films as exposure to scientific racism, and it is difficult to determine when or if this view produced the western, or westerns began producing this view. In either case, by the time sound films became the norm, Indians had almost completely ceased to be depicted as mistreated, noble savages. With the sound western came an on-slaught of celluloid Indian attacks that reinforced the attitudes of view-ers such as the Los Angeles sheriff's deputy.

Owens makes the point that the dominant culture (in this case the white filmmaker) has had no way of really knowing the Native Other and is "not capable of sincerely questioning the epistemological foun-dations of the dominant cultural center . . . and simply cannot compre-hend that 'other' way of knowing."[19] This is the problem with most western films from the first half of the twentieth century. There was lit-tle or no in depth questioning of the rectitude of Euro-American na-tional identity, the stereotypes it manufactures for its Others, or the effects of its inventions. The Indian is defeated before the film begins because Indian and white are allowed to connect, usually violently, but never overlap. Such is the requirement and effects of manifest destiny and the cultural frontier. The celluloid Indians could not be allowed to win. They had to remain consciously Other, and they had to in one or many ways be held as inferior. As Churchill quotes film director Stephan Feraca saying in 1964, "Now those movie Indians wearing all those feathers can't come out as human beings. They're not expected to come out as human beings because I think the American people do not regard them as wholly human. We must remember that many, many American children believe that feathers grow out of Indian heads."[20]

Frozen Time and Pseudo-History

Most films made in America that portray Indians are set in the nine-teenth century. Virtually all westerns take place between 1825 and 1880, a period of fifty-five years, a minute part of a history that goes back thousands of years. There is no pre-white world in these films, and, conversely, rarely a "modern" Indian.

The "pseudo-history" of American Indians is, as Alfonso Ortiz has stated, "so at odds with the facts that Indians often simply ignore it."[21] Ignoring it has been the response until the recent past because Native Americans have had few opportunities to give voice to a counterdis-course of liberation.

The stereotypes fueling this pseudo-history were so ludicrous that most Native American actors of the early westerns found them hu-morous. In 1944 Twentieth Century Fox made the movie *Buffalo Bill*, and Navajos were brought from Tuba City, Arizona, to the Utah mountains to play Cheyennes and Sioux. In a 1944 review, James Denton reported on their activities:

> The Indians lined up before the wardrobe tent, and costumes were handed out. They had to be shown how to wear the feathered head-dress, leather breeches, and fringed leather shirts. They didn't think this was the kind of thing to wear in that summer heat, but they put their costumes on uncomplainingly.
>
> When it came time to have the war paint smeared on their faces by the makeup experts from Hollywood, the Navahos [*sic*] objected at first. They thought this was a bit thick and that Hollywood was overdoing the thing. . . . They laughed and joked over their costumes. . . . When Chief Thundercloud [Cherokee actor Victor Daniels] explained a torture scene in the picture, wherein the Cheyenne proved his bravery by having his back cut, the Navahos [*sic*] laughed uproariously; they thought such action was downright nonsense. There is nothing stoic about the Navahos [*sic*]. They do not bear pain with fortitude nor do they practice self-torture as a sign of bravery.[22]

John Price describes the development of the pseudo-history of white/Indian interaction as a "movie story told by white American producers and directors to a white North American audience, assuming and building the plot from anti-Indian attitudes and prejudices."[23] Native Americans became part of the landscape as the history of the West became an allegorical history, and the western became a system of symbols supporting a fictional history. The American filmmakers did what thousands of years of social evolution and the threat of white encroachment could not do; they created an homogenized Indian.[24]

Northwest Passage (1940)

Americans of the forties and fifties rarely overtly questioned the images Hollywood provided of the American Indian, and movies with slaughters of and by Native Americans were so accepted that they were used to teach children in public schools. For instance, the 1940 film *Northwest Passage* was chosen by the Department of Secondary Teachers of the National Education Association for study because "Rogers [of Rogers' Rangers] comes to personify man's refusal to bow to physical forces, and the success of this hardy band of early pioneers symbolizes our own struggle against bitter enemies in the modern world."[25] The *Photoplay Studies* guide for teachers deals with the novel and its adaptation to the screen, gives some "inside scoop" on the making of the film, and then offers suggestions for using the film in English, history, art, geography, and even in clothing and shop classes.

According to the teacher's guide, *Northwest Passage* is the story of a band of patriotic Americans as they march from Crown Point in New England to the Native village of St. Francis in Canada:

> As this expedition extended from September 13, 1759, to October 31 of the same year, it covers only a very small period of the French and Indian War. However, its military importance was great. From this little Indian town yearly came those horrible attacks upon the New England settlers when so many defenseless farmers and their families were killed or captured. This victory opened the entire interior of New England and promised safety to the pioneers who settled in the rich valleys. . . . Mr. Roberts [author of *Northwest Passage*] has succeeded where so many American writers have failed, for he has more freshness and real humanity in his major characters than most chroniclers. Through his fine assortment of types among his minor characters we glimpse early American characteristics of which we are rightfully proud.[26]

The characters that the guide suggests rightfully deserve praise are men who are in the service of their country; however, as depicted in the film, many (such as the second lead, played by Robert Young) were evidently inducted while drunk. They are attired in colored, fringed buckskin, so they obviously admire the dress if not the culture of the Native Americans enough to appropriate their identities to a large degree, and they look upon their attack on the village as a righteous act. One pioneer even finds a pair of moccasins in the ruins and puts them on his own feet with great glee and no pangs of conscience. They liberate the proverbial white woman captive, and then they burn the village to the ground.

With the exception of the inarticulate guide whom Rogers (Spencer Tracy) is trying to sober up when we first meet him, the Indians are presented as the usual bloodthirsty bunch of heathen devils who get what they deserve for attacking innocent settlers. The only other individual Indian we meet is the boy Rogers "saves" and who becomes part of the group on the trip home. The boy, of course, comes to admire his white saviors, even though he has seen them kill his relatives and burn his home.

To encourage English teachers to use the film in their classes, the *Photoplay Studies* guide quotes the author of *Northwest Passage*, Kenneth

Roberts: "I have a theory that history can be most effectively told in the form of fiction, because only in the writing of fiction that stands the test of truth do falsities come to the surface." It is small wonder that Native Americans either laughed at the images, ignored them, or sat in stunned silence. That their ancestors were used as metaphors for Hitler's Nazis, whom many Native Americans were then fighting, would do little to bolster pride in Native heritage.

In 1940 Americans were especially interested in those "American characteristics" to which the guide refers because World War II was stressing the limits of American physical, emotional, and economic resources, and patriotism and bravery were held as the ultimate American virtues.

Native Americans and World War II

American Indian heroism during the war made it more difficult to think of Native peoples as the savages of *Northwest Passage*. Men such as Major General Clarence Tinker, the Navajo code talkers, and Ira Hayes, who was photographed raising the flag with five others on Iwo Jima, elevated to heroic stature American Indian soldiers in the armed services, which numbered as many as twenty-five thousand Native men and women by the war's end. However, important dimensions of the old stereotypes still prevailed, with the negative image of the blood-thirsty savage becoming positive now that these Americans were employed in defense of the United States.

In 1944 Secretary of the Interior Harold L. Ickes wrote an article for *Collier's* in which he reported that "[t]he Indian . . . has endurance, rhythm, a feeling for timing, co-oordination, sense perception, an uncanny ability to get over any sort of terrain at night, and better than all else, an enthusiasm for fighting."[27] A *Reader's Digest* article from the previous year described the American Indian soldier in similar terms: "The red soldier is tough. Usually he has lived outdoors all his life, and lived by his senses; he is a natural Ranger. He takes to Commando fighting with gusto. . . . At ambushing, scouting, signaling, sniping, [Indians are] peerless. Some can smell a snake yards away and hear the faintest movement; all endure thirst and lack of food better than the average white man."[28]

These descriptions might have been humorous to Native Americans, especially those from Chicago or Los Angeles, unless of course they found themselves in combat under the command of an officer who believed they had *inherited* the ability to smell snakes or see in the dark.

Playing Indian

The homogenized, packaged Indian stereotypes in the films of the forties and fifties, though bearing little relation to reality, were rather interesting in their own right. Because the Plains Indians were well known as warriors, much of the Hollywood Indian's outfit was a costume designer's interpretation of what a Plains warrior would have worn.

The typical Hollywood Indian man of the forties and fifties wore a long, flowing, feathered headdress, a breech cloth (with swimming trunks underneath, of course), and moccasins, and he wielded a fierce-looking tomahawk. His sister the Indian Princess wore a long, beaded and fringed buckskin dress and a beaded headband with one feather sticking straight up in the back. They lived in a tipi, and he hunted buffalo—or settlers—and carved totem poles while she picked berries, slaved away at the buffalo hides, or fashioned pottery. A man described as Sioux might have been found wearing a Navajo blanket over his chest plate, carrying weapons from a northeastern tribe, wearing an Apache bandanna, and standing in front of a northwestern tribe's totem pole.

These individual details of the celluloid Indian were obviously not all figments of a Hollywood imagination. Most of them could be found somewhere in the five hundred separate cultures, but Hollywood was the only place where the whole simulacrum came together.

Native American actors have always had difficulty with these odd, syncretic depictions offered by Hollywood, and they have made their uneasiness known in different ways. Today's actors are often very vocal about what they will and will not do in terms of authenticity, but even in the early days, the actors at times let their feelings be known. Sometimes it was with humor, the sort that is packed with subtext. For instance, John del Valle wrote in the *New York Herald Tribune* on 17 November 1940:

> Since De Mille set the pace with his first filming in 1912–13 of "The Squaw Man"[29] as Hollywood's first feature picture, the red man has had more than his share of work. . . . This offers an anthropological aspect which might not have been anticipated; Hollywood has acquired a permanent colony of representatives of almost all tribes still extant. With the cinema as their melting pot, these expatriates are taking on the semblance of a tribe all their own—perhaps the largest tribal group not on any reservation. One among them, a stalwart of

Cherokee blood known professionally as Chief Thunder Cloud [Victor Daniels], who plays a Cree war chief in "North West Mounted Police," has taken the initiative. With a nucleus of eighteen, and an eligible list running into the hundreds, Thunder Cloud is applying to the Bureau of Indian Affairs for recognition of the "De Mille Indians" as a new tribe composed only of Indians who work for films.

Mr. del Valle evidently saw the humor in the proposition, but the irony of legislated legitimacy for a constructed reality seems to have escaped him.

They Died With Their Boots On (1941)

When Errol Flynn starred as George Armstrong Custer in *They Died With Their Boots On* in 1941, the conventions of invention for Indians in western films were already so deeply engrained that they were virtually unquestioned. As Crazy Horse rides down upon and kills Custer, the audience sees a savage killing machine mowing down a righteous and courageous "real American."

The story was an old one that every child had learned in school—the brave General Custer and his gallant men of the Seventh Cavalry were doing their duty, making America safe for white farmers and their families, when the dastardly Sioux ambushed them and murdered every man. In the film version, low-angle shots produced an image of a Custer of mythic stature, much like the many paintings of his famous last stand. According to a written transition in the film, Custer "cleared the plains for a ruthlessly spreading civilization that spelled doom for the Red Man." The "red man" in this film is represented by Anthony Quinn—who actually is of Tarahumara ancestry—as Crazy Horse, the only individualized Indian in the film, which mainly featured hordes rushing over the Little Big Horn or standing as backdrop for the hero's actions. That Crazy Horse was given any humanity or understandable motivation was very likely done to give the hero, Custer, an adversary worthy of his attention and make his death more tragic and meaningful. The point of films such as *They Died With Their Boots On* was not to tell a new story; it was to reaffirm the righteousness of the nineteenth-century American hero and showcase his heroism against an obvious evil. That evil was conveniently represented by the American Indian because the question of who was right or who would win had been definitively answered. It was "history."

Robert Stam observed in a discussion of *Rambo* (1987) that the film is a "rightest and racist discourse designed to flatter and nourish masculine fantasies of omnipotence characteristic of an empire in crisis."[30] The same could be said of *They Died With Their Boots On*. It was made just before the United States entered World War II, when "masculine fantasies of omnipotence" were selling very well indeed. In November 1941 a reviewer for *Variety* described the film as a "surefire western, an escape from bombers, tanks and Gestapo . . . American to the last man." America of the 1940s was deeply immersed in the war, and filmmakers were producing movies that offered escape from that reality while defining ever more clearly what it was to be an American hero. In much the same way Buffalo Bill's *The Indian Wars* bolstered the American confidence in the righteousness and bravery of the American male entering World War I, *They Died With Their Boots On*, like *Northwest Passage*, portrayed the larger-than-life, courageous, and honorable American male for an America about to charge through another world war.

Stagecoach (1939)

The *Variety* review quoted above said that "In westerns . . . major errors in history and persons . . . mean little to producers or audiences. The test of the yarn is not its accuracy but its speed and excitement."[31] For speed, excitement, and individual fabrication of the American myth, no one surpassed John Ford. His classic western, *Stagecoach*, is an encyclopedia of innovative filmmaking. Many of his sequences, particularly those with fast action, have been duplicated so many times by so many (generally lesser) filmmakers that they have become clichés of American cinema.

As a stagecoach races across the vast expanse of Monument Valley (Ford's all-purpose western setting that stands in for the New Mexico high desert), the scene is shot from a high angle that makes the little island of rambling humanity seem extremely vulnerable. We know that a band of cutthroat Indians is about to attack the stagecoach and that it belongs to Geronimo, because we've already seen the burned-out ranch and the dead white woman, and we've been told that "You're all going to be scalped and massacred by that old butcher, Geronimo." The Indians appear in a low-angle shot as the dangerous villains, and the tension mounts with a closeup of Geronimo (Chief White Horse). Ford's crosscutting of shots builds the tension in the scene as an arrow out of nowhere hits a passenger in the stage and the chase begins. To film the scene, a camera was mounted on a truck that raced alongside the stage-coach at high speed, creating breathless excitement for that early audience. Shots of the speeding stage were crosscut with shots of the passengers within as the white men bravely fought off the attack. Ford's artistic use of the exterior camera was inspired; the filming of the Apaches in low-angle shots showed just how hard they were hitting the ground.

It was apparently irrelevant to audiences that the Apaches would have had to travel for miles across open country to reach the stage-coach—judging by the establishing long shot—and would have been heard long before the arrow appears out of nowhere; or that the archer—apparently the only one in the picture who doesn't have a rifle—would have had to be fairly close to hit the stage. Speed and action were important, not reality, so it was also possible for the hero to knock two Indians off their horses at the same time. The point was not to show a realistic altercation but to show the stagecoach's microcosm of civilized society (with its paradoxes and contradictions) saved by the classic western hero. Ford noted that it would not have done for the Indians to shoot the lead horses instead of firing madly into the air because, "it would have been the end of the picture,"[32] and that's a hard argument to refute.

The film's hero, Ringo (John Wayne), is the ultimate westering hero who carries his own brand of justice, battles against formidable odds, and gets the girl. He has just escaped from prison, where he has been unjustly held while his brother's murderers are living it up in Lordsburg. While the tension over the impending confrontation with the murderers builds, the hero is given the opportunity to prove his worth. He is more than kind to the prostitute (Claire Trevor), whom the others shun, revealing his innocence and his egalitarian value system. During the full-scale attack, he climbs on top of the stage to kill Indians and then jumps onto the rigging between galloping horses to guide the stage, proving his selfless courage. This is all made easier by inept Apaches, who seem incapable of hitting anything except by accident, while every shot fired by a white man not only kills the Indian but knocks his horse to the ground.

Once white valor has been verified, the Indians simply disappear. The frontier having been crossed, the Indians vanish into the landscape, a part of the hostile world only the white hero can tame. While this may be an oversimplification of Ford's accomplishment in *Stagecoach*, it is a fair assessment of the use he made of the Apaches in the

3. From John Ford's *Stagecoach* (1939). Photo Museum of Modern Art Film Stills Archive; courtesy of United Artists.

film. As he stated in a 1928 essay entitled "Veteran Producer Muses," "the director who strives too hard to represent humanity by rubbing down the rough edges of racial and personal traits is likely to make his work drab and colorless."[33]

National Policy of the 1950s

For a while during the thirties and early forties, at least on the surface, it looked as if Native Americans were beginning to receive some respect from the government, if not Hollywood. However, in 1953 House Concurrent Resolution 108 passed, ushering in the Termination era. The resolution, which passed with unanimous votes in both houses, simply "terminated" all tribes within California, Florida, Texas, and New York, as well as the Flatheads of Montana, the Klamaths of Oregon, the Menominees of Wisconsin, the Potowatamies of Kansas and Nebraska, and the Chippewas from the Turtle Mountain Reservation in North Dakota. The idea was that "Indians within the territorial limits of the United States should assume their full responsibilities as American citizens . . . freed from Federal supervision and control and from all disabilities and limitations specially applicable to Indians." The resolution also terminated all agencies set up to serve these people. "[U]pon the release of such tribes and individual members thereof from such disabilities and limitation, all offices of the Bureau of Indian Affairs in the States of California, Florida, New York and Texas and all other offices of the Bureau of Indian Affairs whose primary purpose was to serve any Indian tribe or individual Indian freed from Federal supervision should be abolished."[34] Senator Watkins, the resolution's chief promoter, referred to it as "affirmative action." He felt that terminating the tribal unit would "free" the American Indians and likened the resolution to the Emancipation Proclamation.[35] The national government had effectively overturned the Wheeler-Howard Act and had reverted to the assimilationist policies of the previous century. Whereas the "good Indian" of the twenties was one in contact with the mystical and the natural, in the fifties the best Indians were those that had assimilated. As a *Christian Science Monitor* article noted, "The picturesque, beaded, feathered, and quaint American Indian has just about vanished from the lands of his ancestors. In his place stands Mr. Indian, modern American citizen. Clad in a business suit, his keen black eyes view the passing scene with growing understanding and appreciation."[36]

Termination meant the loss of trust status for the land that went on tax rolls, and American Indian complaints that the land was theirs by right of treaty and therefore not taxable went unheeded. Therefore, much Native land eventually "reverted" to the U.S. government due to unpaid taxes. The resolution also meant the end of tribal government for the 109 tribes and bands with whom Congress terminated its relationship. Many of these tribes had high degrees of stability, tribal constitutions, and a strong desire for self-sufficiency. The aim of the termination program, assimilation into mainstream America, was antipodal to the aim of these tribes to remain cohesive cultural and legislative bodies with power to govern themselves. Matters were made worse by another 1953 law, Public Law 280, that had a tremendous impact on Native self-determination. This law extended state jurisdiction over offenses committed by or against Native Americans in "Indian country," effectively dissolving self-rule by tribes and bands.[37]

The fifties also saw the policy of "relocation" put into effect. Seventeen to twenty thousand Native Americans from reservations were moved to urban areas in twenty different states, with Los Angeles and Chicago receiving most of the relocatees. The government paid their transportation and assisted them until they got settled. News reports of the day ran from an "optimistic" *Saturday Evening Post* article, "Indian Reservations May Some Day Run Out of Indians," to the opposite, in which American Indians were portrayed as victims of a government plot to steal their lands.[38] The end result encouraged the general perception that, for better or worse, Native peoples were indeed vanishing into the melting pot. One way or the other, the effect relocation had on Native cultures and individual Native American families is difficult to overestimate.

With the "termination" of whole tribes and the assumed assimilation of the Native American peoples, it is somewhat understandable that many in the American viewing public might think of the American Indian as a relic from centuries past. The laws above probably seemed like mere Congressional housekeeping chores and the American Indians involved probably seemed like far distant relatives to the "authentic" savages of prior centuries.

The Malleable Metaphor

In post–World War II America, life was good once more. Americans were spending their $140 billion of war-time savings on new cars and television sets (twenty thousand per day by the mid-fifties), and the new suburbs were giving individual Americans a piece of ground they could call their very own. Science and technology offered solutions to old problems like polio and poverty. Religion was a big seller, with Norman Vincent Peale's *The Power of Positive Thinking* riding the crest of the best-seller list and the Reverend Billy Graham a frequent Eisenhower White House guest. Congress attached the phrase "under God" to the Pledge of Allegiance, and Hollywood star Jane Russell said that once you got to know God, "you find He's a Livin' Doll."[39] However, by the early fifties, concern about the possibility of the non-Christian Communists provoking a nuclear war was sending children scooting under desks in bomb drills, and the Cold War was on.[40]

One result of the fear of Communism in America was McCarthyism, a political phenomenon that included but grew larger than the man for whom it was named, Senator Joe McCarthy. Congressional committees were set up to investigate anti-American activities, and blacklists were developed. Among the blacklisted were artists such as Lillian Hellman, Victor Navasky, Charlie Chaplin, Zero Mostel, Abraham Polonsky, and Dalton Trumbo. One result of the blacklists in Hollywood was the shock of suddenly finding oneself among the oppressed. Films of the fifties, therefore, ran the gamut from racist, political propaganda to a type of enlightenment not seen in Hollywood since the days of the early silent films.

As Ralph and Natasha Friar noted about Native Americans in film, "The worst ally and the best enemy the Indians could have is a sympathetic friend."[41] Beginning in the fifties, that was also true of those in Hollywood who were suddenly the American Indians' "friends." As Native Americans became the all-purpose metaphor for any and all oppressed people, Native American identities and histories were buried ever more deeply.

When Hollywood found itself under attack, the film industry reacted by producing films with a startling degree of tolerance. In order to make a point about other types of humanity and their equality to those in power, the filmmakers turned once more to American Indians. It was a logical choice, since filmmakers knew their audiences expected Hollywood Indians to be bloodthirsty savages. Presenting an Indian who was also a respectable human was a good way for filmmakers to shake up preconceptions without getting blacklisted themselves. A significant depiction of this sort is Delmer Daves's *Broken Arrow*.

Broken Arrow (1950)

Consistently cited as an example of burgeoning cultural awareness in Hollywood, *Broken Arrow* was prompted in part by resistance to McCarthyism. Stereotypes were reinvestigated and cultural norms, such as the righteousness of manifest destiny, were questioned. The film even made an attempt to create multidimensional human beings who were Apaches—an unusual idea in Hollywood—but five decades of one-dimensional stereotypes still cast their shadows over *Broken Arrow*.

Jeff Chandler's Cochise is a kind, humane leader with intelligence and military talent—a startling change from the typical portrayal of an Indian chief. He speaks standard English, without "ughs" and without the characteristically rigid body language or fierce scowl. However, Tom Jeffords (James Stewart) states in a voice-over at the beginning that the story will be told in English for the benefit of the audience. Since the conversations between Jeffords and Cochise are understood to be in Apache, it is no surprise that Cochise would be articulate. What is surprising is that the white Jeffords picks up fluent Apache so easily. This is skirting dangerously close to what Bakhtin calls pseudo-poly-

phonic discourse, interpreted by Robert Stam as "one which marginal-
izes and disempowers certain voices and then pretends to undertake a
dialogue with a puppetlike entity that has already been forced to make
crucial compromises."[42] Cochise's voice is not heard in its full force and
resonance, and the interaction in *Broken Arrow* does not consist of a true
polyphony, one that strives to eliminate the inequities and show cultural difference in a positive light. It does, however, at least allow an
American Indian man to speak articulately, with humor, and with some
force. If nothing else, Chandler's Cochise is undeniably human.

The villains in *Broken Arrow* are not the Indians, even though Geronimo (Jay Silverheels) does not want peace, as do Cochise and Jeffords.
The greedy, violent white men are the bad guys in this film, and by the
end of the picture, it is logical even for a Euro-American audience to
think that maybe Geronimo was right, after all. The suggested change
in attitude is made very clear in the film. Jeffords states at the beginning, "I learned something that day. Apache women cried over their
sons and Apache men had a sense of fair play."

Daves also presents Cochise's military skill for the audience to admire. He outfoxes the cavalry officers who have cleverly hidden soldiers in a wagon, and the company is virtually wiped out, except for
General Howard, who becomes a great fan of Cochise. This is very unlike the depictions of Indians as inept fighters in previous films, films in
which they could be defeated by a pack of Boy Scouts (*Scouts to the Rescue*, 1939) or even held off by a woman wielding a pea-shooter (*Bad
Bascomb*, 1946). The Indians in *Broken Arrow* are a force to be reckoned
with, but they can also be reasoned with.

The Apaches are seen as human and noble, but the idea of miscegenation gets the same old treatment. Tom Jeffords falls immediately in
love with Sonseeahray, played by a darkened and contact-lensed Debra
Paget. They are married in a ritual that includes the slicing of wrists and
mixing of blood, an occurrence more likely found in children's pacts
than Indian cultures, and they are deliriously happy. However, they are
ambushed by villainous whites, and Sonseeahray is killed. Jeffords
rides off into the sunset, alone once more. It was a touching love story,
but it could not continue. The same will hold true in films made
through the 1980s and even the 1990s.

The Searchers (1956)

The Ford film that many critics hold up as his most influential is *The
Searchers*, made in the mid-fifties with John Wayne as the hero once

4. From Delmer Dave's *Broken Arrow* (1950). Photo Museum of Modern Art Film
Stills Archive; courtesy of Twentieth Century Fox.

again. More than any other filmmaker, Ford was responsible for the
ideas Americans had about Native Americans, and some critics see this
film as Ford's first attempt to straighten out the distorted portrayal he
had helped create. While it is possible to see the film that way, since it
has a happy ending, more or less, it still perpetuated attitudes about Native Americans that were far from positive.

The film presents the Indians as murderers who kidnap two young
white girls, not an unusual story for a western movie. The searchers are
Ethan Edwards (John Wayne), the uncle of the kidnapped girls, and
their mixed-blood, adopted brother, Martin Pawley (Jeffrey Hunter).
What makes this film particularly disturbing is the attitude of Wayne's
character. He treats the "half-breed" with disdain for most of the

movie, and his goal throughout the film is not to bring the girls back but to save them from their dishonor by killing them. We're left to wonder whether or not he actually does kill the older girl because only he finds her, and he tells the brother not to go look for her. He says this while repeatedly thrusting his knife into the sand as though to cleanse it. The implications of the language and body language are that the Indians have raped, tortured, and killed her, but given the uncle's attitude and his actions, it is not at all certain he didn't slit her throat himself. He is the ultimate Indian-hater.

The younger girl, Debbie (played by Lana and Natalie Wood), has a chance to grow up while the search for her continues for years. These are dedicated searchers. She becomes the wife of Chief Scar (Henry Brandon), the leader of the band of Comanches, and is apparently content to be so when her "saviors" arrive. Killing the chief is a matter of course, but the brother and uncle have an altercation when the uncle wants to shoot the girl to save her from the disgrace she now bears.

Unfortunately, Wayne's character is acting according to the general mores of the day. Some film critics think this was Ford's point, that the audience is supposed to find Wayne's attitude reprehensible and that the film is actually a revisionist western that shows the negative effects of racism. The fact remains, however, that an audience who had little cinematic exposure to favorable depictions of miscegenation would be hard pressed to find anything amiss in their favorite hero's views. As Stedman notes, "Regrettably, because he is John Wayne, because he is so untiringly skillful in the pursuit, his motivation dominates in building audience attitude. Against a bigger-than-life screen figure, the less fanatical approach of the younger partner cannot offer the balance it does in the novel." Even the horror an audience feels when watching the uncle try to shoot down the terrified Natalie Wood character cannot undo the blatantly racist ideas that set up the situation. No in-depth attempt to humanize the Comanches is made in the film, so the "climax of the film says only that at the moment of truth John Wayne cannot murder a *white* girl who is also a close relative."[43]

Miscegenation and Hollywood

Ford turned a harsh spotlight on miscegenation, a subject that from the beginning has haunted Indian and white sexual relationships in film. Laws regulating marriage between white men and Indian women were enacted as early as 1888,[44] and the issue, though generally not as blatantly addressed as in *The Searchers*, has received plenty of attention in

5. From John Ford's *The Searchers* (1956). Photo Museum of Modern Art Film Stills Archive; courtesy of Warner Brothers.

other Hollywood films. In fact, a formula of sorts was developed over the years that is only now beginning to be questioned.

Miscegenation, whether by choice or by force, was a scary proposition to audiences in the 1950s. Philip French sees films such as *The Searchers* as "expressing deep fears about the possible breakdown of American society in the face of an underlying drive toward anarchy and disintegration—a feeling that the inhabitants of America have a tenuous grasp upon their continent."[45] At the end of his life, twenty years before the making of *The Searchers*, Standing Bear of the Sioux voiced the same idea but from the Indian perspective. He said, "The white man does not understand the Indian for the reason that he does not understand America. He is too far removed from its formative processes. . . . The man from Europe is still a foreigner and an alien. And he still hates the man who questioned his path across the continent. But in the Indian the spirit of the land is still vested; it will be until other men are able to divine and meet its rhythm."[46]

Films such as *The Searchers* posed the question of whether or not the prisoners, the white women captured by Indians, could be rehabilitated and whether or not the seekers themselves would remain the same. Would exposure to the land and its inhabitants change them? While later films came up with more palatable choices than *The Searchers* did, most films from the early fifties showed an underlying anxiety about the solidity of American national identity and a need to protect that identity. The anxiety was caused in part by the McCarthy era's witch hunt atmosphere, which made belonging a virtue and difference a disgrace. The result was an interesting shift in the depiction of the film industry's all-purpose Other, the American Indian. For instance, Ford's *Two Rode Together* (1961) contains a plea for understanding for the poor unfortunates who have lived in captivity with the Indians and have been tainted by Indian life. The result is, as Stedman noted, that "*Two Rode Together* really preaches: 'Be kind to poison victims.' The poison itself is beyond consideration."[47]

In Hollywood's westerns, the ultimate solution for a sexual relationship between an Indian and a white was that the Indian would have to die. If the relationship, whether or not it included love, involved an Indian male and a white female, the Indian man must die, and the woman was ruined for life—to the point that she, too, was better off dead. Rather than give in to a sexual relationship, the woman was expected to kill herself; otherwise she was either crazy or a whore and definitely not welcome in the civilized world. If she produced an offspring, the "half-breed" was proof of her lack of virtue and was treated as an outcast. That a white woman might find an Indian man attractive and worthy was beyond thought. This pretty well sums up the ideas in *The Searchers*. The women are ruined or dead, and their mixed-blood (one-eighth Cherokee) foster brother is denigrated as a "breed."

On the other hand, if the relationship involves a white man and an Indian woman, the whole affair actually carries a romantic aura about it, although that relationship is also doomed, and the Indian woman will die, either at the hands of a villain (Indian or white) or by her own hand to save the man from death or humiliation—or sometimes simply inconvenience. In *Broken Arrow*, Sonseeahray's death is tragic but not unexpected. This, of course, implies a gender- as well as race-based value system.

The general assumption of filmmakers for the first three-quarters of a century of filmmaking has been that the male has the dominant role in a male-female relationship, but it was unthinkable that an Indian, even though male, might have dominance over a white woman. An Indian woman—usually a "princess"—could give herself to a white man, but a white woman could never give herself willingly to an Indian man. On the other hand, a white man would be naturally dominant over any Indian *or* any woman, so his seduction and/or love of an Indian woman is tragically romantic and provocative, forbidden perhaps, but therefore titillating.

4

Win Some and Lose Some: The 1960s and 1970s

One of the finest things about being an Indian is that people are always interested in you and your "plight." Other groups have difficulties, predicaments, quandaries, problems, or troubles. Traditionally, we Indians have had a "plight." – Vine Deloria Jr., *Custer Died for Your Sins*

And the Policy of the Day Is . . .

In 1961 the Task Force on Indian Affairs, commissioned by Secretary of the Interior Stewart Udall, issued a report that recommended a shift away from the policy of tribal termination in favor of greater self-determination for Native Americans. This followed the January 1961 preliminary report by the Commission on the Rights, Liberties, and Responsibilities of the American Indian, one of many reports on the subject of Native Americans issued in the early sixties that suggested new attention be given to the issues important to American Indians. The introduction to this report is interesting mostly in that it describes an American Indian value system as the commission perceived it: "Indians believe they have values worth preserving. These are sometimes stated in mystical terms and if related to the Supreme Being, are sometimes kept secret. Nonetheless they exist. Two examples out of many involve their idea of unity and their reverence for Mother Earth."[1] The examples they give are generalizations, but few American Indians would disagree with the gist. What is new here is that the commission itself seemed to value these attitudes.

During the 1960s, for a growing segment of society, particularly the younger generation, the idea of a "mystical" people who valued "unity" and lived in shared communities, who revered the Earth and her creatures and who were (apparently) naturally at peace was very attractive. The contrast between these attitudes and those of mainstream America—"The Establishment," which many young people saw as self-serving and becoming ever more deeply enmeshed in the Vietnam war—produced a longing to "be" American Indian. Communes based on what were thought to be Indian ways of life sprang up all over America. Not that this was necessarily a bad thing for the people who were trying a new way of thinking and living. It was, however, a nostalgic appropriation of homogenized Indian identity, generally that of a hundred years earlier, and it did little to help the causes of contemporary Native peoples.

Again, or perhaps still, America was experiencing a divided and polarized view of Native America. Many were drawn to the advertised mysticism of the American Indian, but others were disgusted by what they saw as a pagan lifestyle. Most of this, however, was focused not on Native Americans themselves but on the "anti-war," "love and peace" set and had little to do with actual Native Americans. Native American experience in the early 1960s was quite different from either of these perceptions.

Native Americans, many of whom had enlisted voluntarily, were dying in Vietnam. At home they were fighting other battles in the courts, on reservations, and in urban communities. A large number of cases were filed against termination and relocation policies. As American Indians moved away from poverty-stricken reservations, tribal cultures were at risk. At the same time, civil rights issues had become a major focus of the media and of legislators, and Native Americans were beginning to be considered one of the oppressed minorities in America.

It was in this climate that in June 1961 Native Americans from seventy-five tribes assembled at the University of Chicago to develop a declaration of purpose. Instead of other people and institutions saying what the American Indian needed or wanted, they were determined to say for themselves what was best for them. The Declaration of Indian Purpose devised by the National Congress of American Indians included recommendations for economic development, health, welfare, housing, education, law, and other topics of interest to the Native communities. The declaration concluded:

> When Indians speak of the continent they yielded, they are not referring only to the loss of some millions of acres of real estate. They have in mind that the land supported a universe of things they knew, valued, and loved.
>
> With that continent gone, except for the few poor parcels they still

retain, the basis of life is precariously held, but they mean to hold the scraps and parcels as earnestly as any small nation or ethnic group was ever determined to hold to identity and survive.

What we ask of America is not charity, not paternalism, even when benevolent. We ask only that the nature of our situation be recognized and made the basis of policy and action.[2]

According to historians Olson and Wilson, the relocation policy of the 1950s and 1960s had a secondary effect of producing more "worldly sophisticated urban Indians who were more independent of tribal strictures, more accepting of pan-Indian ideas, and more politically active and militant than their elders. . . . Activist Native Americans took lessons from the confrontational tactics of black civil rights leaders and proclaimed 'red power' for themselves and their people."[3]

During Johnson's War on Poverty, reservations received massive infusions of money, not because of treaties or other agreements but simply because they were poor. The funds allowed Native American communities to focus a little less on survival and allowed the emerging doctrine of tribal sovereignty to gain some ground, turning the termination era into an era of "self-determination." Some Native Americans, such as Vine Deloria Jr., believe that this was "more potentially destructive of the traditional relationship [between tribal and national governments] than termination, which required all federal debts to be paid before releasing Indians from the tentacles of the national government."[4]

Many Americans of the early sixties, whether wearing beads and fringed leather and protesting the war, fighting for civil rights, or making movies in Hollywood, were predisposed to think well of American Indians. America was a nation charged with emotion fueled by Kennedy's assassination, an increasingly unpopular war, and the resultant public demonstrations, urban riots, and youth protests. The public was in general receptive to change, and reform was the order of the day.

Cheyenne Autumn (1964)

It was in this changing social and political climate that John Ford made *Cheyenne Autumn* (1964), based on a novel by Mari Sandoz. Like *Broken Arrow*, *Cheyenne Autumn* used the American Indian as a metaphor for the oppressed, but the film was also Ford's attempt to correct some of the stereotypes he had helped create. It was perhaps his own personal "reform" movement. Ford tried to present the history of an actual event in this film, which may be one reason it was not very successful—his fictional stories of heroes as agents of civilization were definitely more popular with the viewing public. However willing some in the 1960s were to think of Native Americans as mystical or oppressed, most apparently clung to ideas about the wild west they had received from America's celluloid history, and *Cheyenne Autumn* was a big disappointment to the accountants at Warner Brothers.

The film is based on historical accounts of 286 Cheyennes confined to an arid Oklahoma reservation who tried to return to their traditional hunting grounds in Yellowstone, over fifteen hundred miles away. (In the film, the reservation is obviously in Monument Valley, Ford's favorite location.) They were pursued by a cavalry unit that had orders to return them to the reservation one way or another.

Ford had been fascinated by the story for years, but the only way to sell it to film producers was, apparently, to make it a "blockbuster," another great western in the classic Ford tradition. However, according to a contemporaneous review by V. F. Perkins, what "Ford delivered was a film designed to question that tradition and to destroy the legend which, of all people, he himself ha[d] been most instrumental in creating. Whereas the budget was supposed to have guaranteed an action-packed epic, Ford centered the film on the moral development of a hero too human to be heroic. . . . Thus betrayed, Warners set about bringing the film in line with every philistine's image of what a blockbuster ought to be."[5] Ford was attempting to deliver a film in step with the mood of liberal America, but Warners wanted the product it knew best.

As a result, the musical score was inflated to embarrassingly epic proportion, with stilted, inappropriate overtures and interludes. Evidently uncertain that the audience would notice this very "fancy" music, paintings grace the screen for long minutes while the music plays, with "Overture" or "Interlude" written neatly across the bottom.

The film was edited for action above all else, and scenes that Ford had intended to prune drastically were left intact. For instance, the Cheyennes are briefly incarcerated in a freezing, gruesome prison at a fort commanded by the unyielding, Teutonic Captain Wessells (Karl Malden). The comparison to German concentration camps of World War II is unmistakable and obviously intentional, but the cutting done by Warners places what film critics such as V. F. Perkins felt was an undue emphasis on the similarity.[6] Later, a Polish sergeant sees the Indians' predicament as analogous to the killing of his people by the Cossacks—the U.S. Army exterminating a people only because they are not the same. Although dramatically overdone in the film and obviously making a statement about then current American military attitudes and Viet Nam, the relationship between the events was quite real, and while *Cheyenne Autumn* loses some veracity in the nod to drama, the developing cultural awareness in the film is positive, whatever the motivations might have been behind its making and remaking.

Ford made an attempt to portray the Cheyennes as real people, although his actors were of almost every ethnic background except American Indian. He made an effort to use the Cheyenne language in the dialogue between the Indian characters, and even though a genuine, Cheyenne-speaking Native American might have been confused or amused by the verbiage, it was a great improvement over previous efforts to "sound Indian." To whatever degree of success, Ford's attempt to use the Cheyenne language is one of the most striking and positive aspects of the film.

In *Cheyenne Autumn*, blame for what is graphically depicted as attempted genocide was placed on the system of control over long distance with little or no real knowledge on the part of those in control. The film begins with a rider delivering a message to the reservation, where the Indians wait in the sweltering sun for the "gentlemen from the East." The gentlemen are coming to investigate the promises made by the government, which have gone unkept. They don't arrive—apparently, the discomfort of the journey was too much. Ford emphasizes the distance between those in control and those they attempt to control by holding the shot of the departing rider for a very long time, waiting until he is only a dot on the horizon before cutting to the next frame.

The film's hero, Captain Tom Archer (Richard Widmark), is an admirer of the people he is ordered to chase across the plains after they determine that no help can be expected from the East. He says, "All you've seen are reservation Indians. The Cheyenne are the greatest fighters in the world—fierce, smart, and meaner than sin," but it is only after chasing the men, women, and children across nearly fifteen hundred miles of heat and dirt and snow and ice that he comes to share their determination to get to Yellowstone. He goes to Washington in person and hauls the secretary of the interior (Edward G. Robinson) back to talk to the Cheyennes face to face. Ford is apparently saying that when the image is gone and the reality of a nearly decimated people, the "reservation Indians" of which Archer spoke, comes into focus, respect and justice can finally occur. The problem lies in the image.

That idea is underscored by an episode in which a cowboy shoots down an unarmed Indian who has come to ask for food because he "always wanted to kill me an Indian," and because he is the only one of his friends not to have an Indian scalp. Later, a somewhat heavy-handed scene puts the idea in boldface for any who might have missed the subtleties. A newspaper editor rushes into the newsroom reading out loud the headlines "Bloodthirsty Savages Rape and Pillage." Being a good businessman, he notes that such an idea really isn't news anymore and suggests that now they should "grieve for the noble red man," and sell many more newspapers in the process. In effect, that is what Warners, if not Ford, was doing in making *Cheyenne Autumn*. It is ironic that the film was a box office failure, which suggests that Ford was out of step with his time in portraying the Indians' situation in a more sympathetic light, or that Warners was to blame for changing what could have been a sensitive film into a traveling circus of cowboys and Indians, or perhaps it simply shows that the American movie-goer—whatever his or her political leanings—still preferred the uncomplicated and entertaining Hollywood Indian once the lights went down and the credits rolled.

Civil Rights and the Celluloid Indians

In March 1968 President Johnson gave an address to Congress on the "Problems of the American Indian: The Forgotten American." In that statement, he recognized the need for Native American self-determination: "I propose a new goal for our Indian programs: A goal that ends the old debate about 'termination' of Indian programs and stresses self-determination; a goal that erases old attitudes of paternalism and promotes partnership self-help. . . . The greatest hope for Indian progress lies in the emergence of Indian leadership and initiative in solving Indian problems. Indians must have a voice in making the plans and decisions in programs which are important to their daily life."[7]

One month later, the Civil Rights Act of 1968 passed, titles 2–7 of which had to do with Native Americans. These sections applied the Bill of Rights to American Indians "in their relations with tribal governments, the authorizations of a model code for courts of Indian offenses, and the requirement that Indian consent be given to assumption by state of jurisdiction over Indian country."[8] In effect, the Civil Rights Movement produced changes that had tremendous impact on the legal rights of Native Americans, as well as African Americans and other minorities.

The Civil Rights Movement was defined, by most Americans, as the struggle of black people to gain equal status with the white majority.

However, since much of America in the late sixties and early seventies was apparently not yet willing to pay to see a film about an oppressed African American, one way to tell the story of society oppressing a minority was to make a movie about a Native American.

The images and stereotypes of Native Americans during this period made them ideally complex, sympathetic subjects. Indians were seen as not only poor and oppressed but also mystical and natural. On top of that, add the new separatist militancy provided by the American Indian Movement (AIM) and other groups, and you have a formula that recycles and modifies the image of the noble savage.

Oliver LaFarge, the author of *Laughing Boy*, wrote in a 1961 article that "[t]he temper of American Indians has reached the boiling point."[9] Mary Ann Weston, a history of journalism professor, makes the point that this new militancy was initially reported very positively. "The image sometimes depicted a legendary warrior, fighting a modern conflict to preserve the ancient rights of his people,"[10] and the descriptions of these warriors is very much in line with what a nation familiar with the old stereotypes would expect:

> Tall and sinuous, with fine features, his black shoulder-length hair secured with a red headband, Bridges cuts a flamboyant figure. . . . He has been arrested 21 times since becoming involved in the fishing rights and has a 15-year sentence on appeal; over the years, when few other sources of dignity were available, he has come to take pride in the ability to fight back, as he says, so that it takes three or four of them to get the handcuffs on."[11]

This "legendary warrior" figure is a fair prototype for the character of one of the better-known films about Native Americans to come out of the sixties and seventies, *Tell Them Willie Boy Is Here*.

Tell Them Willie Boy Is Here (1969)

In 1969 Abraham Polonsky returned to Hollywood after two decades on the blacklist. The film he chose to make was based on *Willie Boy, A Desert Manhunt*, by Harry Lawton, which, like Sandoz's *Cheyenne Autumn*, was based on a historical incident. Although there is some disagreement, most critics have found something to like about the film from both technical and social points of view. Susan Rice, for instance, says that "Though *Willie Boy* suffers many of the flaws that working within the framework of myth and allegory invites, it is a dignified, principled movie that evokes a thoughtful, contemplative response."[12]

The story occurs in 1909, at a time when the Indian Bureau had out-lawed Indian dress, religion, customs, even hairstyles. Indians were not allowed to be Indians. That policy is evident in *Willie Boy*, with its Indians in cowboy hats and Levis. Even the female Indian lead has a short hairstyle, although the white Indian agent's hair is fashionably long. At a festival in the film's beginning, the men are playing an Indian game that entails holding a blanket in their teeth, but the bobbing of their cowboy hats makes it seem incongruous and rather sad.

Willie Boy is the story of a tough young Paiute man (Robert Blake), who returns to the reservation in Southern California to reclaim his love, Lola (Katharine Ross). The two have run away together before, but Lola's father and brothers brought her back, and they warn Willie Boy not to try it again. The two lovers meet in an orchard at midnight, but her father and brothers show up, and Willie Boy kills the father in self-defense. The couple takes off across the desert, and Willie Boy tells Lola no one will come after them because "No one cares what Indians do. No one."

He had good reason to believe no one cared. The law generally turned a blind eye on crimes committed against Indians, on or off the reservation. However, three elements converge to prompt an all-out manhunt. The Indian agent wants Lola back so she can make a teacher out of her, some white men of the area miss the good old days of fighting the Indians, and President Taft is making a high-profile trip to the area. Willie's timing couldn't have been worse.

The Indian agent, a white woman (Susan Clark), is a mosaic of well-meaning but misguided intentions. She has multiple advanced degrees, including anthropology and medical degrees, she comes from a wealthy family, and she is an inveterate do-gooder. She believes she knows what is best for everyone, and she orders Sheriff Cooper, "Coop" (Robert Redford), to chase the whiskey runners off the reservation during a festival. She also orders him to bring Lola back when the couple runs away. She only shows confusion, both intellectual and sexual, when the subject is herself. Each time she and Coop have sex in the film, she is emotionally torn. Her ethics and morals prohibit such things, especially with someone like Coop, but she does it anyway, sometimes with tears streaming down her face.

The first time we see her in bed with Coop, they insult each other as he begins to pull on his clothes. He asks, "Who do you think you are?" She replies by rattling off her list of degrees and station, ending with a scornful, "Who are *you*?" She exemplifies the well-meaning people who instituted such realities as the Indian schools to teach Indians how to be white, which they were sure was best for the "poor savages." The point is made when Lola tells Willie Boy that if they go back to the reservation, the doctor/agent will help. He replies in a low, sardonic tone, "Yeah. She's a helper."

The men who insist on going with the sheriff are the typical Hollywood posse—the unshaven lout, the headline-mongering politician, and so forth. In addition, an old friend of Coop's father is along, a man who fought the Indians with the senior Cooper and who never tires of talking about the good old days. Each time he mentions those days or Coop's father, it has something to do with killing Indians. He says, "Your daddy was lucky, Coop. He died while it was still good to live." One can only think that this man dies the way he would want to die, after all, shot by an Indian. But his death is an accident. Willie Boy is shooting the horses of the posse, and the older man, played by Barry Sullivan, simply gets in the way.

Another member of the posse is Charlie, Willie Boy's friend. He's along to see that Willie isn't killed. He is ineffectual, but he does try. Although he is a positive character, he is almost a caricature of the friendly white who tries to help until it really gets tough, at which point he goes home.

Polonsky takes potshots at politicians and the media in the film. Taft comes off sounding (he's never seen) like an obese (he requires a huge chair) racist and a sexist (he tells the agent essentially to take up knitting and leave such problems as the Indians to the men). And the media, lacking a real story—except that Taft is there to dedicate a plaque to Father Serra, an irony in itself—choose to inflate the danger of an "Indian uprising." This is something Willie Boy could not have predicted.

The timing is also wrong for Coop. Instead of "doing his job," he is having sex with the agent when Willie Boy kills Lola's father. He therefore has a personal reason for catching Willie Boy. Even though he is the most rational and well balanced of the white people in the film, he says, "He's mine," and the sadness on his face doesn't dilute the reality of his words.

The scenario that Polonsky creates is a heartrending glimpse of reality. Good intentions aside, however, this film presents a facelift on the stereotype, not an erasure. The society at fault is presented one-dimensionally, the Paiutes serve merely as symbols for the oppressed in America, and Willie Boy acts as a stand-in for the youth culture of the late sixties. If Willie is the rebel youth, his people emerge as the mindless,

6. From Abraham Polonsky's *Tell Them Willie Boy Is Here* (1969). Photo Museum of Modern Art Film Stills Archive; courtesy Universal Pictures.

oppressed masses who have bought the system, or who have at least given up fighting it. As Dan Georgakas points out, the Paiutes in the film are

> faceless, opinionless men. They help neither the sheriff nor Willie. When one Indian-hating sheriff is killed by Willie, they are pleased. When Coop allows them to burn Willie's dead body Indian-style,

they are equally pleased. They are divided over the mysterious death of Willie's woman. One thinks she has killed herself to let Willie escape. Another thinks Willie has had to kill her himself so she would not be captured. Neither alternative is as likely as that the woman would have attempted to stay hidden and if captured would wait until the warrior came for her. Such common sense is very much in line with Indian thinking and very much out of line with Hollywood mythology.[13]

Willie Boy is a rebel with a cause, certainly, but his character is so filled with anger he is unable to interact with anyone, even Lola, in a sustained, even semi-cordial manner. He is Indian only as a device. Lola says, "You can't beat them." When he replies, "Maybe. Maybe. But they'll know I was here," the words are believable from an angry young man of the late sixties but not very believable coming from an Indian of 1909.

Pauline Kael, in a *New Yorker* review, insists that Willie is actually only a metaphor for the militant black men of the era, and "since a Black man (the Indian pretense isn't kept up for long) can't trust any white man—not even Coop—there can be no reconciliation of the races, so he should try to bring everything down."[14] At one point in the film, a posse member says to Coop, "It don't make sense." Coop replies, "Maybe that's the sense it makes." Perhaps, from Kael's perspective at least, that is the sense this film makes.

In some important ways, Polonsky presents Coop as Willie's mirror image in the film. Neither really fits the world to which he belongs. Neither is doing what he wants to do, and both are driven into respective corners by outside forces. Their similarity is emphasized when Coop places his hand in a print Willie left in the mud. It matches. The audience feels pity that Coop, who really doesn't want to chase Willie, must eventually kill him, but that he *will* kill him is really never in doubt. This Indian will have to vanish, too.

Polonsky unfortunately slips into the old Hollywood formula when he positions Coop as the white man who "out-Indians the Indian." At the film's end, the two are in the arid hills, and Willie Boy has the high ground. In a particularly silly segment, Coop dresses some brush in his coat and hat, ties a rope on it and then moves back. When he pulls the rope, Willie shoots at the coat. Why he would want a hole in his coat is unknown, and why Willie—who could see the brush being placed as well as he could see it move—shoots it is unclear. Somehow, this allows

Coop to sneak up behind Willie, whom he finds sitting quietly, perched on top of a rock in broad relief. Coop offers Willie a duel with rifles. The two look into each others' faces, and Willie makes his move, although his rifle is empty. It is, as Georgakas states, "the suicide of the modern existentialist,"[15] and one more Indian vanishes.

The film positions the two men as equal in this man-to-man combat, but this is clearly not the case. The reality is that Willie has only his body, his rifle, and at least one too few bullets while Coop has a horse and a train, traces Willie's movements with help from the telegraph, and has men waiting at every exit point. Although this scenario sounds very much like the real occurrences in white/Indian history (such as the chase of the Cheyennes from Oklahoma to Yellowstone or the seven regiments that ran down Chief Joseph's Nez Percés) and definitely shows the imbalance of power between the dominant culture and an oppressed minority, this film misses the mark by making the Indians, en masse and in particular, stand-ins for other people and other ideas, as did many other films of the era.

Images and Alcatraz

Among the films that used Indian identity as metaphor were three produced in the same year, 1970, a year after *Willie Boy* was made. The films, *Soldier Blue*, *A Man Called Horse*, and *Little Big Man* are each important to a study of the celluloid Indians but for very different reasons.

It is interesting to speculate about how much influence the Native American takeover of Alcatraz Island (which lasted from November 1969 to June 1971) had on the directors' and producers' decisions to make these films. When Richard Oakes and his group took over the abandoned federal prison using a nineteenth-century law that gave Native Americans the right to reclaim unused federal land, they were hailed around the world as the quintessential twentieth-century warriors. The takeover was produced in order to attract attention to Native American issues, and they were initially successful. But instead of treating the protestors as warriors, the government decided to simply wait them out. By the end of the year-and-a-half-long seige, the media had tired of the "cause" and had turned instead to reporting the problems that had developed on the island. When federal marshalls finally removed the last of the Native Americans from Alcatraz, it was almost a non-event.

It was just before and during the early months of the takeover that *Soldier Blue*, *A Man Called Horse*, and *Little Big Man* went into production, a time when a growing proportion of the viewing audience was predisposed to think of Native Americans as twentieth-century American citizens as a result of events such as the Chicago Conference; still regarded them as a mystical/natural people; and admired the new warrior image. It was an audience ready for a "new" western movie experience. Filmmakers could therefore use sympathy toward and notoriety of the Native American to entertain and also to make the statements they chose to make.

Of those, *Soldier Blue* is the most blatant in its use of American Indians as a metaphor for another people, in this case the Vietnamese.

Soldier Blue (1970)

By 1970 the Vietnam War was in its last years, and atrocities such as My Lai were becoming public knowledge. An unpopular war was becoming a national embarrassment. Director Ralph Nelson wanted to make a statement, and he chose as his vehicle the all-purpose metaphor for the oppressed, the American Indian.

Soldier Blue has received a great deal of criticism for being much too violent and much too graphic in its representation of the massacre at Sand Creek. A filmmaker would be very hard pressed to match the actual violence and cruelty of the original, but Nelson's depiction is enough to turn a hardy stomach. His intention was to sensitize the American public to the "plight" of the Vietnamese by relating similar atrocities committed by the U.S. government ninety years before. He was evidently at least somewhat successful in that attempt, but it is unfortunate for Native Americans, since they are once again presented as victims who lost and then disappeared.

The Cheyennes in this film appear only twice. The first is when they attack a paymaster's escort and kill everyone except Honus Gant (Peter Strauss) and Cresta (Candice Bergen), a woman who was captured by the same Cheyennes two years earlier but who made her way back to "civilization." Their escape is sheer luck on his part and intelligence on hers.

The second time the Cheyennes appear is at the end of the film, and we see them welcoming Cresta back with loving, open arms, warm smiles, and laughter. Spotted Wolf, the leader of the raid against the troopers, welcomes her back and asks where the love token is that he had given her. When she admits she gave it to Soldier Blue (Gant), he understands and wishes her well. Now, *that* is civilized. However, the obvious goodness and humanity of the Cheyennes is simply a backdrop that sets off the despicable nature of the soldiers, who seem intent on killing and/or raping everything in sight.

The Indians are hospitable and loving people, so one wonders where Cresta got her foul mouth and horrible manners. She is the only one in the film who curses, but she makes up for them all. She belches, is unabashed about removing her clothes, and shows no remorse when she takes valuables from the dead soldiers. The implication, or at least the understanding Private Gant comes to, is that she learned this "heathen" behavior from the Indians. This does little to enhance the image of the Cheyenne community.

As Honus and Cresta try to make their way back to the fort, they meet three other Indians, this time Kiowas. Cresta, of course, knows just how to handle them. She insults them, which results in hand-to-hand combat between Gant and the leader of the trio. Gant wins, although again by luck, and refuses to kill the man he defeated although the woman urges him to do so. Since he doesn't, one of the Indians leaps down—in a movement that looks more chimpanzee-like than human—and kills his downed comrade. This is Hollywood absurdity. With whites in abundance, killing one's own for losing a fight does not seem a practical way of going about things.

Except for showing that Gant can fight even though he appears terminally stupid, the scene with the Kiowas has little meaning in the film except to provide action. This is not a film about Indian and white relations. It is a film about a man and a woman falling in love, facing formidable odds, and so on—not exactly news. If the scene at the film's end were not so bloody and horrible, this film would probably not have found its way onto anyone's list of "meaningful" films about Indians.

The film ends with the massacre at Sand Creek, and as chilling as the cinematic version is, it would have been even more horrifying if the actual occurrence had been depicted. The film's Colonel Iverson is obviously quite mad with power and glory as he delivers his version of Henry the Fifth's Saint Crispin's Day speech, "You'll be proud to say 'I was with Iverson!'" It is important to realize that his madness places all the horrors of the soldiers' deeds, including dancing around waving severed limbs over their heads, into the category of insanity, while Cresta and Honus represent the majority, the *sane* white people who would never do such a thing.

Iverson's historical counterpart was Colonel Chivington, a preacher, and his soldiers were actually civilian volunteers who hunted down

Black Kettle's band and killed more than three hundred people, over half of them women and children. Chivington is reported to have told his men to "kill and scalp all big and little; nits makes lice."[16] However, it is too simple to say that he was a solitary madman, especially considering that after the massacre he took his men back to Denver, where the performance at a local music hall was stopped and the stage cleared so that Chivington and his men could parade back and forth in front of the wildly cheering crowd and display their trophies—the scalps, heads, and other body parts of the Indian men, women, and children they had slaughtered.

Soldier Blue was not a particularly good film from any point of view, but it is exceptionally distressing that to make his point, Nelson made use of Indians as a metaphor, an exotic one by which an audience could feel sympathy from a distance. Unfortunately, even when the intention and the idea might be positive, the employment of Indians' historical experiences as metaphor dilutes and distorts those experiences and threatens to trivialize their existence.

A Man Called Horse (1970)

An example of a film whose maker seems almost comically unaware of his invention is director Elliot Silverstein's *A Man Called Horse*. It was intended and well publicized as a sympathetic and accurate portrayal of American Indians, and it probably came as quite a surprise to the filmmaker that Native American communities disliked the film so intensely. However, there are numerous reasons for Indians' ire.

A Man Called Horse is a film that must be discussed in terms of reality and authenticity, specifically because it was so widely advertised in those terms. A very popular film, *Horse* played off the recycled American appetite for knowledge about the "real" American Indians and the emergence of the headline-making 1970s warriors that had sharpened public curiosity and an urge by some to go Native.

Considering that a large percentage of the film's dialogue is presumably Lakota, and the film is set in a Sioux village, it is logical to assume that this is a film about the Lakotas, or at least about Lakota–white relations. Instead, it is the story of an aristocratic white man who is captured and treated like an animal by the primitive tribe of Yellow Hand. This treatment runs counter to the Sioux tradition of hospitality. It would have seemed like very bad manners for the Sioux to treat a man like an animal, the entire band standing around laughing while he is tor-

7. From Ralph Nelson's *Soldier Blue* (1970). Photo Museum of Modern Art Film Stills Archive; courtesy of Avco Embassy Pictures.

tured; and leaving an old woman out in the snow to die would have been an abomination—but both of these things happen in this celluloid village.

In the film, when the son of an old, widowed mother is killed in the raid against Horse's camp, she is forced to give away all her belongings, including what she needs to live. The other women tear up her tipi and take all her possessions, and the old woman is left to scrounge for offal with the dogs. It seems that only the white man, Horse (Richard Harris), feels any sympathy for the old woman. In reality, as Oglala Sioux Art Raymond said in a review of the film for the *Sioux Falls Argus-Leader* on 25 April 1970, "[o]ne of the key romantic and emotional parts of the film is Hollywood's alleged desertion of the old people by the Sioux. This simply is not true. In the Siouan culture, the elderly held one special place of honor and never, never, never were deserted. On the contrary, they received very special care."

A myriad of other errors made the widely publicized "authenticity" of this film deleterious to an understanding of Native peoples, past or present. One of the film's major flaws is that the Lakotas depicted are actually the "averaged" and generic Hollywood Indian, only perhaps more so. As Ward Churchill, a Native American activist and author, points out wryly,

> this droll adventure, promoted as "the most authentic description of North American Indian life ever filmed," depicts a people whose lan-

guage is Lakota, whose hairstyles range from Assiniboin through Nez Perc to Comanche, whose tipi design is Crow, and whose Sun Dance ceremony and the lodge in which it is held are both typically Mandan. They are referred to throughout the film as 'Sioux,' but to which group do they supposedly belong? Secungu? Oglala? Santee? Sisseton? Yanktonai? Minneconjou? Hunkpapa? . . . These groups were/are quite distinct from one another, and the distinctions *do* make a difference in terms of accuracy and "authenticity."[17]

The representation of the Sun Dance ceremony in *A Man Called Horse* is a clear indication of paternalistic attitudes found seventy-three years earlier in Griffith's *A Pueblo Legend*. The ceremony becomes a sort of child's game that, although difficult and dangerous, is no match for the superior European-American. In actuality, the Sun Dance was not meant to show off a man's courage or to win a bride, which are Horse's very personal and individual motivations in the film. For the Sioux, this is the most sacred of religious rites and is undertaken to prove a man's humility to the spirits by mortifying his flesh. In that way, it is not so very different from the sack cloth and ashes (physical or metaphoric) of Christian believers. A man undertaking the Sun Dance underwent intense purification beforehand, and his motivation was to prompt a vision that would be of use to his entire tribe. Horse's motivations are purely personal.[18]

The spiritual value of the Sun Dance was obliterated in *A Man Called Horse* by the inaccurate and Eurocentric explanation of its construct and place in Lakota culture. In essence, this sacred ceremony was turned into "a macho exercise in 'self-mutilation,' a 'primitive initiation rite' showing that the Indian male could 'take it.'" In order to gain acceptance by the tribe, marry Running Deer and eventually gain his freedom, Horse must prove that he is as tough as his captors by enduring the pain of a Sun Dance. There is no indication that he does so for any but such self-centered reasons, and there is no doubt he will succeed. As Churchill noted, "Just bloody up your chest and no further questions will be asked."[19] Harris's character does of course succeed, even achieving a technicolor vision that is, again, personal.

The Sioux are called the Vision Seekers because they believe in visions as communications from the spirits, communication for the betterment of the tribe. Horse's vision involves sacred elements, such as an eagle and Wakan Tanka, the white buffalo, but it is more akin to an erotic dream than a Sioux spiritual vision. A rather pretty scene with

Corinna Tsopei, the Greek woman who plays Running Deer, running nude through a stream in slow motion makes up the major portion of his vision.

Horse believes, and is able to convince his ridiculous mixed-blood sidekick/interpreter, Batise (Jean Gascon), that he will soon become a war chief and, by leading a war party through the hostile Shoshone territory, finally make his way back to civilization. The natural superiority of the white man is assumed, apparently unconsciously, by the filmmaker and reinforced in the film when the Shoshones arrive. They come in overwhelming numbers, on horseback, and with the element of complete surprise on their side. It is up to Horse to show the Lakotas how to protect themselves. He, a captive English gentleman, barks an order for the Indians to get their bows and arrows, and the Lakota men jump to do it. He barks another order, and they line up in classic British military shoot-and-reload formation. This is enough to win the battle, drive the attackers away, and give Horse the status of war chief in the tribe, as is shown in the film's final scene, when he leads a group of warriors off into the sunset. As a critic in *Film Quarterly* commented in 1972, "Stripped of its pretensions, *Horse* parades the standard myth that the white man can do everything better than the Indian. Give him a little time and he will marry the best-looking girl (a princess of course) and will end up chief of the tribe."[20] Yellow Hand (Manu Tupou), the previous war chief, is conveniently killed during the attack, as is Horse's pregnant bride, Running Deer, which nicely takes care of the miscegenation problem.

That Richard Harris's character has to show the Indians how to *really* use a bow and arrow to fight a war is curious, but perhaps more so is the fact that this film, purported to show Indians realistically, attempts to do so by scripting a white character to narrate the story of a Native American existence. This is an obvious appropriation of identity, an absorption of an Indian identity into the context of the American national identity. The Native Americans in the film also fall into two familiar categories: those who are the Good Indians—including Yellow Hand, his mother, and Running Deer—and the Bad Indians. The Good Indians have much paler skin and have distinctly European features, which could be fairly realistic, since "Sioux features in fact did range from Nordic to Mongolian and their color from white to copper red."[21] The problem arises in the description of the Bad Indians, who were consistently darker, with flatter, less European features. One could assume that the message is that white is not only beautiful but also mentally and morally superior.

One could also make the case that because Indians are, in relation to the vast majority of the film's audience, the Other, a mediator of sorts is required to make the viewer more comfortable and more capable of developing an understanding; therefore an appropriation of Indian identity by the white hero was desirable. This is probably good economic, ticket-selling reasoning, but the fact remains that Indian experiences are being sifted, interpreted, and delivered through a decidedly non-Indian interpreter.

Yellow Hand's mother, Buffalo Cow Head, is in fact played by Dame Judith Anderson, who wears a dime-store wig and squawks and grunts histrionically, as do most of the Indians. They all seem to be language-deficient, even among themselves. At the film's beginning, the Indians are on screen for a very long time, planning and executing an attack, dividing the spoils and capturing Horse, but they are making their way home with a stop along the way to apply paint before we hear any language from them at all. They seem to manage just fine with childish whoops, squeals of pagan delight, and a little bit of sign language. As Horse begins to "understand" them, they gain some dignity, but the Indians in the film never reach equal status with their gentleman captive.

Batise, Horse's mixed-blood interpreter, is an interesting character in the film. The character was obviously written in to allow Horse an easy way of learning the language, but his presence is disturbing on a number of levels. His father was French and his mother was American Indian, although not Sioux. He hates the French, hates the Sioux, but loves the English. His goal is to help Horse get away so the two of them can go to England. He pretends to be crazy so the Sioux will leave him alone and not expect him to work, but his actions indicate that he might actually be a bit wobbly on his mental base. However, his role as interpreter allows an insight into the way language works in this film. It is, in fact, analogous to the way the film works to translate the Sioux experience to the viewing audience. Although some of his details are correct—he is able to teach Horse to communicate, more or less—his translations are modified by his own experience and his own agenda. During the Sun Dance ceremony, Horse says some very insulting things to his hosts, which Batise translates into a more socially and culturally acceptable compliment. Horse makes him correct the transla-

tion, however, angering the men of the council. This hearkens back to
the days of the early westerns, when the hero showed his bravado and
earned the respect of the less sophisticated Indians by being verbally insulting. If nothing else, however, the interpreter's modification does
show the problematic nature of translation of an alien experience with
an overlay of a culturally foreign, hegemonic discourse. The faces in
this film may look Native American, but the message they deliver is
unequivocally Eurocentric. They represent the Indian soul as white
artifact.

Little Big Man (1970)

Little Big Man also used a white hero to depict an Indian experience, but
of all the films made in the sixties, seventies, and eighties that were
sympathetic portrayals of American Indians, this one has received the
most positive response. It was a well-made film—well acted, directed,
and edited—and it featured an actual American Indian, Chief Dan
George, who portrayed Old Lodge Skins, a Cheyenne man with a mul-
tifaceted personality and a sense of humor. It is, in fact, a very entertaining film.

The film was directed by Arthur Penn and was based on Thomas
Berger's novel of the same name. Berger's story is about Jack Crabb,
who is 121 years of age. He tells the story of his life, which includes being raised after the age of ten by the Cheyennes and drifting back and
forth between the two cultures as an adult. Berger's novel is very funny,
but it is also unique in its even-handed description of two cultures in
historical conflict. In the novel, both whites and Cheyennes do bad and
good things—they are fully realized though thoroughly satirized human beings.

As different art forms, a novel and a film cannot be judged by the
same standards. However, as a film, *Little Big Man* fails in some important ways that the novel succeeds because it attempts to do visually and
quickly what Berger was able to accomplish in words and at length.
The novel is better able, for instance, to elucidate his ideas about the circular nature of the Native American universe as opposed to the linear
nature of the white universe, and it not only describes the Indian belief
in miracles but takes the time and space to make those beliefs understandable.

To understand satire or irony, the audience must understand the object of the satire. Berger is able to satirize both cultures because he
develops in the novel at least an elementary understanding of the Chey-

ennes before he begins to satirize them. The film hasn't the luxury of time, and as a result, only the white culture is satirized well. Another reason for the imbalance in the film may have been that both the screenwriter, Calder Willingham, and the director, Arthur Penn, as part of white culture, felt comfortable transferring Berger's very funny satire to the screen when it came to the white characters. However, they may have handled the Cheyennes with kid gloves to avoid being unintentionally insulting. In the novel, both white and Indian people are quite funny, and both groups are multidimensional. Neither is all good or all bad, and each does basically what might be expected from people facing war, hunger, and ignorance, if not stupidity. In the film, the Cheyennes come out looking much better than their white counterparts, but they are one-dimensional, lacking the depth they achieved in Berger's novel.

The film, much more than the novel, is a search for identity. Jack Crabb (Dustin Hoffman) experiences what today might most closely be described as the confusion inherent in mixed-blood identity. "God knows I thought enough about it and kept telling myself I was basically an Indian, just as when among Indians I kept seeing how I was really white to the core." He shifts back and forth between cultures, trying to find out who he is. It is interesting that in the Indian world his identity remains consistent, but in the white world he tries on personalities and lifestyles like one tries on costumes. If this is really a search for identity, then it is a white identity Crabb is looking for, but each one he tries on ends up unfulfilling because of the hypocrisy, greed, dishonesty, and general craziness of the whites. This appears to be the main idea behind the film, since eleven of his fourteen life segments occur in the Euro-American world.

He is reared until the age of ten by his white family, which includes his sister, Caroline (Carole Androsky). They are the only two left after the Pawnees attack the family wagon on its way west. He states that he never had much use for Pawnees after that. In the novel, it is the Cheyennes who attack the wagon and kill the rest of the family. They are not the angelic people of the film but rather fully realized people reacting to the killing of their own. In the film, however, Crabb carefully differentiates between the "human beings" (the Cheyennes) and the Pawnees, whom he calls "wild Indians" who were "always sucking up to the white men."

After the attack, Crabb and his sister are found by Shadow That Comes In Sight (Ruben Moreno), a Cheyenne, who takes them back to camp. Caroline, a brawny young woman, is dramatically certain the Indians will rape her at any moment, and when they don't, she sneaks out of camp. Crabb says, "Caroline never did have no luck with men." At least this scene, although problematic from a feminist point of view, debunks the stereotype of the brutish, raping Indian.

Just after Crabb has earned the name Little Big Man in a raid against the Pawnees, he, along with a few other warriors and his adopted grandfather, Old Lodge Skins, come upon a camp in which the white soldiers have slaughtered everyone, including women and children. When Little Big Man asks Old Lodge Skins why they would do such a thing, the wise old chief says, "Because they are strange. They do not seem to know where the center is." The old man knows it is time to war against the perpetrators of the massacre, and they do.

The attack on the soldiers is interesting because Crabb's voice-over explains that the two ways of fighting are in total opposition. The Cheyennes hit the soldiers with crooked sticks, counting coup and humiliating their enemy, and the soldiers promptly blow them into the next life with their rifles. While the Cheyennes' method of attack is unrealistic (the amount of prior exposure they would have had to white soldiers' fighting techniques would have altered their own), the scene is an attempt to show the differences in attitudes and values between the two cultures, using the interpretive voice of the twentieth-century Crabb.

After helping Shadow back onto his horse when he is shot, Little Big Man is captured by the white soldiers. The boy shouts "God bless George Washington!" to convince the soldiers he is white, and they "save" him, take him back to civilization, and turn him over to the local do-gooders.

His introduction to white philosophy comes in the form of the Pendrakes, the Reverend (Thayer David) and his lovely wife (Faye Dunaway), who teach him about Christian religion. The good Reverend attempts to beat the fear of God into Crabb without much affect, while Mrs. Pendrake uses her sex appeal, which is absolutely successful. That phase ends when young Crabb catches the virtuous Mrs. Pendrake having sex with the local storekeeper after plunking Jack down to investigate the elephant head soda fountain. He presses the long snout down and "feels" something amiss. When he locates her moans to "stop" and her calls for "help," he quickly realizes it isn't help she wants at all. Her hypocrisy overwhelms him, and he takes up with someone whose total lack of morality he finds refreshingly honest.

Alardyce T. Merriweather (Martin Balsam) is a snake oil salesman with a penchant for losing body parts when caught in one scam or another. Merriweather tells the young man that "two legged creatures will believe anything, and the more preposterous the better." He also says that Old Lodge Skins ruined Crabb by giving him a vision of "a moral center to the universe, and there isn't any." Merriweather is a consummate cynic and profiteer. His role in the film is much larger than in the novel, and most critics attribute this to Penn's desire to make a statement about Vietnam and the immorality of that war; he represents the "fat cats" at home who send others into war for the profit to be made.

The repetition of the idea of "centering"—first introduced by Old Lodge Skins and then repeated with derision by Merriweather—is an apparent attempt by the filmmaker to do what Berger did in the novel, hint at the circular nature of the universe. However, Crabb's philosophical conversation with Merriweather is cut short when Caroline, who still looks like a man, leads the party that tars and feathers the two miscreants. She then recognizes her brother, and he is once again "saved."

His next incarnation occurs because his sister knows what *really* makes a man. According to Caroline, a *man* knows how to handle a gun. In a very funny scene on the river bank, she teaches Crabb to draw and fire before he touches the gun. He's quite good at it—a natural-born gunslinger—so he buys himself a very fancy black outfit, calls himself the Soda Pop Kid, and intimidates everyone around him. Then he meets Wild Bill Hickock (Jeff Corey).

Hickock is a delightful man but always on edge, apparently for good reason. When a man behind him draws, Hickock shoots him. Crabb says in amazement, "Mr. Hickock, this man is really dead." With cool detachment Hickock replies that he "got him through the heart and lungs." This scene is almost a replay of the battle between the Cheyennes and the soldiers—Crabb, with his Indian upbringing, is in effect "counting coup," but Hickock, like the soldiers, is serious and deadly. Crabb isn't ready for the reality of what guns do or this cold-blooded acceptance of violence, so he becomes a storekeeper, much to his sister's disgust.

This is where Crabb encounters white business morality, or lack of it. He thinks his life is going well; he has a sweet Swedish wife (Kelly Jean Peters), a business partner who seems to know what he's doing, and the store is small but busy. But then the business partner cheats him and leaves the couple bankrupt.

As explained in the novel but not in the film, Crabb is able to be swindled because he is still innocent in an Indian sort of way. For instance, in the novel the young Crabb plays a hoax on his Indian friends, proving, as John Turner noted, "his 'manly indifference to pain' by pulling his 'arrow-out-of-arse trick.' The hoax is very funny, but Jack points to its larger significance: 'Maybe you are beginning to understand, when I pulled the arrow-out-of-arse trick, why it didn't occur to none of the children that I was hoaxing them. That is because Indians did not go around expecting to be swindled, whereas they was always ready for a miracle.'"[22] Like the Indian children, the innocent Crabb is not expecting to be swindled and believes he must have made a mistake when he finds his tricky partner's double-billings.

It is at this point in the film that Crabb first meets General George Armstrong Custer, played hilariously by Richard Mulligan. Custer comes across the bankrupt couple in the street and renders one of his many pronouncements of "truth" in the film. He says, "Go West!" and they do, although his wife, Olga, is afraid of Indians.

The next scene takes place in a stagecoach as it races across the plains, an obvious parody of that in Ford's famous *Stagecoach*. Crabb even leaps from horse to horse as John Wayne did, only there is an Indian next to him, perhaps Crabb's alter-ego, also leaping from horse to horse. The two tussle over the lead rein until it is shot in half, and the two fall into a very convenient river before the stage turns over. This is an extremely well done, funny scene, which is in some ways more believable than Ford's scene.

The Indians capture Olga, and Crabb spends three years looking for her before he is attacked by the very people who raised him. He finally convinces them that he is Little Big Man by telling them things only he would know. They are still skeptical, however, because they believe Little Big Man was killed in the first battle with the white army and turned into a bird, which explains the absence of a body. Burns Red in the Sun (Steve Shemayne) decides to spare him, although the thought process gives him a pain between his ears, and they take Crabb back to Old Lodge Skins to find out whether he could actually be Little Big Man.

Chief Dan George does a remarkable job with the standard wise-old-chief role. He manages a beautiful blend of humor and softness that would charm most viewers. However, film critics Ralph and Natasha Friar are not among them. They feel that "Old Lodge Skins, instead of being the character created by Berger, becomes on screen like the Co-chise of *Broken Arrow* (1950) fame—a noble, innocent patriarch who speaks in a quaint manner supposedly conveying an 'Indian' attitude. Berger was able to make the red man quite distinct without such con-descension."[23] They take particular issue with Old Lodge Skins's com-placency and his attitude that all the white men are simply crazy. Since the period depicted, the late 1800s, involved a series of battles, and the white man was a constant threat, viewing the adversary in so simple a way would not have been possible, much less practical. They are also disappointed that Old Lodge Skins appears to be a combination of two real characters, Sitting Bull and Crazy Horse:

> Crazy Horse was a well known visionary. It was his war cry, as he led the Cheyennes and the Sioux, "It is a good day to die," that is given to the peaceful Old Lodge Skins to say repeatedly. Sitting Bull, a great medicine man, was also a visionary. He foresaw the Battle of the Greasy Grass [Little Big Horn] in a dream. The difference be-tween Old Lodge Skins and the real Crazy Horse and Sitting Bull is that the latter two did not have the time for a quaint life in a tipi. They planned; they fought for their lives; they challenged and beat the white man many, many times prior to the Custer affair. While, in the film, the Cheyennes' costumes and customs were fairly authentic, they remained characters, not human beings.[24]

This wise old chief, who knows that the white man will someday pass away as well, is also problematic to American Indians such as Vine Deloria Jr. He envisions another kind of wise old chief, one who says, "'You dirty sons-of-bitches, you lying bastards, you gave your prom-ise and then when we were weak and disarmed, you betrayed us. If I had my ax here I would take a few of you treacherous bastards with me when I go.' No, rather the old chief explains that one tribe follows an-other and the white man himself will vanish. (We all know that ain't true but it does sound cosmically comforting, huh?)."[25]

While the points made by the Friars and Deloria are obviously good ones, credit has to be given to Chief Dan George for rising above the standard role he received. While the humor of "sometimes the magic works, sometimes it doesn't" was a bad directorial choice (as opposed to Berger's ending, where Old Lodge Skins is actually able to will his own death), George makes other sparks of humor flash brilliantly. When Little Big Man tells the old chief that he has a white wife, the old man asks, "Does she show pleasant enthusiasm when you mount her?

I've never noticed it in a white woman." Of course not. White women in prior films were not supposed to allow it, much less enjoy it.

Later, in a darker, more complex vein, the old man grins and laughs as he is led through the carnage at the massacre at the Washita River, believing he is invisible and reveling in the idea. The sight of the old chief walking through the mayhem with a broad smile on his face is unsettling, and it effectively conveys a feeling of how terribly out of sync with logic and humanity the whole attack is.

When Little Big Man is taken to the camp to be identified, Old Lodge Skins tells the band that it is indeed his adopted son who has returned, and they are happy to see him. But Little Big Man still needs to find his Olga, so he becomes Jack Crabb again and attempts to join Custer's army as a scout.

This provides our first good look at Custer, and while he makes us laugh, he is a far cry from the historical man. This Custer is egocentric to the point of insanity. He takes one look at Crabb and decides he isn't a scout but a muleskinner. Crabb has never touched a mule, but he goes along with the general in order to appease his ego and his madness, as does everyone else in the Seventh Cavalry.

The real Custer was also egocentric, but he was certainly not stupid and far from insane—at least not in the way the film depicts his insanity. The historical Custer was politically motivated and ambitious, and he was counting on the American public's fondness for successful generals to launch his political career. He was crafty enough to take mineralogists, reporters, and miners into the Black Hills, the direct result of which was the Indian uprising that was to win him his fame.

The film's depiction of an insane general is not new. Chivington, Crook, Miles, and many others have also been presented as unbalanced. This is unfortunate because, as in *Soldier Blue*, it allows an audience to see massacres such as Sand Creek or the Washita as the result of an individual's madness, not the result of a philosophy of a culture or broader federal policy. Perhaps if Custer had done more in this film than simply render "Custer decisions" that rank next to God's commandments—possibly above—a more realistic statement might have been made about the very real massacres he led. As it is, the film tells us nothing of the loyalty, love, and respect his men had for him or his joy in killing and being wildly reckless.

While Crabb is in Custer's army—short stay that it is—he tells his confederates that he is looking for his wife, who was taken by Indians.

One soldier repeats the old adage that the kindest thing he could do for her would be to put a bullet in her brain. Crabb looks at him in disbelief and mutters, "I don't agree."

Surprisingly, he participates in a raid against a Cheyenne camp, and the soldier leading the charge says, "Spare the women and children. Unless they resist." Crabb takes this command to mean that the women and children will be spared and is unprepared for the slaughter that follows. He tries to intercede and the sergeant fires at him, chasing him across the river. On the other side, he is attacked by Shadow, his old friend. Shadow is about to slit his throat when the sergeant fires from across the river and kills the Indian. Crabb's voice-over narration says, "My worst enemy had just saved my life by killing one of my best friends. Life was just too ridiculous to go on living."

At that point, one is apt to agree with him, but he hears a noise and finds Shadow's very young, widowed daughter giving birth in the bushes. He is enthralled by the process, and protects the woman and child as the soldiers scour the bushes. In the next scene, he is again living in the Cheyenne camp with the woman, Sunshine (Aimee Ecclés), and her young child. She is also very pregnant with Little Big Man's baby.

This camp is "safe." It is on the Washita River in Indian Territory, land deeded to the tribes by the U.S. government. Life is good, and Little Big Man is content. Life is so good, in fact, that Sunshine asks if her widowed sisters can be Little Big Man's wives as well. Cheyenne men as well as white Christian men take only one wife, so Little Big Man is unprepared for the suggestion. He stalks off, walking through the camp with his buffalo hat on his head. He comes upon his old enemy, Younger Bear (Cal Bellini), whom as a young boy he had shamed by bloodying his nose and then feeling sorry about it, whose life he had saved and therefore earned a life in exchange. Younger Bear now seems to need to prove to Little Big Man that he has "made it."

This character is a problem. Earlier in the movie he had become a contrary, a Cheyenne man who does everything backwards. He is terribly disagreeable, which is opposite the role of a contrary in Cheyenne culture. As Dan Georgakas noted, "[s]uch men were usually charged with keeping camps cheerful with their jokes. Special backward ceremonies were also common to emphasize the power of the circle and to note the two faces of reality."[26] Although his character adds humor to the film, this Younger Bear is no joker. He seems obsessed with the dishonor he received, quite accidentally, from Little Big Man.

However, at the Washita Younger Bear has stopped being a contrary, and as per Cheyenne hospitality he invites Little Big Man to join him and his white wife for dinner. The white wife turns out to be Olga. She is no longer the sweet, delicate Swedish girl who was married to Jack Crabb. This woman is a chunky scold who hits Younger Bear over the head with the duck he has shot. Little Big Man decides to pass on dinner, which is another insult to Younger Bear.

Little Horse (Robert Little Star), the homosexual man who grew up with the other two, suggests that Little Big Man eat with him instead; in fact, he invites him to live with him. Little Big Man decides to go home to the four sisters.

The depiction of homosexuality is also inaccurate. Little Horse is a caricature of a drag queen who bats his eyes and dances coyly away. In the Cheyenne culture of that time, homosexual men were revered and feared. "They lived in special parts of the village and warriors might live with them without loss of dignity. At certain times, the homosexuals were sought out to perform specific rituals and other times they were studiously avoided."[27] Little Horse's presence in the film seems to be for comic effect, which is insulting and a disservice to the Cheyennes, to homosexuals, and to Berger's character.

When Little Big Man returns to his tipi, he finds Sunshine going off into the snow to have her baby. A real Cheyenne woman might have gone to a tipi outside the circle of the village, but most women, Indian or not, are too practical to bear children in a snowdrift. That aside, Little Big Man watches her waddle off into the drifting snow and decides that he can indeed husband four women. He enters the tipi and takes off his shirt, asking "Which one of you wants to be first?" It is a tough job, but he manages all three before Sunshine reappears with their new son.

The reunion is touching. She has tears in her eyes, but it is unclear whether she is pleased he has acceded to her wishes or not. We don't have a chance to find out before Little Big Man hears the horses stamping and neighing. Old Lodge Skins has told him of a dream he had in which the horses said they were going to die, so when he hears the horses, Little Big Man runs to find the old, blind man. Thus starts one of the best directed scenes in film history.

Little Big Man kneels and asks Old Lodge Skins what is wrong. The old man says, "Don't you hear that?" Little Big Man looks up and through the snowy mist we can barely see the forms of men riding in from the distance and hear the barely discernible strains of a haunting military tune. The music gets slowly louder, and the forms become clearer until we see that it is Custer's army. What follows would be a typical slaughter scene, with women and children being shot and run through with sabers, except for the almost surreal sense we get from the colors muted by falling snow and the contrapuntal music. In a number of shots, we see a military band standing outside the village, almost like watching ghosts, playing the real General Custer's favorite song, the softly muted but catchy lilt of "Garry Owen." The "voice" of the music brings up feelings of swelling pride at odds with the reality of what the soldiers are doing to the village. The result is eerily disconcerting inner speech.

Virtually everyone is killed, including Sunshine and the babies, except for Little Big Man and Old Lodge Skins, who walk through the carnage as though they are truly invisible.

The scene at the Washita is much less graphic and bloody than the scene of the massacre at Sand Creek in *Soldier Blue*, but it is much more effective. One reason for this is the excellence of the direction. The other is that in *Little Big Man* we get to know the Cheyennes. They are people—not as fully realized as in the novel, but much more so than in previous films. We have heard their voices, laughed with them, and cried with them. We care about them personally, so their slaughter is more heartrending than the butchery of unknowns in *Soldier Blue*. Perhaps that simple fact makes a better point than any other in the film.

However, Penn's depiction of the massacre at the Washita has one striking and disappointing similarity to the Sand Creek massacre in *Soldier Blue*. It, too, is used as a metaphor for Vietnam. No one watching the film at its release could miss the obvious connections being drawn—the greedy, violent white men, the heartless and murderous military, even the Asian look of Little Big Man's wife.

After the massacre, Jack Crabb—and the film—goes steadily downhill. He follows Custer and rejoins the regiment with the plan of killing the general. He enters Custer's tent and has a perfect opportunity to kill the man, but he can't do it. Custer realizes what has happened and on a whim decides *not* to hang him, instead dismissing him like a slightly bothersome insect. This is the ultimate failure and the ultimate insult. This is the type of insult Little Big Man gave Younger Bear, and like his Cheyenne correlative, Crabb is deeply wounded. In fact, he is mentally and emotionally destroyed. The rest of the story depends on characters from the first half of the film who reappear with little or nothing to add to the plot. Crabb goes from being a derelict drunk to a crazed hermit. Then, when he is about to commit suicide by jumping off a cliff, he hears the delicate strains of "Garry Owen" once more and sees Custer's army on the plain below. He decides to join again, presumably for revenge.

Custer recognizes him, but in a formidable feat of inverted logic decides that by doing the opposite of what Crabb wants, he will do what should be done. When his subordinate officer questions his judgment before the battle at Little Big Horn, Custer rants and raves, then spots Crabb sitting on a rock. He asks Crabb what he should do, and Crabb says he should go on down there. Custer says, "Then there are no Indians down there?" Crabb replies that there are plenty of Indians down there. Custer uses this interchange to verify his decision and dismiss the officer's concern. He is frankly mad, and everyone around him knows it.

The real story behind the Little Big Horn is much more complex. Custer was relying on information from General Crook, who seriously underestimated the strength of the opposition. Crazy Horse had just defeated Crook at the Rosebud River five days earlier, and Crook didn't realize that Crazy Horse had already taken his warriors north to join Sitting Bull and the main forces of the Cheyennes and the Sioux. That, added to a sense of white superiority in all things, including war, was the cause of Custer's defeat.

In *They Died With Their Boots On*, Custer dies a heroic death fighting to protect the white American way of life. He is depicted as an admirable man, a formidable opponent, and an American hero. This Custer is his direct opposite, and neither image does justice to the reality of a man who represented the ideals and aspirations of those who believed in the righteousness of their westward expansion, including the death and destruction it caused.

From an American Indian perspective, *Little Big Man* was a film with serious flaws, but it was the best of a new wave of films sympathetic to American Indians. This immensely popular film possibly did more to develop in mainstream America a view of American Indians as human beings than any of the news reports about real Native Americans in circulation at the time, and made it less likely to dismiss contemporary American Indians, including the more militant members of AIM, as exotic oddities.

The American Indian Movement Makes the News

During the 1960s and 1970s Native Americans from a variety of tribes came together to form the American Indian Movement. It was formally organized in Minneapolis in 1968 to protect American Indians from police harassment. In 1972, AIM helped organize and motivate the Trail of Broken Treaties, the demonstration in Washington DC that culminated in the takeover of the Bureau of Indian Affairs (BIA) building, an act of frustration with bureaucracy. For the more militant Indians, a strong stand seemed the only way to fight the continual failure of government to truly address the needs of the American Indian.

One example of such failure is the 1972 Indian Education Act, section 810 of which states, "The Commissioner shall carry out a program of making grants for the improvement of educational opportunities for Indian children."[28] The intention of this piece of legislation was obviously good, although critics such as Vine Deloria Jr. stress that it was designed by Senator Edward Kennedy more to maximize his identification with the oppressed than to actually aid those who were to receive the benefits.

> the act opened a Pandora's box of benefits because it failed to describe precisely the Indians who were to be the beneficiaries of an expanded federal effort in Indian education. Title IV of the act simply made school districts with a certain number of Indian students in attendance eligible for grants and subsidies. The act was hardly a law before school districts discovered a multitude of Indians attending classes where no Indians had previously been suspected. The effort to reform Indian education became a national pork barrel and the forward thrust made by Indians in the sixties collapsed from the weight of its own success.[29]

One step forward, two steps back. It was frustration of this sort, combined with the dismal conditions on reservations, disregard of treaty rights, and the perceived manipulation of tribal governments by the BIA that led to the takeover of the bureau building and the even more militant standoff at Wounded Knee.

In 1971 Dee A. Brown published *Bury My Heart at Wounded Knee*, a best-seller that chronicled the wars of the nineteenth century from a Native American point of view. The public's familiarity with the book, even those who hadn't actually read it, made Wounded Knee a media-perfect choice on which to take a stand. On 27 February 1973, Russell Means (Oglala Sioux), Dennis Banks (Chippewa), and other AIM members and supporters took over the little settlement on the site of the historic massacre at Wounded Knee, in part because of its contemporary notoriety but also because of its location. The Pine Ridge Reservation was under the control of a tribal government led by Richard Wilson, whose administration the AIM group contended was corrupt and subservient to the Bureau of Indian Affairs.

While the takeover was obviously meant to draw the attention of the media, as were the Alcatraz and BIA takeovers, it is unfortunate that the issues presented to the nation were obfuscated by the violence that ensued. The main issues included the gap between the tribal councils and the Indians they were supposed to serve, a gap that had been steadily increasing since the days of the money-infusing poverty programs. Deloria describes the results of this gap: "Reservation Indians saw their tribal lands and resources used by outside interests, who returned a cash income to the tribal government without significantly improving the Indians' lot. Complaints channeled through the regular administrative levels of the Interior Department were turned aside or ridiculed."[30] The insurgents at Wounded Knee were asking for reform of the BIA, enforcement of treaties, and the removal of Richard Wilson, whom they accused of violent harassment, intimidation, and the fire bombing of an AIM leader's home. In other words, their complaints were complex and, as Weston notes, not easily pared down to "short slogans or simplistic stories."[31]

Although complicated, their complaints were legitimate, and the media reports of the siege were, as in coverage of the Alcatraz takeover, initially positive, mostly because it was possible in the beginning for news writers to enter the settlement and see for themselves what was going on. Weston points to John Kifner, one of the first journalists to visit the group, whose story sympathetically described the "noble savage" battling the dark forces of the government: "His story described a young Indian on sentry duty armed with a '.22-caliber rifle with a stock held together by tape' and only one bullet. It described the Indians' armaments as ordinary hunting rifles, small-bore shotguns, pistols, knives, screwdrivers, and Molotov cocktails made from soda pop bottles. This was contrasted with the government's arsenal: 'M-16 and other high-powered rifles, submachine guns, two armored personnel carriers, night-vision Starscopes and powerful searchlights.'"[32] This image would later turn against AIM when, toward the end of the siege, some reporters (who could no longer enter the compound) began to suggest that the then-improved armaments of the Indians indicated they were being supplied by "radicals" and were therefore not only violent but traitors. They suggested that the Indians were being used by the radical left, which insinuated a lack of dedication to their own cause and also presented a less-than-complimentary image of their intelligence. The old bloodthirsty savage was back.

The connection between the stereotypes of the old movies and the reports from Wounded Knee was even spelled out at the time by notable publications like *U.S. News and World Report*, which described the takeover as a "replay of a 'wild West' conflict" and noted that "members of the militant American Indian Movement, held as hostages for two days eleven white residents . . . seized guns and ammunition at a trading post, fired on approaching cars and planes, and sent out a list of demands."[33] This bloodthirsty image was reinforced by the many photos of the AIM leaders brandishing weapons, presumably for the sake of the cameras.

According to Weston, by the time the siege was over, the news media were themselves under fire from all directions, including from within their own ranks, for their representations of the events that finally ended on 8 May 1973. The Indians said the media were totally ignorant of the issues and the history of the issues at stake and accused them of accepting the government's story without investigation. News reporters were incensed at the photo-ops and staged events that they felt were attempts to manipulate the media. The government said the media's involvement prolonged the confrontation.

Whatever one's assessment of the media's role in the actual occurrences, the result for the general public was confusion. Noble savage? Bloodthirsty savage? The new warrior? Who were these people? The sixties and seventies were eventful and sometimes violent for Native Americans, and the media made sure those events were witnessed by America at large. The result was a layering of images, and perhaps the resulting conflicting feelings about Native Americans—of all kinds, not just those making headlines—are what quieted the use of the Native American in films of the late seventies.

The confusion was also felt on Capitol Hill. On 2 January 1975, Senator James Abourezk of South Dakota introduced a Senate resolution for the establishment of the American Indian Policy Review Commission, one more attempt to investigate the relationship between the tribes and the federal government. The commission's formation was a recognition that "the policy implementing this relationship has shifted and changed with passing years, without apparent rational design and without a consistent goal to achieve Indian self-sufficiency."[34] While the intent was laudable, most American Indians were unhappy with the final report, which was compiled by eleven task forces that seemed, to critics such as Deloria, to wander

> aimlessly with no apparent plan for determining a set of policy priorities for Indian programs. The final report of the Abourezk Commission listed more than two hundred recommendations that were basically housekeeping measures designed to enhance certain privileges of the Indian ruling class while making tribal governments more comfortable in their dealings with the federal bureaucracy. . . . It was evident, even to the most casual observer, that federal Indian policy objectives had finally run their course and that any future efforts on the federal level to direct the Indian programs would be merely ad hoc instructions designed to placate the natives.[35]

Hollywood was apparently as confused as the media and the government about how to represent contemporary American Indians, whom the film audience was learning to recognize as more complex than the standard stereotypes would suggest. By the mid-1970s, the major producers had apparently decided that in the case of American Indians, less was definitely more.

One Flew Over the Cuckoo's Nest (1975)

One Flew Over the Cuckoo's Nest was made into a film from Ken Kesey's novel of the same name. The novel uses an Indian, Chief Bromden, to narrate a story through the decidedly Indian eyes of a man trapped, physically as well as emotionally, in a white man's nightmare. While Will Sampson does an excellent job of portraying Chief Bromden in the film version, his part is reduced to a powerful but mostly silent presence. When he speaks, he talks of his predictably alcoholic father in the sort of poetic language viewers have come to expect from wise Indian chiefs. In many ways, he is much like the stoic, silent Indians of the earliest movies, and perhaps for many of the same reasons. In the early days, most American audiences had little or no actual experience of Native Americans, and the nonverbal dime-novel Indian filled the experiential gap. In the seventies many audiences still had little experience, but now they had too much information, some of it contradictory. Chief Bromden's imposing, silent, noble demeanor was perfect for an audience who felt more sympathetic toward Native Americans but didn't want to think too much about them.

The last scenes in the film are some of the most powerful in movie

8. From Milos Forman's *One Flew Over the Cuckoo's Nest* (1975). Photo Museum of Modern Art Film Stills Archive; courtesy of Fantasy Films and United Artists.

history, but they still rely on an audience's limited perceptions of "Indianness." When Bromden smothers the lobotomized McMurphy (Jack Nicholson), picks up the heavy marble water station—which McMurphy had previously used to illustrate the value of "trying"—and hurls it through the window, an audience can't help but feel a resurgence of power and autonomy. The last shot is of Bromden in an easy lope, heading across a wide meadow toward some trees—going back to nature in a literal as well as figurative sense. This scene works beautifully, but only because Bromden is an Indian and Indians "belong" in nature. A white man heading off alone into the woods would more likely have evoked feelings of anxiety and loneliness. The Indian's return to nature is accepted as a flight to freedom.

Like *Little Big Man* (1969), *One Flew Over the Cuckoo's Nest* is an excellent film, but the loss of Bromden's narration and of his full development as a character is unfortunate. It is, however, a fitting portrait of all the "Indian" that Hollywood assumed a mainstream audience could handle after the tumultuous events of the sixties and seventies.

5

The Sympathetic 1980s and 1990s

There's a little bit of magic in everything and then some loss to even
things out. – Lou Reed, from Sherman Alexie, *The Lone Ranger and
Tonto Fistfight in Heaven*

By the 1980s Wounded Knee, The Trail of Broken Treaties, Alcatraz,
and other headline news events made by American Indians were fading
from collective memory. Native clothing, culture, and art were no
longer as fashionable either, as the decade of Volvos, BMWs, and stock
portfolios unfolded. The world's wars were far enough removed from
American life to make antiwar statements, especially through Indian
metaphors, seem outdated. What the public heard or saw most about
Indians was definitely not on the front page and usually had to do with
law or politics. Views of American Indians were becoming much more
connected to contemporary events and cultures than in previous
decades.

By the time Ronald Reagan entered the White House in 1981, Native
Americans had won some major arguments over Indian education,
health, religious freedom, and the taking of archaeological remains.
Self-determination had been assisted somewhat by the Nixon and Car-
ter administrations, and the Termination Policy had become something
of an embarrassment. On the surface it looked as if Reagan would continue self-determination policies. A closer look reveals a program that
has been called "termination by accountants."[1]

In his statement on Indian Policy of 24 January 1983, Reagan acknowledged the initial standing of tribes as "sovereign nations," and
applauded the 1975 Indian Self-Determination and Education Assistance Act. He said the act was a

good starting point. However, since 1975 there has been more rheto-
ric than action. Instead of fostering and encouraging self-government, Federal policies have by and large inhibited the political and

economic development of the tribes. Excessive regulation and self-perpetuating bureaucracy have stifled local decision making, thwarted Indian control of Indian resources, and promoted dependency rather than self-sufficiency. . . . The only effective way for Indian reservations to develop is through tribal governments which are responsive and accountable to their members.

His method of assuring that those tribal governments were "responsive and accountable" was to cut as many federal funds as he could. He continued,

It is important to the concept of self-government that tribes reduce their dependency on Federal funds by providing a greater percentage of the cost of self-government. . . . Development on the reservation offers potential for tribes and individual entrepreneurs in manufacturing, agribusiness, and modern technology, as well as fishing, livestock, arts and crafts, and other traditional livelihoods.[2]

The reservations were already poverty stricken, and the cutbacks were fairly devastating to American Indian communities across the nation. Weston estimates that the amount of federal funds eliminated from Indian-focused programs was ten times greater than that affecting other groups. "For example, according to Stephen Cornell, cancellation of a Comprehensive Employment and Training Act (CETA) program on the Ponca Reservation in Oklahoma eliminated around two hundred jobs virtually overnight. The Navajo tribe reported in 1982 that yearly per capita income had dropped 25 percent from 1980."[3]

The private sector and "individual entrepreneurs" to which Reagan referred were quick to make use of the decrease in funds, the incredibly high rate of unemployment on reservations, and the nation's general recession. The federal government's use of Native land and labor (and the resultant loss of life) to extract uranium was old news, and Euro-American "entrepreneurs" have always invaded Native land, but the 1980s saw an unprecedented wave of private industry hit the reservations.

In 1986 the Academy Award for Best Documentary Feature was given to Maria Florio and Victoria Mudd for *Broken Rainbow* (1985), a film about the forced relocation of the Navajos so that their land in the four corners region of the Southwest could be strip-mined. Shots of Black Mesa being ripped apart, old men and women forced into government housing and then evicted for not paying taxes, livestock slaughtered by the government, and federal tractors plowing under the scrub grass necessary for sustaining stock were emotionally riveting. This film brought into focus for Americans the fact that all the atrocities they had come to know about in *Little Big Man*, *Soldier Blue*, and other films from the sixties and seventies were not isolated horrors from the past but part of an ongoing oppression.

Legally, Native Americans were better off in the 1980s than they had been for centuries, but the incursion of private and government industry onto tribal lands and the exodus of the young to more lucrative areas did not bode well for tribes. In response to these threats, many tribes established gaming industries on their reservations. Many of these enterprises have been successful to an extent, but there has been much contention on and off the reservation about the way profits should be distributed, about whether gaming undermines cultural tradition, and if so, whether it is worth the loss.[4] For the general public, gaming has engendered a new stereotype of the American Indian—that of the rich tribesman who still rakes in the taxpayers' money.

In short, the images of Natives in the eighties were more contemporary, but they were also sometimes grossly modified by new misperceptions. Sympathy for "the Indians' plight" existed, but the Indian was difficult to see as either bloodthirsty or noble.

Stagecoach (1986)

Westerns were out of vogue, and those that were made saw little success. One particularly wretched film of the period is the second remake of *Stagecoach*. The new version was as much a remake of the also wretched 1966 remake as it was of Ford's original 1939 film. In 1982 Raymond W. Stedman had suggested that "one [can] scarcely imagine the frenzy if the logarithmic progression stretches to *Stagecoach III*,"[5] but it was only four years after Stedman's statement that the third *Stagecoach* appeared on the horizon.

Ford's film had presented the Indians as a real and present danger in order to bring his little band together, after which they disappeared. This *Stagecoach* froze the action for long stretches while Doc Holiday (Willie Nelson), who replaced John Carradine's oily gentleman of the Ford film, made speeches about how the Indians have been mistreated and misunderstood. Kris Kristofferson played the Ringo Kid in this one, and to say that he and Willie Nelson brought a new dimension to the story is an understatement. As a result of the sympathy expressed for "the Indian plight," the film's characters were left without an enemy to fear, and if the attempt was to "correct" the prejudices of Ford's film, it was a smashing failure, since the tone went from fearful to patronizing—not a tremendous leap for the better. The film is interesting only in its ladling out of white guilt and its patronizing understanding of the "misunderstood" Geronimo.

As the yuppies replaced the hippies, the cyclical American fascination with the Indian waned, but despite this, at least two fairly decent films from the eighties had Native Americans as their subjects.

The Emerald Forest (1985)

By 1985 the fact that the earth is being seriously damaged by humans was beginning to dawn on many Americans. Those filmmakers who wanted to use their art to educate audiences about the earth's devastation turned to The Indian as metaphor once more. This time it was the image of the natural ecologist they sought, and who better to convey the message than those perceived innocents who lived in perfect harmony with Mother Earth?

Since "natural" and therefore "uncomplicated" Indians that audiences love to love apparently no longer exist in America, and since the deforestation of the rain forests is one of Earth's greatest crises, the story takes place in South America. *The Emerald Forest* is a film designed to show the Brazilian jungle being raped, slashed, and burned by imported white people in the interest of energy, an arguably commendable goal for the filmmakers, and the film did indeed help awaken American consciousnesses to a very serious problem. But those facts alone would be very depressing, and an up-front call to action doesn't sell many theater tickets, so to embellish the story the writer made use of the on-the-spot natural ecologists. Unfortunately, the film's South American Indians resemble the Hollywood Indians of earlier decades— except of course for their dress, which is minimal.

The film gives us long stretches of beautiful scenery and scenes of the dam builder's stolen son learning the ways of his adopted tribe, the Invisible People. These people are peace-loving, innocent, and very likable. There are quite touching scenes in which the boy, Tommy (Charley Boorman), and his wife-to-be (Dira Paes) learn about each other. When Tommy's natural father (Powers Boothe) asks the adoptive father why he stole his son, he replies that when the boy smiled at him, he "didn't have the heart to send him back to the Dead World." It is an emotional scene done very skillfully. But there are some very silly, patronizing scenes as well, such as the drug-induced visions that can be called up at will by anyone (even the engineer from the city), the coming-of-age-by-ant initiation into manhood (which is reduced to a boy's club ordeal), and much whooping and stomping around.

When the dam builder makes his way into the Invisible People's village and is reunited with his son, he sees that Tommy's ten years with these people have changed him. He is as they are—innocent, childlike, and really tough. In fact, Tommy has become a better Indian than the Indians. Sound familiar? He is the "Indian" that is focused upon in the film, which means that the story is being told through an appropriated identity. Even his white, city-dwelling father is a terrific Indian. The leader of the Fierce People says the white invader has "the heart of a jaguar." And, of course, it is the jaguar he sees when he has his turn at the drug-induced vision quest.

The other tribe in the film is problematic in other ways. The Fierce People have invaded the Invisible People's territory because the white dam builders have destroyed their own. This is a good point, one with which Native Americans have been dealing for five hundred years, and it provides the conflict needed in the film—a conflict between the noble savages and the bloodthirsty savages. As is usual with the bloodthirsty stereotype, these people have no compassion and apparently not much brain. They spend their time whooping, dancing wildly (even when just moving along a path), drinking, killing people, and possibly eating them.

While the peaceable Invisibles are taking Tommy's white father back to civilization, the Fierce People invade the village and kill everyone except the young women, whom they kidnap. They sell these women, including Tommy's new wife, to the dastardly white brothel owner in exchange for alcohol and machine guns. Tommy goes into the city to find "Daddee" and enlist his help. While this is logical, since the women have been taken into the white world, it also suggests that without the white leader, the Indians are still helpless. It is a bloodbath as the white and Invisible crew rescue the young women, a scene that is made heroic in large measure by the contrasting depictions of the low-life, drunken white men inside the brothel and the Fierce People outside—climbing in a drunken frenzy over each other, whooping and bouncing with body language much resembling that of excited monkeys.

John Boorman, the film's director, deserves credit for depicting a problem that needs all the publicity it can get and for producing a well-crafted, beautifully paced and scenic film. It is simply unfortunate that the Hollywood Indian in both noble and bloodthirsty guises was imported for the film. The new Natural Ecologist stereotype is unfortunate as well. Even though it is a positive image, it is still an image that obscures the face of the real people.

War Party (1988)

Halliwell's Film Guide describes *War Party*, a 1988 film directed by Franc Roddam, as "[a] mundane excuse for a not very interesting modern-day western." The editor of this encyclopedia of film also quotes film critic Julian Stringer, who stated that the film's "message is that it takes danger and excitement to release the pent-up, dulled emotions of both the Indians on the reservation and the white men in town. The result is a straightforward celebration of action-movie clichés."[6]

These assessments are unfortunate because they have so completely missed the intent of the film. There seems little doubt that Roddam and screenwriter Spencer Eastman carefully researched the stereotypes of the American Indian in film in order to produce a movie that makes an attempt to deconstruct them. Though white audiences raised on Hollywood westerns might agree with Stringer's assessment, for an American Indian audience it is a very different film.

Although *War Party* was not produced by an all-Native crew, the actors playing Indians are mostly Indian, and some of the casting is an inside joke for Native American audiences. The main character's father is Ben Crowkiller, a very assimilated tribal leader who, as his son says, is an "ass kisser" desperately trying to appease the white mayor and governor. This is funny to an Indian audience because the character is played by Dennis Banks, the well-known, very political American Indian Movement leader. For Indians, it's a bit of a relief when, toward the film's end, Crowkiller/Banks joins his people against the white bureaucracy.

The music in the film is cleverly chosen, particularly the very slow, melodic tune that opens and closes the film. This repetition is important because the film itself goes full circle, ending with a scene almost identical to the first. The story's circularity underscores what the main character, Sonny Crowkiller (Billy Wirth), says, "Same old shit. Nothin's changed in a hundred years."

The film opens with a shot of blood running down a stream onto the body of an Indian chief (also played by Dennis Banks) who is lying with his eyes open and his torso partially submerged. In his hand is a tomahawk. A cavalry lieutenant takes the weapon from his hand and gives it to his commanding officer, who is wearing a buckskin jacket reminiscent of Custer's. In the film's closing scene, a National Guard lieutenant takes the same tomahawk from the hand of the chief's great grandson, and as he turns and looks back, the frame freezes and the credits roll. There is no reason to see him take the tomahawk to the National Guard major; we know he is going to because that's what happened before. Sonny is right. Nothing has changed.

Not even the horses. After the major takes the tomahawk in the first scene, the men line up for a photograph, and the flash startles the horses—a buckskin, a paint, and a dalmation-spotted Appaloosa. It's impossible to miss that these are the horses that appear throughout the film, the horses that we follow as they run up a hill and into the twentieth century. They stop to graze just as Sonny Crowkiller drives by in his red truck. It is a pretty piece of directing and photography, but it also fits with the Native American sense of time as circular rather than linear. It makes good story sense.

Music introduces and comments ironically on the film's change of world. Last century's slaughter is behind him, and Sonny drives his truck into the settlement as the radio plays "It's All Right Now," past run-down houses and through impressive potholes that show how little funding there has been for civic improvement. As he waits for his friend, Skitty (Kevin Dillon), Sonny changes stations long enough to hear "Can you feel it? The power of the glory of God." Although most American Indians today are Christians, this little vignette is almost certainly a jab at the missionaries of Zane Grey's description.

A great deal of drinking goes on in this film, but there is only one alcoholic Indian, Freddie Man Wolf (Saginaw Grant). The other members of the tribe treat him rather badly, brushing him off and being disrespectful, even though he is an elder and a medicine man. Freddie has lost touch with himself, perhaps, but the others' treatment of *him* shows that his people have lost touch with their culture. In one rather too obvious scene, when things are looking very bad, Freddie hands his bottle to Ben Crowkiller and suggests that maybe now he will turn to drinking. Ben says there has been too much of that already and pours the whiskey onto the ground. Part of the message is obvious—that alcoholism is a problem in most Indian communities—but more interesting is the film's point that most of the Indians are *not* drinking to excess and do not approve of it.

War Party also challenges the Hollywood idea of mixed-blood identity. While Sonny and Skitty picnic with their girlfriends, Skitty looks around at the countryside and suggests they "take it back." Sonny jokingly calls his best friend a "crazy mutt." Skitty responds with "Hey, I'm three-eighths Indian," and Sonny replies, "Yeah. And five-eighths nuts." The Hollywood formula for a mixed-blood would call for someone mean, duplicitous, or just stupid. Skitty is none of the above. He is bright, friendly, and funny. He is given numerous occasions in the film to be a "Hollywood half-breed" jerk, but he never is. For example, when the young men are on the run, they capture a sheriff's deputy and tie him to a chair. They have every reason to be furious with the law, but Skitty is genuinely empathetic toward the deputy and even asks after his sister. He's simply a very nice young man with a good sense of humor.

To be the action-movie wannabe that Stringer feels this film is, *War Party* must have a crisis, and it does. It seems the town's mayor (Bill McKinney) wants to reenact the massacre at the Milk River as part of the Labor Day celebration. The location and the description of the massacre make it sound very much like the massacres at Sand Creek or the Washita, and most of the Indians in the film (as well as those in the audience) are not initially thrilled with the idea of a reenactment on its one-hundredth anniversary. However, Ben Crowkiller says it's good for the local economy, and the business that employs most of the reservation has offered the day off to anyone who participates, so the motion carries. According to the mayor, it will be "one hundred Blackfeet braves, greatest horsemen of all time—against an equal number of cavalry in full uniform . . . a classic plains battle reenactment."

It will all take place in front of the stands at the fairgrounds with the governor and his son in attendance. As the mayor says, it will "give those Winnebagos another reason to get off at exit thirty-nine."[7]

The only person to voice dissent over the plan is Freddie Man Wolf. He stands up, swaying, and asks, "What about the women and the children and the old ones?" He sees nothing entertaining in the slaughter of his people, but his objection loses weight when he continues with a litany the people in the room have obviously heard many times before and that seems a non sequitur in this context. "It is better to die in battle than to grow old, but no one hears these words any more."

The white mayor responds to Freddie's outburst with "Nobody's out to open old wounds or to rewrite history. All we want to do is put on a good show." How anyone could think that it would not open old wounds is a mystery, but his lack of understanding and his focus on the "show" is very much what this scene is about—ignoring the reality of the people, both historical and contemporary, for the sake of the show.

Whites in this film generally do not fare well. The one-dimensional stereotypes so familiar to Hollywood have been reserved for the white population of Montana, who are depicted as insensitive at best and racist criminals at worst. The trouble all starts because one of the "good old boys" of the town, Calvin (Kevyn Major Howard), cheats an Indian, Louis (Matthew E. Montoya), out of a twenty-dollar pool bet. Louis cuts his cheek slightly and Calvin, of course, vows revenge.

That revenge occurs during the reenactment of the massacre, for which the young men have taken great pains to dress authentically. Sonny will even carry the tomahawk we recognize from the first scene, which he and Skitty have liberated from the local museum, something an Indian audience might not condone but would very likely see as a justifiable reclamation of a family heirloom and a piece of their culture. As Skitty says, "If the museum didn't steal it, it'd be hanging on your living room wall." That Skitty takes the major's pistols as well is his own form of mixed-blood retribution. When the sheriff tells the mayor about the robbery, the mayor asks him to treat it like a bank robbery. "We don't want that stuff getting out of town." The tomahawk, like the bead dresses and other artifacts of the Blackfeet culture housed in the museum, is a commodity to the mayor, just like the bloody history that he uses to advertise the town.

Leading up to the reenactment, both sides appear to be having fun, onlookers and participants alike. There is much drinking going on, and Calvin is swigging straight from a bottle of whiskey. But the staged battle quickly and predictably degenerates into real violence. The most striking aspect of the battle scene is Roddam's direction. It begins with a long shot from behind the Indian camp and looks very much like battle scenes in countless other movies, with the cavalry riding hell-bent-for-leather from one side while the screaming Indians rush in from the other. What makes this scene unusual and eerie are the jaunty-looking carnival rides that rise into the sky behind the onrushing cavalry. It neatly places the battle out of time and place, making the whole thing seem like a nightmare scene in a fun-house mirror. As the battle progresses, the camera moves in closer and closer, effectively pulling the audience into the violence. And it does, of course, get very violent. The cavalry have been issued blanks, but after one of Calvin's friends accuses him of being afraid of "prairie niggers," he loads real bullets into his gun. He puts one of those bullets into Louis's forehead, and Sonny gives him a very real tomahawk chop to his forehead in return. Sonny, Skitty, Warren (Tim Sampson), Bubba (Perry Lilley Sr.), and Dennis (Monty Bass) then take off on horseback, and the chase is on.

Julian Stringer's point that the excitement of the killings releases "pent-up, dulled emotions of *both* the Indians on the reservation and the white men in town" is much amiss. In this film, the young men run for their lives, and the other Indians behave with calm and reserve until Dennis has been shot and Bubba, who was returning to town to get the others an attorney, is brutally scalped by one of the posse members.

In an aerial shot of the boys riding through open country, we see a John Ford landscape from the opposite point of view. The boys look like they belong to this country, and it is more than a little disconcerting that our angle of vision is that of the men chasing them in a Cessna, with one man leaning through the open door and shooting at the boys. When the man in the Cessna shoots Dennis, Sonny begins firing back with his bow and arrow, the only long-range weapon he has. It may be a bit hard to believe that a young 1980s man like Sonny would have the necessary skill to shoot one arrow, much less two, into the cabin of the plane as it goes over, but he does. In a lucky shot, he hits the pilot in the throat and the plane goes down. Hard to believe but dramatic, this scene leads to a statement by Jay Stivic (Jimmie Ray Weeks), one of the white vigilantes, that sums up the idea that is swimming in the group of rednecks' heads and fed by the only slightly suppressed racism to which Stringer referred. "I believe in the Bible, and it's real Goddamned simple. An eye for an eye. Let's go."

This same man later shoots Bubba off his horse and then scalps him while his cohorts watch and presumably approve. An interesting point is made in the scalping scene. Scalping is an act of violence from another century, one that the men have no trouble calling up in the present, but Bubba is wearing a set of Walkman earphones around his neck as his hair is lifted.

If mainstream audiences find such racially motivated violence a bit exaggerated, Robert Redford's documentary *Incident at Oglala* (1992) might change their minds. It depicts the bloody events on Pine Ridge Reservation leading up to the trial of Leonard Peltier and two other men accused of killing two FBI agents during a shoot-out at the reservation.[8] Atrocities such as these and worse can not be relegated to the distant past.

In *War Party*, besides the redneck posse, the saner sheriff, the tribal police, and the National Guard, a white tracker is hired to find the young men. He appears slightly unbalanced and thoroughly ego-ridden, and the real tracking is done by his man Friday, a Crow Indian (Rodney Grant) whose name we never hear. The chase gives the white tracker, Colin (M. Emmet Walsh), a chance to posture as scout extraordinaire. For instance, when one of his hired men shows him a stick from the young men's campfire and tells him it's still warm, Colin asks for a horse apple. He takes the chunk of manure in his hand and breaks it up, pronounces it warm, and says they are not far ahead. The man with the stick is understandably perplexed, since he just said the same thing—without getting his hands dirty. Colin is a blustering fool who enjoys the limelight, saying he can "track an eagle if it shits often enough."

The real tracker, the Crow, is the more interesting presence in the film. Native audiences probably wouldn't find it at all strange that an Indian tracks the other Indians. It is an explicit reminder that "Indians" cannot be lumped into one category any more than Danes and Greeks. Still, it is disconcerting when the Crow shouts gleefully that "the wounded Indian's dead. It's the big one—the big Blackfeet." He whoops happily as he takes the stolen pistol from the not-quite-dead Warren's hand, and it would be difficult to feel much sadness when Warren fires a bullet into the Crow's forehead.

Freddie's character is more disturbing to American Indian audiences. He is a medicine man and should therefore be revered, but he is a drunk and a derelict. He is, as Sonny will come to understand, the only one still holding on to the traditions and the strengths of their people, but even he has been damaged, perhaps beyond repair. Portrayals such as this one are disturbing because alcoholism is a serious problem, and no matter how right characters like Freddie are in other ways, they don't exactly make good role models.

As the young men run from the law and the lawless, it becomes clear that they know depressingly little about their culture. They had been quite at home trying on light blue tuxedos with ruffley shirts for Sonny's planned wedding, but when they are on the run and decide to make a war party, they don't know how. Skitty suggests that they need to have a sweat and then maybe cut their thumbs a little bit and mix the blood. The sweat might be a good idea, but the rest is straight out of Hollywood and has nothing to do with Blackfeet culture. It is only the gentle, soft-spoken Warren who seems to have a clue. "You don't need to do that. Just make up your mind, say the words. But it ain't something you do lightly." They do say the words, vowing to stick together no matter what.

Warren is killed before the National Guard offer the trapped men, at the suggestion of the governor, "just a couple of years of probation." Had Warren been alive at that point, he might have had an answer, but Sonny and Skitty don't know what to do, so they ask that Freddie Man Wolf be helicoptered to them. Skitty asks, "Think that old drunk has some answers?" and Sonny replies, "If everybody would've listened to that old medicine man, none of this would have happened." Of course he is right. It was Freddie who was against the reenactment. It is Freddie who still holds on to the Blackfeet traditions, although the alcohol has made his hold more than a little slippery.

Freddie arrives, and the audience is offered a bit of hope that these two young men will survive after all. Sonny tells him that they "made a war party—spoke the words," and then asks him to "tell us what to do, fight or surrender." Freddie spreads his medicine bundle and begins to chant, and a still sky darkens and lightning flashes ominously. Freddie is ecstatic. "I did it," he says. "I made great medicine. Let the bastards laugh at Freddie Man Wolf now." This response is bothersome. That the uninitiated young men would ask for spiritual guidance is understandable and commendable, but that this medicine man is more interested in his personal reputation than their problem is upsetting. A perplexed Skitty asks, "Did the great medicine say anything about *us*?"

As Richard Hill points out, "[t]he Indian as mystic medicine man is another new version of an old image. In the new film Indians we see an increasing reliance on spirits to solve the dilemmas Indians find themselves in. . . . No matter who the Indians are fighting—and all the films feature fighting Indians—we see the power of the Indian spirits make dramatic devices work."[9] This is simply a different kind of *deus ex machina*. Hill points to *War Party* specifically as one of the films that perpetuate this dramatic device, but there may be another explanation in this case. Perhaps the filmmakers were attempting to address New Agers, who tend to pirate Native American spirituality, by showing that the answers rarely come in a flash of lightning.[10] Freddie does give the two advice, but it is nothing he hasn't said to them many times before. "It is better to die in battle than to grow old," he says, and continues what seems very much like a charade, saying, "Napi is a man of few words. If one dies the other should surrender. One man does not make a war party."

The young men are understandably upset, since they were expecting the answer to what they should do *now*. At this point Freddie changes. He drops the persona he has been trying to fit into, the mystical, magical, miracle worker the fugitives want him to be. He becomes instead the knowledgeable elder that he should always have been. He says, very logically, "Sonny, you'll probably get twenty years. Skitty, ten—at least five. They lied to you like they lied to our people so many times before. You've acted as warriors in doing what you have done. You make me very proud of you." Freddie is reclaimed, but his advice to the young men will lead them to a suicidal charge on a crowd of well-equipped National Guardsmen. Dressed again as nineteenth-century warriors on horseback, they charge the lines and are blown to bits, and the music we hear is the music we heard at Sonny's great-grandfather's death. The film ends where it began.

War Party is not a perfect film. The love stories between Sonny and Crystal (Jackie Old Coyote) and Skitty and Dolly (Dianne Debassige) seem included simply because that's the way it's done, and the pushy news correspondent (Peggy Lipton) just sweeps through in a condescending rush. However, the film is worthwhile on two levels. It is well crafted, with excellent cinematography by Brian Tufano, and it depicts American Indians that are very recognizable to the American Indian community, with stereotypes constructed but also explicitly deconstructed. In the end, the Blackfeet people of this film turn out much the way Sonny and Skitty describe the museum photograph of Sonny's great-grandfather. Sonny says, "Got the eyes of a warrior, don't he Skitty?" Skitty replies, "Yeah. Real vulc-like. A natural hunter."[11] Sonny retorts, "Yeah, but my grandfather said he never had any luck. Wrong place at the wrong time."

Powwow Highway (1989)

Powwow Highway is an odd little film that almost everyone likes for one reason or another. It's been called a comedy, a thriller, a road film, a western, an action film, a buddy film, even a mystical movie, and each of these fits at least to a small degree. The film's shape-shifting is intentional and very effective in taking apart the old stereotypes of the American Indian.

Jonathan Wacks directed the film, Toyomichi Kurita was the cinematographer, and together they created a film that is both beautiful and not so beautiful, but it always seems natural. The landscape shots are spectacular, and as one reviewer noted, "[T]he movie was shot entirely on location, and the set decoration, I suspect, consists of whatever the camera found in its way. (If this is not so, it is a great tribute to the filmmakers, who made it seem that way.)"[12]

9. From Franc Roddam's *War Party* (1988). Photo Museum of Modern Art Film Stills Archive; courtesy of Hemdale Releasing.

The "sets" include poverty-stricken reservations, a ratty poolroom, a high school gym, a middle-class Denver suburb, as well as road shots and location shots in Santa Fe, New Mexico. One reason this film was so well received by American Indians is that they *recognized* it all, the story, the people, and the places, a rare thing in depictions of Native Americans.

The two buddies in the film are Buddy Red Bow (A. Martinez) and Philbert Bono (Gary Farmer). Buddy is a Vietnam vet, an AIM member who was part of the Wounded Knee altercation, a volatile young man who is not shy about expressing his point of view, verbally or physically, and a respected member of his tribe. Chief Joseph (Sam Vlahos) says that "everybody knows Red Bow's got his own way of doing things, but he's done more for this tribe than anyone." His way of doing things is confronting trouble head-on. In short, he is a recognizable "type" in Indian communities, and like the real AIM members, he is respected by most but certainly not all of that community. His cinematic predecessor is Willie Boy.

The other buddy, Philbert, initially seems like Buddy Red Bow's absolute opposite. Phil is a big man with a sweet smile, a soft look, and an open sincerity that seems, at first, very simple. His simplicity is easily misunderstood as simplemindedness, but he is actually quite bright.

He has chosen the "old way" and moves to a different rhythm. In many ways, he is like the "traditionalists" who choose the way of their ancestors. Usually, the Hollywood Indian who makes that choice, rare though that is, behaves as though he has had a lobotomy and forgotten that he actually lives in the twentieth century. Philbert has no such problem.

Philbert lives in both worlds, but he chooses to privilege the traditional Cheyenne way, though he is misunderstood and laughed at even by the old aunt he goes to for advice. He is on a quest to become a warrior—not the way Buddy has become one, by fighting in Vietnam or Wounded Knee, but the old way. He is "building power" throughout the film, finding the four tokens that have special meaning for him and which will help him earn his warrior's name, Whirlwind Dreamer. Whirlwind Dreamer is a good name for Phil. The world of the film goes round in a violent whirl, but Phil remains centered and calm, no matter what goes on around him.

Powwow Highway begins with a sepia-toned image of a Cheyenne warrior riding a pony over a hill. Rodney A. Grant is the rider, and although Grant never looks totally at home on or near a horse, he makes a splendid-looking warrior, the kind Philbert yearns to be. The camera shifts to a contemporary reservation filled with shacks and wrecks. Inside a bar, Buddy is playing pool. As he leaves, he squeezes past Phil, who is coming in. Phil sits at the bar with his beer, watching a commercial on television.

The white man selling cars in the ad is dressed in a suit and wearing a large headdress. He announces, "We got mustangs. We got Tontos, and we got Pintos. . . [He holds up his hand, palm out.] 'How' folks. This old cowboy's on the warpath with heap big savings—all our choicest stock. Come on down off the res or the ranch and check out your pony today." This is the sort of appropriation and denigration that would immediately raise Buddy's temperature, but Phil sees it as a sign. To be a warrior you need a pony, and he likes the idea of the car being a pony and decides he must have one. He doesn't go to the slick salesman in town to buy it, however. He goes to a junkyard and says to the owner, Fidel (Del Zamora), "I want to buy one of your fine ponies." He looks through the dirty window and imagines a herd of horses running across the plains. The camera follows a beautiful pinto and then cuts back to a dilapidated wreck of a '64 Buick. Fidel looks incredulous when Phil says, "That brown one's a nice one." Instead of buying it "normally," he trades whiskey, a packet of something that could be marijuana or sweetgrass, and a few bills. He has gotten his pony the old way, by trading for it.

He is ecstatic as he sits in the old car, which he names Protector the War Pony. He whoops, laughs, takes the plastic Madonna off the dash, and casually tosses it out the window.

The next scene is a tribal meeting where Sandy Youngblood (Geoffrey Rivas) is trying to sell the reservation community on allowing his employer, Overdine, to strip-mine the land. Red Bow speaks up, pointing out that the reservation's 75 percent unemployment figure isn't going to change if they allow the corporation to strip off what's left of their natural resources. He says, "This ain't the American dream we're living. This here's the third world."

This scene sets up the plot of the film. The corporation is in cahoots with the "feds," who want the contract to go through so badly that they frame Red Bow's sister, Bonnie (Joannelle Nadine Romero), so that Red Bow will have to leave the reservation and travel to Santa Fe to get her out of jail, and the fly will be out of their ointment long enough for the vote to go their way. Aside from pointing out that the American Dream and the American law do not always work for the Native American, the plot is not overly stimulating, and that's okay. As Roger Ebert pointed out in a 1989 review, "The plot is not the point. What 'Powwow Highway' does best is to create two unforgettable characters and give them some time together."[13]

This time together is part of Phil's warrior quest, and though he does succeed, it is Red Bow who learns the most. In the beginning, Red Bow thinks he is pushing Phil around, as he did when they were kids, using him because he has a car—more or less. Throughout the film we see him making the decisions, which Phil casually and good-naturedly ignores completely.

In one of the movie's best scenes, Phil talks on the CB to a trucker named Light Cloud (the voice of Floyd Red Crow Westerman), who is surprised that Phil recognizes his name as that of a prophet. "Nobody picks up on that," the trucker remarks. "Nobody cares about history these days." Phil says something about seeing a Cheyenne Chief on *Bonanza* (noting that the chief was played by a white guy, but . . .), and the trucker says, "*Bonanza*? That's not where you learned about Light Cloud." Phil says, "No. My Uncle Fred told me about Light Cloud."

This little scene is absolutely packed with meaning. Farmer does a remarkable job of conveying the multilayered issues. There's the fact that many American Indians have moved away from the old ways and the old stories, the obvious reference to history via the media, in this case television, and the jab at those who routinely cast "white guys" to play Indians. But Phil is a trickster figure, and as such he always turns the expected into the unexpected. The beneficent trucker assumes that Phil is one of those learning his history on television, and "Uncle Fred" comes as a pleasant surprise.

An uncle is exactly what Bonnie Red Bow's two children haven't had. They are mixed-bloods who don't even know what tribe their mother is from. While this is unlikely in real life, the point it makes in the film is that one's culture can slip away.

The trucker and Phil talk about Light Cloud and Sweet Butte, where Light Cloud had his vision, and the trucker says to Phil, "You gotta go there. Just keep on going straight into sunrise. Can't miss it." For Phil this is a sign, and instead of turning south on Interstate 25, he heads for the sunrise.

Buddy has been asleep in the car, and when he wakes he finds himself not in Colorado, as expected, but in the Black Hills. Phil has hiked to the top of the butte and left an offering (a Hershey bar) with the other prayer ties. He tumbles down a hill toward Buddy, whooping gleefully. Buddy is angry because he is on a mission of his own—to save his sister. He grabs Phil as he goes by, and Phil picks him up off the ground like a toy. "Nobody grabs me no more." It's true. Phil is gathering power, and no one will push him around, but it certainly doesn't mean he gets huffy about it. He smiles pleasantly when a young Sioux couple tells them there's a powwow at Pine Ridge that evening. Buddy is in a hurry, but for Phil the trip itself is important, not just the getting there. There's no discussion; Phil simply heads for Pine Ridge.

Buddy is again upset when Phil stops the car, wades into a wide stream, and sings into the sunset. However, he joins Phil and they sing together, Buddy getting better as they go along. This music is part of the culture and the people that Buddy has been fighting for all his life, and Phil is reminding him of that. They are by then wet and cold, and they stop at the house of an old army buddy of Red Bow's to warm up and dry out.

Wolf Tooth (Wayne Waterman) greets them with a gun aimed through a window opened by a previous bullet. He lives on the Pine Ridge Reservation, the site of the "incident" that resulted in Leonard Peltier's imprisonment. The "goon squads" are apparently still there, and they have recently wrecked Wolf Tooth's machine shop. He and his wife, Imogene (Margot Kane), have decided to leave because, as Imogene says, "There's a shooting a week. It's like living in Belfast." Phil offers them a ride to Denver. Buddy doesn't like the idea because he thinks they should stay and fight it out. Phil doesn't make a judgment of any kind.

The powwow at Pine Ridge is held in the high school gymnasium, which makes sense since the film's time is mid-December. They aren't specially dressed for the occasion, except that Buddy is wearing a traditional bone choker. This pleases Phil, and he asks what the rosetta is. It is Buddy's Purple Heart, and the two elements together provide an excellent description of who Buddy Red Bow is.

Philbert is happily singing with the drummers, when Wolf Tooth is accosted by Bull Miller (Adam Taylor), the crooked Pine Ridge tribal leader and goon-squad commander. Buddy breaks in and insults Miller. He is about to be beaten by Miller's men when a very large knife sticks in the wall by Miller's head. Miller and company leave, and the camera pans to the bleachers, where we see the man who threw the knife. It is an old war buddy of Red Bow and Wolf Tooth's.

Wolf tells Phil that the man, Jimmy (Graham Greene), was held in a tiger cage for thirty-one months until he managed to escape by slitting four throats. This exposition is a little clumsy, but it helps the audience understand why the vet stutters uncontrollably and weeps. Buddy goes to sit by him and tries to make conversation. Jimmy tells him to dance. Red Bow scoffs, "Look at these people dancing around a basketball court. You'd think a few feathers and some beads was a culture or something." In a highly charged moment, Jimmy chokes out, "No. You got mean."

Obviously, Buddy has never thought of himself as mean, especially not where his people were concerned. It comes as quite a shock to Buddy to think that Jimmy might be right. Buddy moves to the dance floor and begins to dance, slowly getting into the rhythm of it and finally smiling broadly.

A welcome change from the "wise old chief" stereotype is the Cheyenne tribal leader, Chief Joseph (Sam Vlahos). He is calm like Phil, savvy like Buddy, and gets things done. For instance, he drives to Santa Fe when he hears about the problem with Bonnie. At the jail, the federal agent asks him if there is a six-foot-tall, three-hundred-pound man from his reservation, and Joseph replies, "No." This is an obvious lie made more obvious when he hears Phil gunning Protector outside. He peeks through the shades and sees Phil, who has hitched a rope to the jail bars and to Protector's axle in order to make a jailbreak. Joseph

10. From Jonathan Wacks's *Powwow Highway* (1988). Photo Museum of Modern Art Film Stills Archive; courtesy of Warner Brothers.

smiles, leaves the jail, and follows the crew (which now includes Bonnie, her kids, and Bonnie's friend, Rabbit) as they head for Pueblo land. The inference is that once on Indian land they will be safe from the federal agents, corporation employees, and sheriffs that are chasing them (which probably seemed odd to all the Indians for whom this has never worked). But Chief Joseph follows them, and it is his releasing cattle onto the road that stops the pursuers and allows the group to get away. He also has a truck to take them home after Protector the War Pony crashes and burns.

There is a great deal to like about this film, but there are problems as well. One of the most obvious is the casting. A. Martinez does a splendid job in his role, but he is not American Indian. Since Buddy Red Bow is the lead character in a film that consciously deals with appropriation of identity, a Native American actor would have been a better choice. The film has excellent American Indian actors in minor roles, but you have to look fast to find them. For instance, Graham Greene's Vietnam vet is wonderful, but his entire role takes up about a minute of film time.

The other major flaw is the character of Rabbit Loyton (Amanda Wyss), Bonnie Red Bow's friend. It is plausible that Bonnie would have a good friend who is, as Buddy says, a "Texas Twister." Unfortunately, someone must have felt that the film needed a little sex thrown in, so she wears jeans that are amazingly tight and pursues Buddy in no uncertain terms. It is as if she sees him as the exotic Cheyenne warrior, and the ghosts of all those lusty Hollywood Indians come back to haunt us.

The Last Decade of the Twentieth Century

The presence of Native Americans on television and in news stories escalated during the 1990s. From popular television shows like *Northern Exposure* with its very likable Natives to heated discussions about sports mascots, Native Americans appeared everywhere and in many forms. The old stereotypes were represented, but new images appeared as well. Partly, this was caused by the increasing presence of American Indians in law and politics, as business leaders on and off reservation land, as journalists, and as filmmakers.

A look at some of the news stories of the nineties shows some interesting developments in the activities of and attitudes about American Indians. For instance, the first few years of the decade saw disputes between Native peoples and non-Indians over spearfishing rights in Northern Wisconsin. The courts had validated the treaty-given right of the Chippewas to spearfish, and sometimes violent disputes erupted over what some non-Indian people thought of as unfair treatment. The question was, "Why the hell can they do it and we can't?" The response from Tom Maulson, spearing leader of the Lac du Flambeau band, was that they must exercise their rights or lose them forever.[14] The courts upheld the Native rights, and by 1995 the conflicts had virtually disappeared. The treaty rights were accepted by the non-Indians, and the Chippewas made an effort to exercise their rights in a way that had less impact on daily limits for others.

In 1973 AIM members had pressed for Indian rights at Wounded Knee. In 1990 Wounded Knee was revisited, this time by four hundred people who braved minus twenty-five-degree temperatures and icy winds to attend a releasing-of-the-spirits rite. Birgil Kills Straight, one of the spiritual leaders who led the dawn blessing of the site, said, "We are here to wipe away the tears, to mourn the dead . . . something that should have been done 100 years ago."[15] Unlike the 1973 siege, this was not a media event but a nonpolitical, spiritual ceremony. In fact, the media-attracting presence of Russell Means and Dennis Banks (AIM leaders during the 1973 encampment) caused a bit of a rift, with some Indians refusing to ride with them.

When Leonard Peltier made his 1993 bid for a new trial, it made national news—and a fair number of Americans across the country actually knew who the newscasters were talking about. (This is due in part to Robert Redford's excellent documentary, *Incident at Oglala*.) In 1995 the Kickapoo Nation was welcomed back to its home in Illinois.[16] And Russell Means published *Where White Men Fear to Tread*, an autobiography that didn't earn him many friends but did bring some attention to the "whys" of American Indian actions. In short, attention was focused on American Indians from many directions.

When old prejudices did surface in the media, Indian communities often strongly voiced their objections. For example, the 1993 outbreak of the hanta virus in New Mexico was initially reported as "Navajo flu" spread by rodents (implying that the Navajos were at fault for being unclean). News writers were made to pay attention when the Navajo people strenuously protested that depiction as well as the invasion of their private mourning of their dead.

Perhaps the best-known furor of the nineties was over team mascots. In 1991, fans of the Atlanta Braves introduced the tomahawk chop and a war whoop, and it didn't set well with Native Americans. As an editorial in the *Minneapolis Star-Tribune* requested at the time of the World Series, "Please, Georgians, leave your tomahawks, chants and headdresses at home. It's simply wrong to mock another people, to use their cultural symbols crudely, to resurrect hurtful old stereotypes." And Nick Coleman of the *St. Paul Pioneer Press* said, "I hate to use a term like 'redneck,' but Atlanta deserves abuse. A city of white folks wearing Indian costumes and waving toy tomahawks is a city in danger of getting such a good smiting from on high that [Gen. William T.] Sherman's outing will look like a backyard barbecue."[17] Even with such scolding the tomahawk chop continued, and demonstrations were held at the next World Series as well. Since then many teams, including those from Stanford University, Dartmouth College, Western Michigan University, as well as many high schools have changed their team names and mascots. But that fight goes on. The legal arm of the Coalition Against Racism in Sports and Media has gone to battle with the University of Illinois for its mascot Chief Illiniwek, with Bradley University for its Brave, with Florida State for its Seminoles, and with the professional teams—the Washington Redskins, the Kansas City Chiefs, the Cleveland Indians, as well as the Atlanta Braves.[18]

You would think that with all these problems over the old names, new products would steer clear of offensive handles. However, the

Brooklyn-based Hornell Brewing Co. has begun marketing "Crazy Horse Malt Liquor."[19] The company and their supporters can't understand why American Indians wouldn't find having one of their greatest heroes gracing bottles of beer a compliment.

Sometimes the press tried to get it right, but their long-held stereotypes got in the way. For instance, in 1994 the birth of a white buffalo was hailed in the *Washington Post* as "The Great White Hope." That story earned its author the "Columbus Award" from the Native American Journalists Association for "perpetuating ignorance and stereotypes about Native Americans."[20]

That tribal law is seldom accepted by Americans unless it coincides with their own ideas of justice is also evident in the 1994 story of two Tlingit boys who were banished to an island for a murder they committed. The Associated Press dispatch read, "There were no lawyers, no oaths, no objections. The twelve judges drank the juice of a thorny plant, wore deerskin tunics and had the courtroom cleansed of evil spirits. This was justice, Tlingit style."[21] The cultural and spiritual contexts were excluded from the story, leaving an impression of the Tlingit elders as exotic primitives. This story made national news headlines, as Weston points out, while the press virtually ignored the fact that the Tlingits were battling against termination efforts by the federal government at the same time. Sometimes choosing which story is more newsworthy is the most effective way to perpetuate cultural biases.

Some legal goings-on received so little public recognition that only last-ditch efforts were able to save American Indian nations from disaster. In July 1997, with almost no debate and no public hearings, a Senate subcommittee approved two measures that would have drastically changed the way tribes are governed in the United States. The measures were cleverly buried as riders on a spending bill that provided funding for the National Endowment for the Arts and for new park lands (which included buying a gold mine that threatens Yellowstone and a grove of old-growth California redwoods about to be axed). The first measure would have forced tribes to waive sovereign immunity from civil lawsuits or lose up to $767 million, nearly half the budget for daily operations on Indian land. The second rider stated that tribes could be denied federal money if their income rose above a certain level. This rider could have resulted in bankruptcy for Indian nations.

The second measure was a direct response to the impression current in America that Indians are getting wealthy from gambling casinos. It would have instituted means-testing, whereby tribes would be denied federal money if their incomes rose above a certain level. Only a small percentage of the Indian tribes with casinos make money; in fact the Lummis of Washington—the home state of Senator Gorton, architect of the riders—closed their casino in 1997 because they were losing too much money. As John Blackhawk, chairman of the Winnebago tribe of Nebraska said, "If Senator Gorton would ever be willing to come to a reservation, he would see that most tribal governments are barely getting by as it is. These two riders are outrageous. They are a total departure from the government-to-government relationship the tribes have always had with Washington."[22]

Most Indians and many of Senator Gorton's fellow senators saw his actions as part of a long-standing vendetta against Indians. The feud started in the mid-seventies when Mr. Gorton lost a landmark Supreme Court case, known as the Boldt decision, which recognized the Lummi Indians' right by treaty to 50 percent of all the salmon caught in the waters of the Northwest. In 1995 he led an effort to cut $200 million from the $1.7 billion budget for Indian tribes. "He's an Indian-fighter," according to Darrell Hillaire of the Lummi tribe. And he says that he will continue to fight, and that he will use his position as chairman of the committee that oversees spending for the tribes to "overhaul" Indian affairs.[23]

Fortunately, intense lobbying by the tribes and fellow Republicans induced Gorton to drop his riders. In exchange, however, the Senate agreed to hold hearings on the immunity question and to bring it to a vote by spring 1998. It also authorized a study of whether future payments to Indians should be based on need instead of the current population formula. Senator Gorton's response was, "I have not gained the goal I set for myself, but we are going to be able to debate these issues intelligently over the coming year in a way we haven't done in this Congress."[24] It seems that Native Americans are still under attack, even in the late 1990s.

On the other hand, many Americans still see Native Americans as mystical and in tune with the universe. The result of this affection is, as often as not, the all-too-familiar appropriation of culture. An August 1997 article in the *Washington Post* describes one of the many instances of this kind of thing. The article begins, "Very few Indians live here anymore. They left for parts west long ago, but some of their teachings remain. Many of those in the East who follow the Red Road of spiritual practice of one tribe, the Lakota Sioux, are white people. . . . 'They aren't here, but their teachings are,' said Nancy Alves, owner of White

Buffalo, and American Indian crafts shop in Carmel. Ms. Alves, 46, is of Greek and Portuguese descent."[25] The author of this article seems unaware of what she wrote: that Ms. Alves and her husband opened a shop to sell Indian spirituality through crafts and sweats. She goes on to write that Mr. Alves, also of Portuguese descent, is the "sacred fire keeper. He keeps the rocks hot." The article gives a blow-by-blow description of a purification ritual à la *Native Wisdom,* a book on the spiritual practices of Native Americans. (To say that the book is unappreciated by many Native Americans is an understatement of epic proportion.) It is disheartening that the article was printed in one of the nation's leading newspapers in the 1990s.

Hollywood had little to say about Native Americans for a decade or more, but the 1990s saw the celluloid Indian back in the saddle, literally. Multiculturalism became one of the buzzwords of the nineties, and Hollywood filmmakers were ready to "set the record straight" on the American Indian. But it wasn't as easy as it seemed.

Dances With Wolves (1990)

Dances With Wolves was hailed as a landmark film because it treated American Indians as fully realized human beings, and it does make a serious attempt to do so. Kevin Costner (director, producer, and star of the film) chose to use talented Native American actors from the United States and Canada for the Indian parts, with the result that they are believable, likable, and interesting. The gentle humor of Kicking Bird (Graham Greene) and his fellow Lakotas is a refreshing change from the one-dimensional Native American characters in the westerns of previous years.

The Lakotas are presented as intelligent, happy, loving people who can and will fight if necessary. The Pawnees, on the other hand, don't fare as well. Given that the film is partially told from the Lakotas' point of view, it is understandable that their enemies would not be presented in an altogether positive light; however, the Pawnees are not allowed to surface as anything but vicious killers. The one minor exception is a warrior who says (about his confederate who insists on attacking a white muleskinner's camp), "He won't stop until he gets us all killed." But, of course, they do attack. We still seem to be facing the noble savage/bloodthirsty savage stereotypes—they simply inhabit the same film.

Every positive trait of the Lakotas has a correlative opposite trait in the white world of the film, a world represented by the Union Army.

Whereas Ten Bears (Floyd Red Crow Westerman), Kicking Bird, and Wind In His Hair (Rodney A. Grant) are individualized, and respectable, intelligent men, the cavalry officers are misfits at best and psychotics at worst. Costner's character, Lieutenant John Dunbar, begins the film as one of those with his screws a bit loose. He has received a wound to the right foot that the surgeons, without much thought, are about to amputate. Unable to tolerate the idea of living without a foot, he decides to sacrifice himself.

His injury is serious enough to necessitate amputation but not to prevent him from walking to the front line, where the Union Army faces the Confederate Army across a small field. He gets on a horse and gallops across the field in front of the Confederate sharp-shooters, who miss him. This is miraculous enough, but then, to make the point even clearer, he does it again, this time dropping the reins and holding his arms out in an obvious replication of Christ on the cross, saying "Forgive me Father" as he begins his run. The Rebels still can't hit him, and the Union soldiers are so encouraged by his heroics that they take to the field and win the battle. When the smoke has cleared, General Tide (Donald Hotton) leans over Dunbar, who is still thinking about his foot. The general promises that he will be allowed to keep the foot and tells his subordinate to bring up his private ambulance because, "We've got an officer who's worth something here." Suicide was apparently an admirable ambition for cavalry officers of the time.

Given his choice of assignments in payment for his bravery, Dunbar chooses to go west. He wants to see the frontier "before it is gone." As Louis Owens has noted, "'Frontier' in this context—and in most American contexts—clearly means 'Indian.'"[26] He is another white hero going in search of the Vanishing American.

Dunbar's first stop is Fort Hayes, where the commanding officer, Major Fambrough (Maury Chaykin), responds to him as a king to a subject, but this king is from some bizarre fairy tale, hallucination, or perhaps Conrad's *Heart of Darkness*. He is obviously mad. The last words he says to Dunbar after sending him to "the farthest reaches of the realm" are, "I've just pissed in my pants, and there's nothing anyone can do about it." Why this character is mentally disturbed is never answered, except perhaps to underline the unnatural existence of Euro-Americans on the "frontier." His reference to himself as a monarch is a clear allusion to his European roots, and his seeming inability to become Indianized, as heroes such as Natty Bumpo and Dunbar are able to, is perhaps his undoing. It is the hybridization that occurs to Dunbar that allows him not only to survive like an Indian but to actually become more Indian than the Lakotas who adopt him. The commander's lunacy also serves to set in high relief the wholesome sanity of the Lakotas.

As Dunbar rides away from the Alice in Wonderland world of Fort Hayes with the white muleskinner, Timmons (Robert Pastorelli), they hear a gunshot as the commanding officer puts a bullet into his own brain.

Timmons is another fine example of white manhood. He is foul-mouthed, filthy, and disgusting in every conceivable way. Watching him eat pickled eggs and talk at the same time is enough to make an audience gag, and that is one of his lesser flaws. He is exactly what the striking and impeccably groomed Wind In His Hair is talking about when he describes white men as stupid and dirty. The only saving grace for Timmons are his last words to the Pawnees about to scalp him, "Don't hurt my mules. Please don't hurt my mules."

After Timmons, it is a long time before we see any white men other than Lieutenant Dunbar. In the meantime, we get to know the Lakotas very well. Owens has noted that the scene of first contact between Dunbar and the Lakotas is a "seminal moment in American film fantasies about the Indian, and it tells us much about contemporary America." He points to the pond, where Dunbar has been bathing after the intensely difficult task of cleaning up the wasteland left by the former army men, as a baptismal pond:

> Costner, as Dunbar, rises stark-naked from his baptismal pond to confront the splendidly dressed and very startled figure of Kicking Bird, a Lakota warrior and holy man. . . . Millions of people around the world had a good laugh over this scene. On the surface Costner appears to be playing subtly with comic inversion: The very proper "civilized" Indian meets the naked White savage. Close beneath this comic veneer, however, lies a more disturbing reading, for this scene illuminates the crucial Euroamerican fantasy of being inseminated with Indianness, of absorbing and appropriating everything of value in the indigenous world as a prelude to eradicating and replacing the actual Native. . . . It is, in fact, the very nakedness of Dunbar that frightens the Indian warrior, as well it should, for Dunbar will soon be clothed in Kicking Bird's Indianness. Like a psychic vampire, the Costner character will from this moment on in the film become more and more Indian until, in the final absurdity, he is a better Indian than the Indians themselves.[27]

The Lakotas are presented as friendly, warm, affectionate, and humorous with a love of stories and laughter and a very definite sense of justice. Dunbar quickly adapts to their lifestyle, and we are allowed to watch his learning curve soar. For instance, when he loses his hat during a buffalo hunt, and a Lakota man picks it up and puts it on, Dunbar learns how to deal with it in a Lakota way. At first he asks for it back rudely, and gets nowhere. Wind In His Hair intercedes and tells the Indian man, "If you want to keep it, that's okay, but you must give him something in exchange." The others nod in agreement, so the man in the hat gives Dunbar his hunting belt. Dunbar has the good sense to take it, and Wind In His Hair, who is also learning white ways, says in English what Dunbar had said to him earlier, "Good trade."

The Lakota lifestyle and sense of justice are in total opposition to those of the white soldiers who finally arrive at Fort Sedgewick, long after Dunbar has become a Sioux. These men are stupid as well as ignorant; they lie, cheat, and steal; they are inherently violent. When Dunbar returns to retrieve his journal, they kill his horse, Cisco—which the audience has come to love—for no good reason. They beat Dunbar and treat him worse than they would treat an animal. They accuse him of being a traitor and refuse to listen to him. They take turns shooting at Two Socks—Dunbar's pet wolf, which the audience has also learned to love—and finally kill him, too. The slaughter of the two animals was well planned to wrench the emotions of the audience and make the soldiers into one-dimensional villains. It is more effective, in fact, than the scenes of slaughter in *Soldier Blue*, although the victims in this film are animals instead of people. The point is that they are mercilessly killed innocents, as were most of the Indians in *Soldier Blue*, but these are victims we get to know well. They work beautifully as metaphors for the Lakotas in *Dances With Wolves*, because we know that "the People" will be killed with as little thought as the horse and the wolf.

The only member of the white crew that is in any way admirable is the other lieutenant, Lieutenant Elgin (Charles Rocket), whom we can easily see going the way of Dances With Wolves given the same experiences. His positive presence lets us know that there but for the grace of the Sioux goes Dunbar. When his Indian friends rescue Dances With Wolves and the soldiers are killed, the audience is well prepared to cheer the action, even the lieutenant's death, a complete reversal of the old "the only good Indian is a dead Indian" theme.

Given that the film attempts to undo in a little over three hours stereotypes developed over hundreds of years, it is understandable that

11. From Kevin Costner's *Dances with Wolves* (1990). Photo Museum of Modern Art Film Stills Archive; courtesy of Orion Pictures.

the characterizations of the white people in the film are one-dimensional, but it unleashes other stereotypes that are equally unfair. Not all white men of the 1800s were stupid or cruel, and not many were crazy. The mentally unbalanced officer is quickly becoming the new stereotype in films attempting to be sympathetic to the Indians or Vietnamese or other oppressed groups. This is a problem because in relating violence and cruelty to the madness of a few, it releases the general public from responsibility.

The main flaw of *Dances With Wolves*, however, remains the problem of appropriation of identity; John Dunbar is the white narrator of an Indian existence who, when the white men become so loathsome to him he can no longer stand being identified as one of them, shouts "I am Dances With Wolves!" Like Horse, he slips into the Indian world easily and skillfully, and like Horse, he marries a woman from the Sioux camp. The difference is that she does not die at the film's end. Instead, they ride off together, selflessly leaving "the People" so that the soldiers won't look for the renegade Dunbar in their camp. (How the soldiers are supposed to know he has left is unexplained.) The love affair, however, continues. This would have been a breakthrough for miscegenation in Hollywood films, except that Stands With A Fist (Mary McDonnell) is a white woman saved by the Lakota as a young child, so the taboos apparently still exist in Costner's film. In fact, when Kicking Bird asks his wife, Black Shawl (Tantoo Cardinal), what the people think of the match, she responds, "They like the idea. It makes sense. They're both white."

The film is also set within the "comfort zone"—that fifty-year period of cinematic Indian existence in the "Wild West." As Jan Elliott, editor of *Indigenous Thought* states, "Indians are the only minority group that the Indian lovers won't let out of the 19th Century. They love Indians as long as they can picture them riding around on ponies wearing beads and feathers, living in picturesque tee-pee villages and making long profound speeches. Whites still expect, even now, to see Indians as they once were, living in the forest or performing in the wild west shows rather than working on the farm or living in urban areas."[28] Elliott's description fits Costner's invention very nicely. They are indeed picturesque, like a favorite snapshot in a very old album.

Dances With Wolves is also, to some extent, a take-off on the theme of the Great White Hunter in league with the Natural Ecologists. That is one reason many Native Americans are not particularly enamored of the film. Ward Churchill, in fact, calls it *Lawrence of South Dakota*, a reference to the colonialist themes underlying *Lawrence of Arabia* (1962) and such films.[29] This is underscored by Dunbar's obvious imitation of Christ as he spreads his arms wide and rides back and forth in front of the Rebel army, and his symbolic purification of and by the waterhole before he immerses himself in the Indian culture. However, Costner (as director and producer) did make a serious attempt to portray the Indian experience from the Indian point of view. In addition to the fact that Indians were played by Indians, he made a serious attempt at getting the Lakota culture and even the geography right, used the Lakota language with a remarkable degree of success (although the men were inadvertently taught a feminine inflection), and presented in the gentle, irrepressible humor of "the People" a wonderful contrast to the one-dimensional savagery in so many other films.

The use of the Lakota language is one of the most positive, though not unproblematic, aspects of *Dances With Wolves*. Subtitles have been used, with varying degrees of success, in a number of films with American Indian characters. Since few members of mainstream audiences would understand Lakota, subtitles were necessary in this film. These were more successful than most, artfully constructed and therefore relatively unobtrusive; however, they still represent reported speech, the word of the Other through the medium of an alien language. Translating one language into another is not a simple matter of finding the corresponding words. Language is based in experience and culture, and when one culture tries to explain another, the language is likely to be inadequate. The result is that the translator must settle for the best possible choice, and in the case of *Dances With Wolves*, the choices were informed by people from the Lakota culture, so we can assume that the translations were approximations of good quality, and the juxtapositioning of the two languages, especially the gradual change as Dunbar learns Lakota and the Lakotas learn English, allows them to illuminate each other, with an emerging plurality of voices that does not fuse into a singularity. As Bakhtin stated, "Languages throw light on each other: one language can, after all, see itself only in the light of another language."[30] Whether this juxtapositioning allows insight into the Other culture is, in *Dances With Wolves*, questionable, but the attempt is a positive one.

The film's closure is more bothersome for Native Americans. The audience reads the scrolling statement that by thirteen years after the story's end, the Sioux had been defeated completely and had surrendered to live on reservations allotted by the white man's government. The implication is that the people we have come to know no longer exist. Vanished. End of story—end of film. While the history may be basically correct, the implication of extinction is, as Mark Twain said of the report of his own death, highly exaggerated. *Dances With Wolves* falls into the same final slot—it reinforces the sad but unavoidable "truth" that real American Indians are gone, and it's just a damn shame.

Though not perfect, this film deserves a few points for presenting the Lakotas as a unified culture with a national identity of their own, one independent of that which the white intruder brings, and at least attempting to present Indians as wholly realized human beings. In this way, at least, it is a successful revisionist film.

1492: Conquest of Paradise (1992)

1992 was the quincentennial of Columbus's "discovery" of the Americas, and Hollywood jumped on the revisionist bandwagon with two major films and numerous television specials on Columbus the hero or Columbus the villain. None of these were particularly successful, possibly because American audiences seemed unwilling to accept Columbus as either hero *or* villain. Although the concept of Columbus as hero is deeply entrenched in American mythology, by 1992 it was a well-publicized fact that the Taino Indians, who numbered in the millions when he arrived, had ceased to exist within a very few years due to forced labor, starvation, disease, slavery, and slaughter.[31] That knowledge has made it difficult for American viewers trying to be "politically correct" to accept Columbus as a film hero. Judging by box office receipts, most viewers in 1992 apparently chose simply not to deal with him at all.

Ridley Scott's *1492: Conquest of Paradise* is possibly the most revisionist of the productions. The directing in this film is excellent in flashes, with incredibly beautiful scenes of the little fleet at sea, the island breaking through the mist, frightening Inquisition burnings, and lavish court scenes. Although the pacing is generally tedious, an unusual problem for the director of such action films as *Blade Runner* (1982) and *Thelma and Louise* (1991), the rich texture of the film almost overcomes that flaw. The acting is also of top quality. Gérard Depardieu as Columbus (with a French accent?), Armand Asante as his nemesis, Sanchez (a conflation of King Ferdinand and Torquemada), and Sigourney Weaver as Queen Isabel bring immense talent and believability to their roles. The other supporting actors are also excellent, so the failure of the film does not lie in the talent assembled. The problem is that Scott tries to walk a razor's edge between depicting the national myth and revising that myth. The result is that no one is particularly pleased.

In his article, "Cinema's Conquistadors," Peter Wollen places the films about Columbus, particularly Scott's, in the realm of the western genre. He believes that at the "heart of Hollywood lay the myth of the West, the evocation of a world in which 'knights of the true cause' were set against the forces of evil and 'pagan savagery' represented by the Indian." He refers to a 1955 essay by Eric Rohmer, who saw the depiction of the American hero and the American West as the act of inventing a tradition—in short, constructing a myth. "[T]he classical elegance and efficacy of the American cinema came precisely from the historic role of the Americans as a colonising people like the Ancient Greeks, . . . there was a clear parallel 'between the first colonisers of the Mediterranean and the pioneers of Arizona.' Typical American heroes are members of 'a race of conquerors, which opens up the land, founds cities, is in love with action and adventure, and in spite of or perhaps because of this is more determined to preserve its religious or moral tradition.'"[32]

Columbus not only fits the description of a western film hero, he is actually the prototype of the invention's various incarnations. Wollen believes that for most Americans, he represents the nation's "first adventurer, the first immigrant, the first prospector, the first pacifier of savages, the first missionary to the heathen, the first law-maker, the first town-builder, the first merchant and entrepreneur, the first slave-taker, *the first modern American*" (emphasis mine).[33] This representation is as old as Euro-America itself, since the myth developed as a result of the new settlement's need for its own identity, its own heroes.

In 1792, only a few years after the American colonies declared their independence from Britain, the tricentennial of Columbus's mission to the New World became the perfect focus for the national myth builders. King's College was renamed Columbia University, Columbus was called the "new Moses," and the nation's new capital was planned for an area newly named the District of Columbia. Washington Irving's popular three-volume biography of the man helped to firmly entrench him as America's first hero, a "romantic genius and an embattled underdog, harried by flat-earthers and envious hidalgos, betrayed by perfidious royalty."[34]

By the 1892 centennial, Columbus Day had been established as a national holiday, and an extravagant ceremony was planned for the anniversary. It was so ambitious an undertaking that when the World's Columbian Exposition finally opened in Chicago, it was 1893. There were no Tainos left, so the exposition's developers brought in Navajos, Kwakiutls, Haidas, Apaches, and Penobscots, along with some Arawaks, who at least spoke the language of the Tainos. The result was an exhibition much like the wild west shows popular at the time, except that the scenes were domestic instead of violent.[35]

By 1992 idolizing Columbus was not such a simple matter. Apart from a general loss of idealism about America, mainstream audiences had been conditioned by films like *Tell Them Willie Boy Is Here*, *Soldier Blue*, and *Dances With Wolves* to see Indians as victims. Columbus was no longer clearly a heroic "discoverer" or founder of a better world. He was as likely to be judged the bloodthirsty savage and the Tainos the truly civilized.

This is the milieu into which Scott fits his film, albeit uneasily since his star—the protagonist—can't emerge as the villain. The film was based on the well-researched book by Green Party activist Kirkpatrick Sale, which places responsibility on Columbus's "fanaticism" for the damage done to the peoples and the environment on the continent he "discovered." The book makes Columbus into a personification of the sadly deteriorated value system of fifteenth-century Europe, but Scott's film emphasizes Columbus's single-minded courage and makes Columbus a quietly rebellious observer of that value system. The result is a more acceptable hero for the nineties, a man who values Indian cultures, appreciates the bounteous natural world he has stumbled upon, and is a victim of churchmen and politicos motivated by greed.

A more believable description of Columbus is that of the "Admiral of the Mosquitoes," as one of the malevolent Spanish noblemen in the film disdainfully refers to him. According to Tzvetan Todorov in *Conquest of America*, that would be a very mild epithet to come from one of his men. Todorov describes a Columbus who has little in common with a John Wayne character or Costner's Lieutenant Dunbar, but one who was apparently not the gold-hungry explorer he is often made out to be, either. His journal is filled with references to gold or the search for gold, but Todorov believes this was to appease his readers, the royalty of Spain. Gold was the primary reason he received financing, and he was duty bound to find it. According to Todorov, the Tainos understood and used Columbus's political and economic needs. They repeatedly told him of *other* islands where there was more gold than sand, and "[t]hus Columbus wanders from island to island, for it is quite possible that the Indians had thereby found a means of getting rid of him."[36] Todorov sees Columbus's fundamental motivation to be religious, not monetary, that "[i]nfinitely more than gold, the spread of Christianity is Columbus' heart's desire," and that he envisioned himself as the man chosen by God to bring the true faith to the New World's savages.[37]

Perhaps true faith is what gave him the courage or confidence to sail beyond the known limits; he thought he had the answers even before the questions presented themselves. He never swerved from believing he had found Asia, a "truth" he already possessed. Evidence of his single-minded need to reaffirm this "truth" exists in copies of the oath he insisted his men take as they searched the island of Cuba for the "civilized" people he was certain lived there. Each man had to state that

> he had no doubt that this was the mainland and not an island, and that before many leagues, in navigating along the said coast, would be found a country of civilized people with some knowledge of the world. . . . A fine of ten thousand maravedis [Spanish currency] is imposed on anyone who subsequently says the contrary of what he now said, and on each occasion at whatever time this occurred; a punishment also of having the tongue cut off, and for the ship's boys and such people, that in such cases they would be given a hundred

lashes of the cat-o'-nine-tails, and their tongue cut off ("Oath sworn regarding Cuba," June 1494). A remarkable oath, whereby one swears that one *will* find civilized inhabitants![38]

It is no wonder his men were continually on the verge of mutiny, his settlements were a disaster, and he was finally dragged back to Spain in irons.

Columbus was neither the egalitarian Scott presents, nor was he the daring knight of Western myth. Wollen suggests that Scott would have been better off starting from scratch with a fiction than attempting to cram a very square Columbus into the circular understanding America is trying to develop.

Although the Indians in Scott's picture are secondary to the plot, such as it is, they are something of an embarrassment. The dress, body paint, and so forth are as authentic as Hollywood gets, but the people are portrayed as childlike until they finally fight back. At that point, they cease communicating in language, and make only unidentifiable noise. A review of the film in *Sight and Sound* stated that the noise was electronic, but it sounds very much like that made by a wild animal, specifically a large cat. In short, Scott presents the Tainos as human as long as they are communicating and going along with the invaders, but when they strike back, they become less than human. Perhaps this was the only way to make the hero of this film appear justified in killing them, although the film's Columbus seems to kill more of his own men than Tainos.

Clearcut (1993)

Richard Bugajski's *Clearcut* takes place on the other side of the continent from the islands of *1492*, and five hundred years later. The film is based on the novel, *A Dream Like Mine*, by M. T. Kelly, which is derived from current news stories of Native land rights disputes. It was filmed shortly after the Mohawks and Lubicons had particularly violent altercations with the Canadian government, and there is an unmistakable sense of reality to the interchange between the groups in the film—and a particular sense of déjà vu to those who were involved in the Lubicon Lake conflict.

By the end of October 1990, a logging company, Buchanan Lumber, commenced logging operations on unceded Lubicon lands, even though the Lubicon people had made it very clear that they would fight to protect their lands. After much legal wrangling but while the matter was still far from settled, Buchanan's sister company, Brewster Construction, was caught bulldozing logging roads on Lubicon land. On 8 November 1990, Lubicon Chief Bernard Ominayak released the following statement:

> After years of unsuccessfully trying to protect Lubicon land rights through the Canadian Courts and around the negotiating table— during which time unauthorized resource exploitation activity in our unceded traditional territory has continued at an ever accelerating rate, doing great and growing damage to our traditional society and way of life—the Lubicon people have regretfully concluded that we have no choice but to once again enforce our legitimate jurisdiction over our unceded Lubicon traditional territory and to defend ourselves and our lands as best we can.[39]

A similar standoff happened that year between Quebec police and Mohawk warriors at Oka, Ontario. In an interview with Tony Hall, a specialist in Native American Studies, Maureen Pendergast noted that "[m]any Indian leaders across Canada say the legal and political system has repeatedly failed them." Hall responded,

> The begrudging reluctance of [Prime Minister Brian Mulroney's] government to intervene in this blossoming crisis is indicative of a far deeper failure at the root of virtually all the festering controversies surrounding Aboriginal land claims throughout Canada. . . . The current crisis can be seen as a symptom of a prolonged failure on the part of the national government to fulfill its constitutional obligation to protect Aboriginal lands. Whether we are talking about a golf course in Oka, or major hydroelectric works in northern Quebec or northern Manitoba, or polluting pulp and paper mills in Alberta, or logging in BC or Ontario, all of these developments—and many others like them—are proceeding under the auspices of provincial governments. And most of this activity is going ahead with stunning disregard for Aboriginal claims or for the environmental or social devastation that this kind of exploitative development often presents for Aboriginal societies.[40]

This sounds like a plot synopsis for the film *Clearcut*. Unfortunately, however, the film offers a strange Indian man as the Native line of defense once the negotiations fail, which is a far cry from the sort of organized, well-articulated, and powerfully presented defense of the Mohawks and the Lubicons.

Clearcut starts with eerie sound effects that introduce the film as more nightmare than dream. Film critic Geoff Pevere states, "[f]rom the first [wilderness horror movies], it borrows the sense of latent mysticism and brutality that a secular, largely urbanized world suspects lurks beyond the treeline, and from the second [Yuppie panic cycle movies], the sense that that same urbanized world, and all the values it represents, is constantly vulnerable to the violent rage of those ploughed under by 'progress.'"[41]

This very odd film stars Graham Greene as Arthur, an Indian man who shows up after the Indians have lost a case against a logging company. Pevere characterizes the film as a "clearly serious movie dealing with a pertinent but troubling issue—native rage," and Arthur is apparently the enraged arbiter of payment for the crimes against his people and the environment. Discussing the character in an interview in *Maclean's*, Greene said, "Arthur is a spirit of nature who shows human beings, 'This is what you're doing to us and this is what I'm going to do to you.'" Greene added that he thought Arthur was "hilarious."[42] While it is true that Arthur can be very funny, the humor is as dark as it can possibly be, and the intensely violent nature of the film produces laughter only as a release of tension.

The Native community in the film is quietly contained in its rage except when trying to physically block the progress of bulldozers, after they have exhausted all legal avenues. *Clearcut*'s Indian characters exhibit the stoicism of the stereotypical Native American, and the raw rage in this film is embodied in only one man, who is difficult to understand from either a white or Native point of view.

As in the real events, the logging company is clear-cutting the forest, and all legal efforts to stop them have failed. The white attorney for the tribe, Peter Maguire (Ron Lea), arrives just as the bulldozers start ripping the land once more, and as he watches helplessly, he notices Arthur briefly walk through.

In the novel, Maguire is described as a journalist, one who reports on the goings-on, but in the film he is transformed into the attorney, and as such he is inextricably linked to the problem. The film suggests that his concern is generated by "white guilt" and that he sees himself as the liberal savior who has let these childlike people down. A tribal elder (Floyd Red Crow Westerman) asks him the most pertinent question in the film, "Who do you feel most sorry for, us or yourself?"

Later, when Maguire confronts Bud Rickets (Michael Hogan), the mill owner, he notices Arthur in the background for the second time.

When the ubiquitous "wise old elder" of the community takes the attorney to the other side of the lake, Arthur hitches a ride in the small boat. During the trip across the lake he banters in an almost childish manner with Maguire, making fun of the attorney's "book-learned" knowledge of Indians. When the attorney fluffs his macho feathers and says he would like to skin the mill owner alive, Arthur cocks his head at him and says, "You think that's a good idea?" Just when he seems to be making sense, he sits up and says, "We have an oral tradition." The attorney says he knows that. Arthur then takes a small snake out of his bag, lets it flick its tongue in the attorney's face, proceeds to bite its head off, and throws the body in the lake. "Now that's oral tradition," he says and laughs. The purpose here is evidently to let the attorney, and the audience, know that there is more to Native Americans than can be learned from books, but the message is lost in the senselessness of the action. Arthur is quickly emerging as an unpredictable psychopath and the white attorney's worst nightmare.

Arthur later arrives unannounced at Maguire's hotel, while the people in the next room are making noise. The attorney asks them to stop, and they laugh at him until Arthur bursts through the door with a very large knife. He uses duct tape to immobilize the revelers and forces the mortified attorney to help him. This scene appears to convey the idea that Arthur sees what is wrong and fixes it, dispensing his own brand of justice—in this case duct tape across lips, hair, and eyes as well as wrapped around the body. He is apparently a self-appointed avenging angel, and the attorney is on his list of people who have to pay. This is in contradiction to Maguire's vision of himself as liberal do-gooder trying his best to help, but Arthur apparently sees him as part of the white world—specifically the white legal system—that is destroying his culture.

Earlier in the film, the elder had invited Maguire to participate in a sweat ceremony, during which the attorney had a vision of blood, petroglyphs, and Arthur's face. This is not a film that would be likely to grant a significant vision (which is generally of benefit for the entire group) to this white man who has earned so little respect. It can be supposed, then, that we are to deduce either that Arthur is causing the vision or the attorney is calling on Arthur-the-Spirit to dispense a justice he has been unable to attain through the white legal system. Either way, the attorney's vision and the sweat in general represent a bastardization of what is supposed to be a cleansing or healing ceremony.

Arthur kidnaps not only Maguire but also the mill owner and takes them up the river into the wilderness. It is evidently Arthur's job to show the attorney what justice is by dispensing it to the mill owner in front of him. The story might have had possibilities if Arthur's brand of justice had not been so reprehensible. He flays the skin off the mill owner's leg and cauterizes the wound with a burning stick. He refers to it as "debarking." He explains that it is in retribution for a history of genocide and environmental waste. He says, rather casually, "You know that soldiers used to play catch with the breasts of Navajo women. They were slippery and hard to hang onto. This is nothing—this is one man's leg." The mill owner's penalty does fit his crime in an extreme way, but Arthur's demeanor throughout the film makes it seem more like the action of a psychotic criminal than an avenging angel, although the horror of the history he recites is unsettling and causes a definite stutter-step for an audience appalled at his actions.

Brian Johnson calls Arthur a "version of the trickster spirit of Indian folklore . . . a ghost from the past."[43] While it is true that a trickster is an unpredictable manipulator who allows people a look at themselves, this "trickster spirit," with his deadly war club and bloody revenge, is downright psychopathic in his rage. By making him appear so mentally imbalanced, the positive results of the "trick" are lost. If the screenwriter and director intended Arthur to represent Native physical prowess, the "Native rage" Pevere refers to, the natural ecologist, or the Native trickster, they failed rather badly. Arthur, in the last analysis, more closely resembles the hillbillies in *Deliverance* (1972) than the tricksters of Native American tradition. He is simply a terrorist.

The most unfortunate aspect of this character portrayal is that audiences might extend it to the real Natives who were fighting real bulldozers. While the Mohawks, Lubicons, and other Native nations are serious about protecting their interests—even when pushed to extremes—they do not bite the heads off snakes or involve themselves in senseless cruelty as a matter of course.

Black Robe (1992)

In his essay, "Hostiles," Geoff Pevere compares *Clearcut* to a film that was released at the same time, *Black Robe*, directed by Bruce Beresford and based on a novel of the same name. Pevere states that they are "two nearly identically themed movies," which is, at first glance, a rather strange remark.[44] He isn't referring to the time or place, since *Clearcut* is set in contemporary time on the western edge of Canada, and *Black Robe* is set during the 1600s in the Great Lakes area of Quebec. Both are

overly simple plots that dispense white guilt, but while the main characters in *Clearcut* are a white attorney and a probably psychotic Indian,
the protagonist in the Beresford film is a Jesuit priest, Father LaForgue
(Lothaire Bluteau), who has come to help civilize the savages, although
he has seen the damage they can do (he learns of the tribes from a priest
whose fingers and ear they have cut off).

Maguire and Father LaForgue have one thing in common: they each
want to "help" the Indians, one by saving their land and the other by
saving their souls. They are both do-gooders who fail in their missions,
feel guilty about things that are and are not within their control, and
misunderstand the people they are trying to help. They do, in fact,
cause harm.

Pevere sees *Black Robe* as a film that

exploits and assuages contemporary guilt by making damned sure
not only that we know that what is about to happen is and was
wrong, but by making equally sure that its central character knows
the same thing. From the moment we see LaForgue, he is clearly
bearing the weight of all our rear-projected knowledge and pain.
Etched in Bluteau's drawn face and watery dark eyes is the back-
ward-flung knowledge of impending and ineluctable cultural atroc-
ity. And he, as befits our moral ambassador in history, feels bad about
it already.[45]

While it is true that LaForgue is the white man through whom the
audience is supposed to view the Indian world, which results in a softly
muted appropriation much like that of Costner's Lieutenant Dunbar,
the priest "feels bad" about almost everything—not just the Indians.
His eyes are always "watery" because he has apparently taken on the
burdens of the universe. He is serious to the point of becoming boring,
and he doesn't allow himself to think or feel anything that might shake
his religious foundations, although the sexual activity in the Indian
camp is particularly difficult for him to bear. Bluteau's portrayal of the
priest is so restrained that it leaves one wondering what all the fuss is
about. As Johnson pointed out, "The movie's most obvious shortcom-
ing is that LaForgue's spiritual torment—which serves as the backbone
of the book—is almost invisible. In the novel, he suffers such agonizing
lapses of faith that his mission seems absurd; in the movie, his faith is
unshakable and the irony is lost."[46]

LaForgue is accompanied by a lusty young Frenchman, Daniel
(Aden Young), who finds the Indian world very attractive. This young

man falls in love with an Algonquin woman, appreciates Indian sensibilities, and is even willing to be open-minded about their view of the after life, saying to the priest, "Is it [the spirits of the dead hunting spirit animals at night] any harder to believe than sitting around on clouds looking at God?"

When an Indian man asks the priest for some of the tobacco he knows is in the priest's baggage, the priest says no, because it is for trade with the Hurons. The man walks off in disgust, and Daniel tells the priest the man doesn't understand because "they share everything without question." The priest responds that they *should* question—they plan nothing further than the moment. Later, the priest tells the band's men that there will be no need for sexual relations in Paradise, and Daniel says, "They don't look too happy." The priest replies, "They *should* be happy. I've told them the truth." Father LaForgue believes he knows what *should* be in any given situation. In this way, he is less interesting than his counterpart in the novel but more representative of the westering white population, many of whom felt that any situation or lifestyle not similar to their own was to be changed. He manifests their "sacred duty" to change the savage world, to save the savage soul, and use the "unused" landscape. Father LaForgue is ultimately successful, although it costs the lives of the whole band of Algonquins (save one girl) given the task of transporting him the twelve hundred miles to the Huron village. He does manage, with help from the diseases brought by his predecessors, to convert the Huron village to Christianity, and as the credits at the end make clear, it is a conversion that proves fatal for the whole tribe.

Pevere's irritation with this film is justified in that it makes very clear that the Indians were doing fine before white people, blackrobes especially, came. It is truly heavy-handed in its depiction of the rightness of the Indians' lifestyle and the rigid ignorance of the priest.

The white people in the film are supposed to be French, although they speak in English, and the Natives speak their own languages, which are subtitled. So why would the Indians need to speak in Tonto-talk? They, like their Hollywood brethren, seem to be infested with the bug that takes away the use of pronouns, which in film generally indicates a lower mental capacity. There is also a scene in which the Indians sit in hushed silence waiting for "Captain Clock" to chime. While a clock would certainly have been an impressive novelty for Natives of the sixteenth century, the film's depiction of them as wide-eyed innocents waiting for the "god" to make a noise isn't meant to elevate the audience's view of their intelligence. The scene makes it easy to forget that these are people who were master navigators, who mastered multiple languages, and who used muskets in other parts of the film.

However, the film does have some positive qualities. For one thing, it is beautiful. The countryside, Quebec's Saguenay River area, is fabulous and the cinematography exquisite—it would be worth watching with the sound completely off. Also, this is one of the few films in which white men don't end up being better Indians than the Indians, although only the white men and one young Indian woman survive the trek.

The costuming is well researched and authentic, with the exception of shaved heads, something the Algonquin apparently did not do. Beresford makes it very clear that costuming is important at the film's start when the Algonquin Chief Chomina (August Schellenberg) is seen putting on his paint, feathers, and other regalia. The scene is spliced with cuts of the same goings-on in Governor Champlain's quarters. Both men's costumes come to seem bizarre and overdone, which is a refreshing point of view. It is rendered especially humorous when two white officers discuss the look of the natives in less than complimentary terms, and it is impossible not to notice that their mustaches are twirled and the plumed feathers in their hats sit at rakish angles.

This film also scores a point on miscegenation. Daniel and Annuka (Sandrine Holt) leave the priest to his mission and go off to live together. We know the Huron village isn't going to last, but we don't know about the couple at the film's end, so it is at least possible to think they might live happily ever after.

Brian Johnson summed up the differences between the two Canadian films of 1991 very well: "*Black Robe* is a dignified spectacle, visually stunning yet strangely lacking in consequence. *Clearcut* suffers from an overkill of consequence."[47]

Last of the Mohicans (1993)

In 1993 director Michael Mann took on the daunting task of making James Fenimore Cooper's *Last of the Mohicans* into a new film, and it is generally an improvement over the first four movies that were made of the novel. Fortunately, Mann resisted the urge to reproduce the earlier versions, all of which exhibited even more exaggerated colonialist ideals than the book. He also ignored much of the book itself, which is not necessarily a bad thing either, except perhaps for a Cooper purist who would probably be surprised to see his Natty (always Nathaniel in the

1993 film) Bumpo involved in a love story, which is exactly what Mann made of the script. Much of Bumpo's motivation, including his stay at Fort Henry during the battle, is driven by his love for Cora, which probably has Cooper revolving in his grave. Cooper's rough backwoodsman has become a very smooth operator with the ladies.

Central to the great American myth of Nathaniel (Hawkeye) Bumpo is his rejection of the white culture that spawned him, a desire to be part of the Indian world, a world where he will always be set apart. He has shunned the pious White existence and has adopted the wilderness as his home. Mann's Bumpo is a "new age," sensitive guy. Although he is a white man raised by Indians, he is still quite white, even aristocratically white. Once more, the Indian experience is depicted through the interpretive presence of a white protagonist. Film critic Gavin Smith sees Nathaniel as the "living embodiment of proto-American identity, synthesizing the values of his two cultures while remaining separate from nationalist allegiances."[48] This is a good description of the typical western hero and a good definition of the appropriation of identity that is common in films containing American Indians.

In Mann's film, Nathaniel behaves just as his Indian brother and father behave, and his values appear clearly Mohican, or at least as much so as those of the Indians in the film. As is common with white heroes in films with Indians, however, he is better at everything than they are. While the respect they hold for each other is made obvious, Nathaniel is the one who gives directions and makes decisions. Yet, he is also stronger, smarter, more honest, and more philosophical than his white acquaintances. Perhaps this is the "synthesis" of which Smith speaks.

Nathaniel's Indian brother and father are admirable types with good senses of humor, and they are obviously trustworthy. One of the first scenes in the film establishes their total acceptance by the white colonists. Russell Means as Chingachgook and Eric Shweig as Uncas play affectionately and good-naturedly with the white settlers' children; however, they remain firmly in the background. Only the final scene makes a real statement about Indians, unless you count the stereotyped images of the "great tracker who never steps on twigs" or the "bloodthirsty savage" as represented by Magua (Wes Studi), who, incidentally, is smitten with stereotypically white desires for furs, gold, and whiskey. Unfortunately, the one direct statement about Native Americans is that they are doomed to vanish. This film is about the British, French, and white Americans, with the Indians as colorful backdrops and sidekicks for the hero, and in the end, as the white Bumpo and his adoptive Indian father stand on a mountain and look over the wilderness, we hear only that he is the "last of the Mohicans." It would be a poignant scene, except that it seems a fitting ending for some other film.

A major problem in this film is that the Native Americans are so visible that it leads audiences to think they are also "heard," that there is a real interplay of voices and perspectives. Actually, the Mohican and the Huron experiences in Mann's film are relayed through the alien and dominant white voice and white perspective.

Also a problem is the idea that although Nathaniel has lived all his life with the Indians, it is the white woman he stumbles upon who immediately becomes his soul mate. As previously stated, mixing emotions, mixing blood, and mixing identity are actions quite likely to provoke violence in Hollywood movies. Although miscegenation is and was a fact, apparently it is an easier idea to deal with in film if presented as a tragic possibility rather than as a possible reality, even in the nineties. Cinematic examples are numerous, including previous films discussed, such as Horse's Indian wife, Running Deer (nicknamed Freedom), who dies carrying their unborn child, and Little Big Man's Sunshine, who dies along with their newborn baby. When an Indian woman is loved by a white man, she is almost certain to die. But Nathaniel (Daniel Day Lewis) and Cora (Madeleine Stowe) in *Last of the Mohicans*, as well as John Dunbar and Stands With A Fist in *Dances With Wolves*, show that white men and white women are destined to be together, even if one or the other has lived with Indians most of his or her life. Perhaps this is why Mann's Cora is all white, while Cooper's was of mixed white and black parentage.

In *Last of the Mohicans*, there is also a more traditional twist on the dynamic. Cora's younger—white—sister and Bumpo's adoptive—Indian—brother are in love with each other, which results in his glorious death trying to rescue her, followed by her choice to commit suicide. The American identity requires separation from the Native Other, and it seems that any way it is arranged, miscegenation is a very risky business.

Geronimo (1993)

There is no love interest at all in Walter Hill's 1993 film *Geronimo*, aside from almost casual mention of wives who have been killed or left behind.

12. From Michael Mann's *The Last of the Mohicans* (1993). Photo Museum of Modern Art Film Stills Archive; courtesy of Twentieth Century Fox.

There is not a hint of miscegenation, but most of the other old conventions for depicting American Indians have been followed to the letter.

Geronimo is played by Wes Studi, an Indian actor of considerable talent, but like most Hollywood films, this one is moderated, interpreted, and relayed through a white man, the sixth Cavalry's Second Lieutenant Briton Davis (Matt Damon). In fact, as the list of actors appears on the screen at the film's start, Wes Studi is the first Indian but the fourth actor. The main character in the film is not Geronimo but Lieutenant Charles Gatewood, played by Jason Patric. This is a film about the white man's experience of Geronimo, not about the man or his people.

Lieutenant Gatewood, like Dunbar, Horse, and the other white heroes, "knows" the Indians he is chasing. Davis says at the film's start that Gatewood has a "sympathy and knowledge of *all* things Apache." For a man as young as the lieutenant appears to be, with a past that includes fighting for the South in the Civil War, a four-year stint at West Point, and time to marry and produce two children in the East, it is amazing that he has obtained so much sympathy, much less so much knowledge, which includes an excellent command of the Apache language. His knowledge is so in-depth that he, like his film brothers

Dunbar, Bumpo, and Horse, makes a better Indian than most of the Apaches. For instance, when a column of Apaches parallels Gatewood's column with only a shallow arroyo between them, one suicidal Apache man streaks across to meet Gatewood *mano a mano*. Gatewood tells the naive Davis that the man is showing his bravery to his comrades, which, considering the situation, seems a bit redundant. Any Indian who rode with Geronimo against the odds they faced already had plenty of opportunity to display courage. It would also seem that the Apache was taking a great deal for granted—that the cavalry would sit still while their leader went out alone, that the lieutenant would know what was going on in his mind, and that he could out-joust the "white knight" of the Southwest. He rides straight at Gatewood, firing his pistol wildly and hitting nothing, much like the Indians in old grade-B movies. In a move that appears much more (stereotypically) Indian than cavalry, Gatewood pulls his horse to the ground and uses him as a shield while he calmly aims and fires his carbine, sending a bullet neatly through the Apache's heart. The roles have been reversed, and Gatewood's appropriation of an Indian identity is firmly established.

The lieutenant's demeanor also fits the stereotypical idea of how an Indian should behave. He is a soft-spoken, quiet, strong, and stoic man who is difficult to read. He comes from a Southern family and therefore also has reason to "hate the blue coat," which makes his choice of profession rather puzzling. Most of his dialogue in the film exists to explain to Davis, and thereby the audience, what is going on. Gatewood is so "cool" it would be unlikely that he would tell this story, *his* story, at all. This explains the existence of the younger, more loquacious Lieutenant Davis.

The Apaches in the film speak more than they are allowed to in most films, but the fluidity and linguistic control of their speech is orchestrated to fit their status. The Apache scout, Chato (Steve Reevis), who rides with Gatewood, is very quiet, and when he speaks, it is in the stilted English of the old western tradition. His most interesting and poignant scene occurs when he is dismissed from the army and herded into a cattle car with the rest of the Chiricahua Apaches. He is a man who helped the white invaders track his people, ostensibly because he believed it was best for them, a man who has believed the "white lies," and who is devastated when his rank, his gun, and his identity are taken from him. He says, "I am *Sergeant* Chato. Scout." Later, in the cattle car, he will tell Geronimo, "You were right to fight the White-Eye. Everything they said to me was a lie."

Of Geronimo's band, the warrior we get to know best, although not well, is Mangas (Rodney A. Grant). He is a dignified man with absolute ideals. During the brief time Geronimo's band is detained on the Turkey Creek Reservation, the white Scoutmaster, Charlie Seiber (Robert Duvall), asks him to be a scout like Chato. He says simply, "I will stay here." In the cattle car, after the war has been lost, he will tell Chato that he hates him—that he will always hate him. Mangas is a loyal and ethical man but his character is not multidimensional, and neither is his language. That he speaks a simple but more fluent English than Chato is an indication of his morally elevated rank.

Geronimo is a more complex character than the others, he has much more dialogue, and he is the only one who exhibits a sense of humor. In a scene toward the beginning of the film, Gatewood and Geronimo are holding out against a posse that wants to hang Geronimo. The posse stops quite a way from the two, who are taking cover on the mountainside. Geronimo fixes the sight on his rifle and shoots the whiskey jug one of the white men raises to his lips. Gatewood says, "Great shot." Geronimo replies, "Not so great. I was aiming for his head." The whole scene, improbable as it is that the posse would simply turn tail and run after losing the jug, is a bonding experience for the two men. Gatewood gives Geronimo his field glasses, and Geronimo gives him a hunk of turquoise in exchange.

When Gatewood comes to take Geronimo back for the second time, the warrior asks him if "they" have taught him how to lie. Gatewood rips the chain with a silver cross from his neck and places it in Geronimo's hand. "My god is a god of peace," he says, "a god of life, not death." Geronimo is touched and reminds Gatewood that he gave him the chunk of turquoise, implying that the stone functions as a symbol of the Chiricahua's "One God," just as the cross symbolizes Gatewood's Christian faith. While it is true that the Apaches believe in a single creator who had twelve helpers,[49] the differences between the two systems of belief are a bit diffused in this scene. Audience sympathy for the Apaches is likely to be high by this point in the film, so the implication is apparently that Apaches are not so different from white people. Both believe in peace, and both are killing each other as fast as possible. The difference—in the film—is that the Chiricahua are fighting to preserve their lives, and they are truthful. The duplicity and hypocrisy of the whites is underscored immediately after the discussion of belief; the Chiricahua, including women and children, are seen being herded onto the railroad cars that will take them to the prisons in Florida. The audience hears the sorrowful strains of a hymn as the defeated people shuffle off to confinement.

White hypocrisy finds corporeal form in General Nelson Miles (Kevin Tighe). He appears on the scene, historically and in the film, when he comes to replace the more benevolent, intelligent, and honorable General George Crook (Gene Hackman). After dismissing the Apache scouts and Crook's line officers from field duty, Miles sends five thousand men out into the desert to bring in Geronimo. The result is predictable, especially since Gatewood and Davis went alone to bring him in the first time, and it was made quite clear then that Geronimo could only be found if he wanted to be found. After five months of chasing shadows, Miles calls in Gatewood. He orders Gatewood to find Geronimo and make him the offer Crook had made earlier—if they surrender, they will spend two years in Florida and then be returned, with their families, to Arizona. Gatewood says he doesn't believe Miles or the U. S. government means to keep the bargain, but Miles says it is an order. He also says, "This conversation never happened." As the scene ends, Miles turns out the lamp and his face goes into shadow, the only remaining light coming from behind and below. The effect is sinister, making Miles look very much like a devil. Although this general is not obviously mad, as was Custer in *Little Big Man* or the commanding officer of Fort Hayes in *Dances With Wolves*, he is disastrously stubborn, emotionally impoverished, and morally corrupt.

The two major Indian characters in *Geronimo* are Ulzana (Victor Aaron) and Geronimo. Both men speak fluent English, and even their Apache has a more rhythmic sound to it than Mangas's or Chato's. In a somewhat puzzling scene, shot inside a tipi in a wash of deep red light, Mangas, Geronimo, and Ulzana talk. The elder Ulzana speaks first. "Before the White-Eye came we had a good life. Now we are forced to stay on this little piece of land. The White-Eye do not understand the way of the Apache." Mangas continues the disjointed conversation, saying, "The medicine man at Cibeque is called the Dreamer. He says the dead chiefs will rise. He says the Apache are the true keepers of the land." It is then Geronimo's turn to add, "I will go to him. I want to hear his words. Today while Gatewood talked with me, I looked into my power. I saw a white horse running. I saw signs of war."

As each speaks his piece, in Apache with subtitles, he looks directly into the camera. This is an interesting choice for a director to make, since it is startling to an audience to be looked at so directly. But if the attempt was to make the speeches more "meaningful," the scene is a failure. It simply appears out of place, staged, overly dramatic, and heavy handed. Instead of the Indians appearing dignified and deserving of respect, they seem just a bit silly, and it takes some piecing together to realize that Geronimo is planning a trip to Cibeque to speak to the Dreamer.

The Dreamer (Pato Hoffman) leads the people confined on the reservation in the Ghost Dance, which the cavalry officers see as an attempt to foment violence. As noted in chapter 1, this is a misreading of the meaning of the dance, and the film makes this point when the officer in charge shoots the medicine man. Geronimo and his followers quickly respond, and the result is a renewal of conflict and the band's flight into the mountains of Mexico.

While on the loose, Geronimo's band takes what it needs from the settlers and miners of the area, killing people and stealing horses and supplies. At a mining camp, the Apaches surround a group of miners, and one miner pleads for mercy. Another shoves him back and says, "Quiet, damn it. He's going to kill you anyway." Then he looks at Geronimo and tells him the miners have a right to be there, that they "make things outta this country. There was nothin' here before us and there'd *never* be nothin' if we left it to you." In the context of the film, the expression of the idea that land not put to agrarian, mercantile, or mining use is unused, wasted land and that white people have a righteous duty to overcome the barbaric hordes that simply move over the face of it sounds simplistic and unenlightened. Thus when Geronimo's men do indeed slaughter the group of miners, with the exception of the one who was brave enough to confront Geronimo, the audience is not likely to shed a tear.

Unfortunately, like many of the new, sympathetic films about Native Americans, this film depicts Indians in the past tense. The final scenes, although historically accurate, emotionally wrenching, and beautifully filmed, are perhaps the most damaging of the lot. Sitting with the diseased, defeated remnants of his people in a cattle car on the way to Florida, Geronimo says, "For many years, the One God made me a warrior. No guns, no bullets could ever kill me. That was my power. Now my time is over. Now, maybe, the time of our people is over." The implication is that the Apaches, like the Mohicans and the Lakotas of other films, have vanished. The point is further stressed during the ending credits, which roll over a very long shot of the train as it makes its way across the vast expanse of the now-empty Southwest.

Cheyenne Warrior (1994)

A recent film that earns a few decent marks is *Cheyenne Warrior*. In this 1994 film directed by Mark Griffiths, the subject of miscegenation is central to the story. Although a white woman is used to tell half the tale, the other half belongs to the Cheyenne warrior who becomes her lover and her friend.

The young, pregnant Rebecca Carver (Kelly Preston) is left alone at a trading post after a buffalo hunter kills her husband and the owner of the post, Mr. Barkley (Dan Haggerty). The buffalo hunter is about to rape Mrs. Carver when a Cheyenne man, also wounded by the hunter, kills him. Soars Like A Hawk (Pato Hoffmann) has a broken leg and a bullet in his body, and since Mrs. Carver had been introduced to him earlier by Barkley, who was married to a relative of Hawk's, she overcomes her fear of Indians and treats his wounds. While he is mending, they get to know one another.

The film is well directed, with a well-paced and charming musical score, but its main two assets are excellent actors and a solid, simple script. It is also mercifully free of the white guilt that weighs heavily on most contemporary films sympathetic to American Indians. There are no apologies on either side, simply a look at people from two cultures, some good people and some bad people, but just people.

The political issues are there, certainly. For instance, the film opens with the wholesale slaughter of buffalo by white hunters, the same hunters that kill Mr. Barkley and Mrs. Carver's husband. And toward the end of the film, a white wagon master (Bo Hopkins) and Hawk fend off attacking Pawnees, and he tells Hawk he thought all Indians were brothers. Later, Hawk asks him if he fought in the white man's war (the Civil War). He says yes, and Hawk says, "I thought all white men were brothers." Occasionally, Hawk and Mrs. Carver talk of his need to fight for his people against the white invasion. The political issues are important to the film, but what makes this film different is that there is no blame cast on either side. There are no victims, only people doing what they believe to be the best thing at the time.

The love affair between Hawk and Mrs. Carver is tender, comfortable, and seems strong enough to last a lifetime, if only they existed in the same world. This film, like all the others, assumes that white and Indian cannot live together, but at least neither of them dies as a way out for the screenwriter. Hawk watches for a long time as the wagon train Mrs. Carver has joined moves across the plains toward Oregon, and the scene is poignant because of the love between the two, not because it was a tragic mismatch.

This film is refreshing in its respectful treatment of white and Cheyenne characters. The only one-dimensional characters are the Pawnees. Once more, they are depicted as bloodthirsty savages who kill indiscriminately even when unprovoked. The Pawnees seem to have replaced the Sioux and Apaches in recent years as the all-purpose Bad Indians. In *Little Big Man, Dances With Wolves, Cheyenne Warrior,* and many others, they are the ruthless killing machines of the plains.

Pocahontas (1995)

One of the most popular films of 1995 was *Pocahontas,* an animated film by Disney Studios.[50] In an interview with the *New York Times,* Eric Goldberg, the film's co-director, said, "We've gone from being accused of being too white bread to being accused of racism in 'Aladdin' to being accused of being too politically correct in 'Pocahontas.' That's progress to me."[51] Mr. Goldberg's idea of progress could benefit from redefinition. Instead of progress in depicting American Indians, this film takes a step backward—a very dangerous step because it, like *A Man Called Horse,* has been so carefully glossed as "authentic" and "respectful."

Robert Stam has argued that even in such cases, in which an ethnic group has been denigrated by historical inaccuracies, a positive approach "would emphasize the role of choices, of representation, of mediation, defining the issue less as one of fidelity to a preexisting truth or reality than as one of a specific orchestration of discourses in relation to a theme." However, he also says that "we want to reserve the right to suggest that certain films are false or pernicious . . . to reserve the right to judgment on questions of realism is especially appropriate in cases in which there are historical antecedents or real-life prototypes for a film."[52] Each film about or including Native Americans should reserve that "right," but it is particularly so for *Pocahontas* because it appears on the surface to be such an innocuous little children's movie. It is specifically the "orchestration of discourses" and their "relation to a theme" that are the problems with this film. Very few biographical filmmakers have felt the necessity or the justification to change not only the surrounding facts of a person's life, but her age, motivations, physical makeup, and life history.

Disney Studios evidently holds that an animated film needn't adhere to the guideline of "truth" or reality. To a certain extent, they have a point. The cute, fuzzy little animals in the film aren't realistic, and no one cares about that. However, the visual tends to be more immediately, emotionally compelling than the written word, as well as more accessible, and since few people will ever read about Pocahontas, this film's pseudo-history will exist as "fact" in the minds of generations of American children. They will believe in the Romeo and Juliet story set in the wilds of North America that Disney presented, which, as Robert Eaglestaff, principal of the American Indian Heritage School in Seattle, has said is much like "trying to teach about the Holocaust and putting in a nice story about Anne Frank falling in love with a German officer."[53]

Debating the authenticity or reality of an animated film in which a tree speaks words of wisdom and the protagonist guides her canoe over a deadly looking waterfall without mussing her hair would seem an empty exercise, which would be the case if this were a story about a fictional character in a fictional situation. However, Pocahontas was a real woman who lived during the pivotal time of first contact with the outside force that would ultimately decimate her people. Although we know of her only from the English reports, and some of the details are a bit hazy, there are some facts that are well supported. For one thing, she was not a voluptuous young woman when she met John Smith but a ten- to twelve-year-old girl, and John Smith was a thirty-something mercenary who more resembled a tree stump than a blonde superhero.

Smith's report of Pocahontas's brave act in saving his life was nowhere to be found in his initial description of his capture by Powhatan in 1608, only surfacing eight years later in a letter to the Queen. There are at least two possibilities to explain why that might have been. He could have been embarrassed, given the "macho" community of Jamestown, to admit a child had saved his life. Or he might have stolen the story—possibly from an account that was published around the same time of Juan Ortiz and the Utica woman who saved him, an incident that occurred in Florida about eighty years before Smith met Pocahontas.[54]

Assuming she did save his life, it could have been her idea, or it could have been her father's. If Powhatan had his own reasons for wanting Smith to live, he might have instructed her to do as she did to save face. Smith's report said she wanted her father to keep him alive but in captivity so he could make bells and beads for her, which, according to John Gould Fletcher (*John Smith—Also Pocahontas*, 1928), would have provided a cover story to eliminate the censure of the tribe for Powhatan's benevolent act and which would have been in keeping with their traditions.

Assuming Smith stole the story, he could have done so because he eventually turned to chronicling his adventures in the New World after it became clear he was not going to be able to return to America to have more of them. He tried repeatedly to find his way back, but even the first settlers in New England, who were happy to accept his advice, steadfastly refused his company.

What we do know of Pocahontas is that she met John Smith in 1608, was probably responsible for some trading between the settlers and her people, was kidnapped and raped by the English but later married a tobacco planter named John Rolfe, had a son in 1615, and sailed to England in 1616. She was introduced to Ben Jonson and made such an impression that he wrote her into one of his comedies, *The Staple of News*; she attended a court masque that he wrote and evidently impressed the King and Queen as well. She attempted to return home but became ill on the voyage and had to turn back to England, where she died, probably of smallpox or pneumonia, at the age of twenty-two. We have no idea how she or her people felt about any of this, except that some of the contemporary reports said she died "of a broken heart." Her son, Thomas Rolfe, finally traveled to America, where he led military expeditions against the Indians.

That is a rather interesting story, but not really the sort of thing animated Disney films are known for. For one thing, it is much too violent and sad. But according to James Pentacost, the film's producer, the changes that were made for the film were decided upon because Pocahontas's real story was simply too long. He said, "We decided to dramatize what we felt was the *essence* of Pocahontas."[55] The logic of that reasoning may be difficult to follow, but evidently to depict her "essence" they needed to change her age and her body, and give her a motive for her actions that boils down to falling desperately in love with the first white man she sees.

Ignoring for a moment the very non–politically correct, non-feminist content of these changes, there lies within them a very old stereotype of Native American women. In hundreds of films made during the last century, Indian women have been seen sacrificing themselves and their tribal communities for their white lovers. The irony is assuredly unintentional in *Pocahontas* as she paddles her canoe along, having just refused to marry the stereotypically stoic and noble Kocoum, singing about the change that is waiting "just around the river bend." The change that awaits is another man and another culture in the form of John Smith. The bigger change around the bend will occur to the land she sings so happily about, as well as her people, who will soon find themselves dealing with invaders from another land.

The Disney folks have made much of the fact that Pocahontas is the driving force of this movie, which presumably means it makes some sort of feminist statement. She does sing to John about living naturally in tune with the Earth—also skirting dangerously close to the Natural Ecologist stereotype—but she does it in an off-the-shoulder, form-fitting and very short dress. The physics of her body are improbable; she resembles a Barbie doll with hips. Glen Keane, the supervising animator on the film, researched the paintings of the real Pocahontas but wasn't very impressed, so he made a few "adjustments." Besides her beautiful "more Asian" eyes, he gave her a body with a waspish waist, sexy hips and legs, and breasts that are truly impressive. He says, "Some people might see her as sexy, but she's not Jessica Rabbit. I think she looks rather athletic." Perhaps. Mel Gibson (the voice of John Smith) put it more succinctly when he said, "She's a babe."[56] The only woman on the creative team was scriptwriter Susannah Grant. She said, "I've had some nightmares that I've let some antifeminist things slip into the movie accidentally when I wasn't looking."[57] Her nightmares have probably increased lately.

To give the Disney team their due, they apparently made some effort to be inoffensive, hiring Native Americans to work on the film and to act as consultants. Unfortunately, there seems to have been some miscommunication of concept. The Disney people were making an animated film about a fictional character. They knew she was fictional because they created her. The Native Americans on the team had other interests. Russell Means, the voice of Powhatan, likes the film, even though they were willing to take his advice about details—such as her father referring to Pocahontas as Daughter instead of her name—but were unwilling to change important aspects of the image of the Indians as warlike, as established by the return from war at the beginning of the film. He says, "There are scenes where the English settlers admit to historical deceit. . . . [T]heir animated settlers say they are here to rob, rape, pillage the land and kill Indians. This is the truth that Disney is entrusting with children while the rest of Hollywood won't trust that truth with adults."[58]

American Indians are concerned with disclosing the facts about the colonization of America, but establishing another stereotype is not the way to go about it. Even given that Disney's animated characters are by nature larger than life, the English in the film are extremely one-dimensional in their bumbling greed. As Terry Russio, a screenwriter for Disney, said, "You can judge the sentiments of the country by who you can confidently make fun of. Nowadays the ultimate villain, I suppose, would be a fat, white male terrorist who ran a Fortune 500 company on the side."[59] That fairly well describes the governor in *Pocahontas*, a description that "renders the history of first contact literally cartoonish."[60]

Disney also hired Shirley Little Dove Custalow-McGowan, a Powhatan who travels through Virginia teaching the history and culture of her people, to work as consultant for the film. When she saw the early rushes, she said, "My heart sorrowed. . . . Ten-year-old Pocahontas has become twenty-year-old Pocahontas. The movie was no longer historically accurate."[61]

According to the film's producer, James Pentacost, the Native Americans' interest in historical accuracy is somewhat irrelevant. He believes that "Nobody should go to an animated film hoping to get an accurate depiction of history."[62] While that may be true about a film such as *The Lion King* (1994), it does not hold for *Pocahontas*. Most of the adults who view the film do not have the background to judge whether it is accurate or not, and since the media hype has been focused on the "political correctness" of the film, they will logically be more apt to trust it than not—and those are the adults. What about the children? As Linda Woolverton, screenwriter for *Beauty and the Beast* (1991) and *The Lion King* said, "When you take on a Disney animated feature, you know you're going to be affecting entire generations of human minds."[63] In this case, the effect is one more misconception advertised in the guise of authenticity and respect for Native American values.[64]

As Custalow-McGowan said, "History is history. You're not honoring a nation of people when you change their history."[65]

Last of the Dogmen (1995)

The Last of the Dogmen is a seriously depressing film for those who hoped for an upward trend in American Indian depictions by the mid-nineties. Not that the scenes that actually show Indians are badly done; in fact, the Cheyennes in the film are generous, warm, strong, and fairly accurately described, thanks in part to the advice given by the not-for-profit group American Indians in Film.[66] The problem is that they have been lifted from the old, time-frozen nineteenth century and plunked into the late twentieth century with virtually no change. The film's Cheyennes have been hiding out in the wilderness area of the Oxbow in Montana, and doing very nicely, it seems, until the heroes of this film find them. As usual, it's a lucky thing for the Indians, since the white hero saves them from disclosure and assumed assimilation/annihilation.

As usual, the film tells the story of an Indian—with the message that Indians *really* know how to live—through the medium of a white protagonist. In this case there are two white protagonists: an anthropologist, Dr. Lillian Sloane (Barbara Hershey), who speaks fluent Cheyenne, something not all modern Cheyennes can do, and a super-tracker, Lewis Gates (Tom Berenger), who is commissioned to hunt down escaped convicts in the Oxbow wilderness area. Gates stumbles upon a band of Cheyenne Dog Soldiers whose generations have remained hidden for the last hundred and twenty years.

The film is disturbing because it wallows in the fashionable New Age pangs of white guilt. Dr. Sloane gives three lengthy monologues about the "plight" of the Indians, first telling the story of Black Kettle's band and the Sand Creek massacre—evidently the band they find are descendants of survivors who escaped—and later saying, "We owe them a tremendous debt. What happened was inevitable; the way it happened was unconscionable." While the inevitability is debatable and the unconscionability absolute, her flat-footed recitation is almost as condescending as her later comment that her "work has just begun." She wants a "living record set down—a memorial to the last of their kind." Since she has decided to give up the white world and live with the Cheyennes, a living record seems an absurd idea. Does she intend to leave the record hidden under a rock? Or is she planning to deliver that final paper to her anthropologist peers? The more important point is that she sees the Cheyennes as vanishing and feels the need to catalog them for future museum use.

As a box-office attraction, the film was a nonevent, probably because the story it tells of the white people in the film is simply silly. The voice-over narration is downright embarrassing. In an effort to make the movie seem like a real Western western—a gravelly male voice (evidently the bartender at the story's beginning) tells us what's going on, but he tells us nothing we don't find out simply by watching the film. In addition, the idea that Lewis Gates told the story originally to the narrator is highly unbelievable both logistically and psychologically because Gates kept his secret even when facing a possible prison term; it is unlikely he would spill everything over a beer. The narrator repeatedly says the heroes are searchers, wanderers, lost souls looking for something. That "something" turns out to be the life of a Cheyenne Indian of the last century. This sounds familiar. Just as *Dances With Wolves*'s Lt. Dunbar wanted to see the frontier—meaning the Indians—before they were gone, Sloane and Gates lust for the Cheyenne life. And like Dunbar, Horse, and the hundreds of other "friends of the Indian," these protagonists immediately set out to change them. They bring penicillin to cure an infection, they use dynamite to seal off the route to the camp, and Sloane tells them about airplanes, walking on the moon, and other "magical" things. An infection has been introduced to these Cheyennes, and it looks like Dr. Sloane may be right. They may be the last of their kind.

Getting Closer

The abysmal offerings of 1995, *Pocahontas* and *Last of the Dogmen*, might have strained audience optimism about the future of Native representations. However, 1996 produced two films that provided new hope. The first is a decent film, *The Sunchaser*, directed by Michael Cimino and starring Woody Harrelson and Jon Seda, and the second is a great film, *Dead Man*, directed by Jim Jarmusch and starring Johnny Depp and Gary Farmer.

These two films have very little in common except that each includes a Native American as one of the two lead characters, and each represents that character as a fully realized human being with a culture of significance that is neither denigrated nor glorified.

The Sunchaser (1996)

Michael Cimino is best known as the director of one tremendous success and one tremendous failure; *The Deer Hunter* swept the Oscars in 1978 and *Heaven's Gate* swept United Artists into financial ruin in 1980. An interviewer for *People Weekly* asked Cimino how the disaster of *Heaven's Gate* affected him, and he replied that "It was really a great trauma, as everyone knows. Since then I've been unable to make any movie that I've wanted to make. I've been making the best of what is available." He says he thinks of John Ford, who took "endless studio assignments so that when *The Quiet Man* (1952), the film he most dearly wanted to do, finally came along, he was ready to make the most of it."[67] The implication seems to be that *The Sunchaser* was one of those he did while waiting for the one he wanted to do. If so, that is unfortunate because *The Sunchaser* is a relatively important film that breaks out of the mold and the moldy stereotypes and shows what other films seem unable to—a contemporary Native American existence.

Evidently, the folks at the Cannes Film Festival saw it that way, since it was one of the films selected to be shown there in 1996, but other critics did not. Reviews of *The Sunchaser* were mostly unfavorable, some downright vicious. Lisa Schwarzbaum's is typical: "Michael Cimino, the daredevil director for whom the tidy story is never worth shooting—pokes around interesting themes . . . but really doesn't know what he finds. Nothing jells."[68] John Polly was less tactful: "The movie plays as a straight white man's view of life beyond Bel Air: the minority gangster characters talk about their lives in the 'hood;' the women are either shallow trophy wives, slutty waitresses or trashy shop clerks; Native Americans are earthy and wise in a cheesy New Age way; and some homophobia is employed to spark a boring barroom biker brawl. But the main victim of the film's offenses is any audience who would be forced to endure it."[69]

Polly is correct in some ways; *Sunchaser* is certainly not a "perfect" film. It still tells the story through the white male intermediary, and at least one scene is thoroughly hokey from a Native point of view. As for the stereotypes, however, Polly seems to have missed the attempt to deconstruct them.

The film has been dubbed an "intergenerational buddy movie," a "holistic road movie," and a "psychological thriller" by other reviewers, but these designations also seem rather shortsighted. So, what is it?

In a nutshell, it is the story of the emotional, psychological, and spiritual awakening of a very successful Los Angeles surgeon. His growth occurs because of his forced immersion in a totally opposite existence, courtesy of a young Navajo cancer patient who kidnaps him and forces him to drive from Los Angeles to Shiprock on the Navajo Reservation. There are plenty of guns and fast cars, a fist fight, an abduction, and a chase across three states, but the film still doesn't deserve the term *thriller*, which seems to imply lightness of content.

The film's protagonists are a successful Los Angeles oncologist (Woody Harrelson), whose biggest problem at the film's start appears to be whether or not to pay two million dollars for a house, and a sixteen-year-old half Navajo (Jon Seda) in jail for murder. The doctor places great stock in his professional status and money, has a beautiful wife who spends her days at the hairdresser's and in meetings of the

Zoo Board, and is slated to become the new Chief of Oncology at the hospital. The young man is a tough case, his language profane and his actions often violent, but he holds onto his Navajo heritage, both real and imagined, as his only hope for spiritual and physical salvation. That's the short version. The film's reality is much more complex, sensitive, and interesting.

The first few scenes are intercut shots of the two leads as their lives head toward each other. The young man, Blue, is shown being shackled and driven in a police car to the hospital, while the doctor, Michael Reynolds, drives there in his new $176,000 Porsche 911 Turbo.

At the hospital we see the doctor dealing with the three main communities in his life in a series of vignettes that could be entitled "Doctor at Work." He is charming but rather condescending with his coworkers. He tells two young doctors their ideas are garbage, says that the school of dentistry is across the street, and walks off chanting, "Hip bone connected to the leg bone." The young doctors don't seem to mind, but as an audience we can't help but feel this is a man with a God complex made palatable only by a charming personality. He visits one of his cancer patients to discuss the man's CAT scan. Later, Blue will accuse him of not knowing how his patients feel because of the emotional distance he keeps from them, saying he doesn't "have the balls for it." This seems to be true, since Reynolds leaves in the middle of breaking some bad news to a patient in order to take a personal call. He excuses his absence by saying the hospital is a madhouse and that they are understaffed. That may be true, but that certainly isn't the reason he left the man sitting alone and feeling "not so good."

The telephone conversation with his wife is also disturbing. The house they want—the one "with the pool Spanky swam in"—is slipping away because they didn't bid two million dollars. His wife, Victoria (Alexandra Tydings), wants to bid higher, and when he resists she says, "If you don't want the house, you don't love me." Feminists in the audience might lose their lunches over that one, and it seems an odd thing to place in this film. On closer inspection, it makes some sense. This is a film about emotional and spiritual growth, and in very subtle ways, the audience is a part of that growth because we are part of the doctor. Everyone else is seen objectively; it is only the doctor's mind we are part of; we hear about Blue's past but it is only Reynolds's memories we *see* in artfully done flashbacks. It makes sense then that our experience of Victoria would owe much to his attitude toward her. She is the "perfect" wife for a prominent physician, the "trophy wife" to which

Polly referred. She is lovely, she is on charitable boards, she is a good mother, and she tries to please him. He is The Doctor, a fact he repeats often in the film. He is a nice man, a good man, a charming man with an absolute faith in science and the empirical, which he believes posits his position as superior. He treats Victoria with condescending "instruction," and she responds with a slightly childlike acceptance.

However, as the doctor changes through the course of the film, so does our experience of Victoria. By the time Reynolds has been hauled across two states, beaten up, and bitten by a snake, he is a much more understanding human, and the audience sees a much stronger Victoria. This is clearly represented when the police question her about her husband and insinuate that the kidnapping was somehow his fault. They ask if he has been treated for any kind of "emotional problem" and whether there is any part of her husband's life that he doesn't talk about. They treat her with syrupy sweetness and condescension, much the way Reynolds treated her before. She looks them straight in the eye and responds, "I'm not intimidated by police technique, Mr. Collier, so please don't treat me as you do everyone else." He says, "It's information I need, Mrs. Reynolds," and she responds, "My husband is a healthy, rational, loving man. The only emotional problem he has is the gun that's been put to his head." She is a woman with strength and intelligence, not at all the bit of fluff we saw in the film's beginning.

So too do the doctor's attitudes shape to a certain extent how we see Blue. We do, however, get an introduction to Blue before he sees the doctor. He is sixteen, but his face shows a toughness many years older, a toughness gained on the streets of Los Angeles. But he has another side, and as he sits in the back of the squad car he clutches a book, *The Man Who Travels* by Dib Nitsaa, and looks with longing at a painting of a sacred mountain inside the front cover.

When the nurse gives Reynolds Blue's chart, he hands it back and says the boy should be in pediatrics. But Pediatrics can't handle him because he's too dangerous—he's locked up for murder. Reynolds tries to give the case to someone else but is ultimately forced to take it, and their first encounter is a test of wills. Blue is sitting on the table smoking a cigarette, which is obviously against the rules in the hospital, especially the oncology section. Their exchange is tense, but Reynolds actually handles it well, better than we would expect, perhaps because he keeps that emotional distance intact throughout. Blue says, "You're looking at me like I'm an animal or somethin', you tight-ass, suit-wearing motherfucker. . . . You do just as much damage as anyone else. You

just hide your shit better, right?" Reynolds responds, "No, that's lawyers. I'm a doctor." It's a joke, of course, intended to ease the tension,
but by the midpoint of the film we will have heard him say he's a doctor a number of times. He wears it like a Good Housekeeping seal of
approval.

In this scene we also see Blue's attitude about the dominant culture
and its premier representative (for him), the doctor. Blue is dying and
he knows it. He's afraid but won't show it, and he won't "go into that
fucking oven again like some kind of hot dog." He has no faith in the
treatments or the people who administer them. When Reynolds says
they will just do a CAT scan and chemo, Blue calls him a liar, and when
the doctor touches the scars on his chest and asks what they're from, he
answers "bullets" as though it were a very stupid question. Reynolds
asks if he saw them coming, if he had any warning, and Blue points out
that if you're going to shoot someone, you don't warn them. Reynolds
seems to have lived a very sheltered life, at least in comparison to Blue.
Reynolds asks Blue to cough, but the coughing gets out of control, so
Blue throws back his head and howls like the animal he knows the doctor thinks he is. Their differences are more than ethnic. They are gener-
ational and, more importantly, classist.

The next scene takes place in an upscale restaurant where Dr. Reynolds and Dr. Byrnes (Matt Mulhern) are dining with their wives.
Reynolds sends his salad back because he asked for goat cheese, not
mozzarella. This is the first of many times we will see him being fastid-
ious about what he ingests. Byrnes says Reynolds is a shoe-in as Chief
of Oncology, but Reynolds says he doesn't think so, and the other man
takes it to mean he's modest. Mrs. Byrnes says, "There's no such thing
as a modest surgeon," and Victoria says, "Michael's not modest; he's
just superstitious." This is a very interesting point for her to make,
since everything else we've seen of Reynolds thus far seems to point to a
total focus on the scientific and tangible. This perhaps foreshadows his
need to believe in something.

Byrnes mentions Blue, and Victoria asks what he did. Reynolds answers, "I read his records, hon, not his rap sheet." While his reluctance
to discuss the gory details of Blue's past is admirable, at this point he is
still being condescending to his wife, treating her like a little girl, and
she looks as though she's had her hand slapped.

Byrnes has no qualms about spilling everything, so he describes
Blue as a "sixteen-year-old gangbanger with a rare high-grade peri-
toneal sarcoma" who "blew his stepfather's brains out." This is exactly

the kind of description Blue would expect. While the medical evaluation is correct, Blue is not a "gangbanger" and we will learn later that he did kill his *foster* father, but for understandable reasons. Byrnes isn't interested in the truth of who Blue is, so he chooses to depict him as a subhuman, patricidal rapist.

Not that Blue is an angel. He makes no bones about the fact that he has killed. He's been on the street for a long time, and he has survived by playing the game. But while Reynolds is conversing by candlelight, Blue is throwing up in a dreary little cell. As he collapses on his narrow cot, he looks through the bars at the moon and quietly recites the Navajo Beautyway Chant.

Using part of a ceremony in a film could easily become a problem of improper appropriation, but at least when Blue recites the chant it is with deep respect, and we clearly see that it means a great deal to him. He longs for beauty, both physical and spiritual. Both types of beauty are at the heart of this film. We will hear him recite the chant two more times, once when he tells the story of the Sunchaser to the doctor, and again as he runs into the sacred lake that has been his goal from the beginning of the film. In this way, the Beautyway Chant forms a framework for the action and a meaning for the act. Beauty is what both men long for; Blue knows it, and the doctor discovers it.

We next see Reynolds kissing his little girl good night. She is snuggled in a cloud of soft pillows and fuzzy toys, and both her mother and father obviously adore her. This is the absolute opposite of Blue's life. Blue is on the doctor's mind, and Victoria knows it. He brushes her off when she asks about it, but we are taken into a flashback from Michael's childhood. It is beautifully filmed in black and white, and it is sensitively played by John Christian Graas as the young Michael Reynolds and Christopher Kennedy Masterson as his older brother, Jimmy. Jimmy is lying in a hospital bed while machinery keeps him alive. He is bald, like Blue. He gives his signature ring to Mike and asks him to turn off the machine. "For me, Mikey. Mighty Mike." The connection has been made in the doctor's mind between his brother and Blue.

The significance of this connection will become clear later in the film, when the doctor has finally had enough of the cross-country ordeal and throws his wallet in an oil can to prevent Blue from filling the car. Blue gets into the backseat behind Reynolds and holds the gun against the back of his head. He asks for the ring, presumably to trade it for gas. Reynolds refuses. We see the rearview mirror, across which an American flag is reflected, as Blue says, "Make that fifty rads. Put the motherfucker in and pull the switch," and he shoots the mirror. Reynolds still refuses to give up the ring. Blue shoots twice more, but Reynolds still refuses. Realistically, this would have made them both deaf for life, but all the shooting and tension are included to make it possible for Blue to tell the following story without boring the typical audience. The story is one told him by a "full-blown medicine man," Webster Skyhorse (Victor Aaron), around the campfire when Blue was a kid:

> There were two brothers, one big strong one and one small weak one. The weak one got weaker and weaker until he couldn't walk. Medicine men came from all around, even Utes and Apaches, but no one could do anything about it. Beetle comes up on the boy's bed, tells about Sunchaser, who chases the sun when it comes up. He says, "follow me to the lake on the sacred mountain. If you swim in its waters, it will cure you of all your disease." Shit. For four fucking days, Sunchaser comes at sunrise and for four days said his prayers and made his promise, but nobody believed the boy when he told them about the Sunchaser's promise, nobody except finally his brother. He was small, but he was tough, *cabron*. He was the only one who was really helping his brother. So at the next sunrise, the younger brother rode with his brother on his horse. They went from sunrise following the Sunchaser. They rode for fucking days until they reached that mountain, and when they did, Younger Brother, he climbs up that mountain with his sick older brother on his back. You understand? And he put him in the water, and he started to swim, and there was nothin' wrong with him no more. Nothin' at all. I learned a lot of shit from that old medicine man.

The camera then focuses on an extreme close-up of Blue's face; we only see his eyes as he once more recites the Beautyway Chant. Reynolds doesn't give up the ring until the story's end, when he tosses it to Blue, saying, "We made it." Little brother is, in fact, giving it back.

The story of the Sunchaser is intercut with the flashbacks of Reynolds's brother asking him to turn off the machines. This flashback goes further, and we see that "Mighty Mike" did do what his brother asked. He ended his brother's pain, but in doing so he gave himself a very deep wound. This film is the story of brothers who believe in one another, who carry one another, who heal one another. But at this point, Reynolds has much to learn before he can say to this new brother, "Thank you for saving my life, Blue."

The brotherly tie is made in the film, but Reynolds doesn't become

"Indian." He doesn't even want to. He learns to see himself through his association with Blue, but he sees *himself,* not an Indian wannabee.

Blue's character also avoids stereotypes. He is absolutely contemporary—nothing of the time freeze here. He is also that seldom heard of though common entity, the urban Indian. He's a mixed-blood and violent, but the violence is engendered by the situation he lives in, not by blood. As he and Reynolds are driving away from the kidnapping scene, they pass through a neighborhood Blue calls The Hazards. This is familiar territory to him, and he doesn't seem surprised by the police lines and the eleven bloody bodies lying on the sidewalk, the result of gang warfare.

His father was Navajo, and Blue spent some of his childhood at Shiprock. We find later that the last time he saw the medicine man was when he was only eight years old—half of his lifetime ago. Since then, both parents have died (his mother died in jail), his brothers are all in jail for one reason or another, and his sister is raising two kids alone. There is no romanticizing of his life. He has been far away, but his experiences on the reservation are the ones he holds dear. He tells Reynolds that Skyhorse sent him the book about the sacred mountain and the sacred lake and that he is waiting for him. This is not the truth; he has had no contact since he left the reservation. He leaves messages on Skyhorse's answering machine, but he doesn't talk to the man. However, he has faith that the medicine man will know him, will know he is coming, and will help him when he gets there. He means to get to that mountain, and he tells Reynolds, "If you think you're going to stop me, you're dead wrong. You ain't deep enough."

Blue speaks Navajo, but some of his ideas about what being Navajo means have obviously been influenced by his Los Angeles environment. When the doctor is bitten by a rattlesnake, Blue takes care of it by using jumper cables to send electricity through the leg to neutralize the venom.[70] He then tells the doctor that "Indian people believe you get bitten by a snake it's because of something bad you did to someone else. There's something crawling around inside you. Your mind ain't in tune with your heart." He hits the doctor's problem on the head, but he shows his separation from his native roots as well. Navajo people do not connect snakebite with doing bad things. Later, he will say that being sick is payback for doing wrong, and that he's "done a lot of bad shit," also not exactly in line with the Navajo spiritual belief system. This is a gross oversimplification of a complex philosophy, one Blue might have gotten from an old *Bonanza* episode. The fact that he says

"Indian people" is also a giveaway. This lumping together of tribal identities is definitely not something he learned at Shiprock. Native audiences would probably see this as evidence of the harm done when young people are taken away from their cultural centers and then grasp at something only partially understood in their search for something "deep enough."

The Sunchaser is partly about deconstructing stereotypes. We learn that there is more to Victoria than the "airhead" doctor's wife she first appears to be and much more to Blue than the "sixteen-year-old gangbanger" Byrnes has labeled him. We also get a look into other stereotypes, one of which turns into an object lesson for the doctor.

They have pulled into a deserted Mohawk station (a nice touch) so Blue can call Skyhorse again. He leaves a message on the machine, which is answered by a feminine voice. Reynolds has begun to soften toward Blue and offers to forget the whole kidnaping and not press charges if Blue will let him go. Blue finds this funny. He tells him, "You're dumb as two bricks," and the audience has to agree. Reynolds himself has told Blue he has less than a month to live and so must have realized the boy has nothing to lose. Irritated, Reynolds says, "Next time we stop *anywhere,* this whole thing is finished." Blue says thoughtfully, "Anywhere, huh?"

The "anywhere" Blue chooses is a redneck biker bar. The breakfast special is to the doctor a heart attack on a platter, but Blue eats ravenously as they "conversate." Reynolds talks about his wife and daughter, and they get along relatively well for a while. Blue talks about his foster father, who used to beat him and the other kids every night with the buckle end of a belt. "Sick motherfucker, man. I should've peeled his cap a lot sooner. It was always 'you little half breed. You little bit nigger.'" The doctor goes into the bathroom, and Blue begins to fold over in pain. Seda does a terrific job of showing the agony of abdominal cancer and Blue's "bluff" as he walks through the gang of bikers to the bathroom, where he folds up and throws up again. He then hears Reynolds talking on a telephone, calls him a liar, and leaves. As he passes through the bikers he cries, "Help. Help. He wanted to suck my dick. I was hitching a ride back to the res and he promised to buy me breakfast." This outrages the bikers, and they begin beating up on the doctor as soon as he emerges from the bathroom. They throw him through the front window just as Blue screeches up in front, slamming into the motorcycles parked there. Reynolds flings himself through the car's open window and they take off, chased and shot at by the livid

13. From Michael Cimino's *The Sunchaser* (1996). Photo Museum of Modern Art Film Stills Archive; courtesy of Monarchy Enterprises B. V. and Regency Entertainment U.S.A.

bikers. In short, Reynolds gets a crash course in what it means to be known as a "faggot."

Reynolds also fights his own label. When the stolen Trans Am runs out of gas on the rim of the Grand Canyon, Reynolds walks to the edge and says, "beautiful." He tries to console Blue by saying he wishes there really was a sacred mountain and a sacred lake that would make him well, but there isn't. No magic will cure him. Blue tells him he's "full of shit." Reynolds tells Blue he needs medical attention, but Blue says he needs more than that. Reynolds begins to lose patience and says Blue needs *him*, but that he doesn't trust him because of all the "stereotypes you have of white people." This little turnaround amuses Blue, who responds, "I'm in the jungle and you're in the hills looking down on me, and you think that my life depends on you. Fuck you." He asks, "Isn't anything sacred to you?" This touches close to home and outrages the medical man, and he bursts into a condescending litany of sacred mountains, Disneyland, Dorothy, and the Tin Man. That's when the snake bites him.

The snakebite scares Reynolds, as it would anyone. He immediately feels his neck, muttering about tachycardia and cardial hemorrhage, and is amazed when Blue takes care of the bite with electricity. Blue's response to his amazement is, "Why? Because you thought I was dumb?"

Reynolds is still firmly hanging on to his belief in the rational. When he and Blue are picked up hitchhiking in the Yavapai Wilderness by what he might call a hippie (Anne Bancroft), he is repulsed. She believes in the power of the spirit, she likes Blue, and she finds the doctor lacking. He introduces himself as "Michael Reynolds. DOCTOR Michael Reynolds." She responds with "Renatta Baumbauer. DOCTOR Renatta Baumbauer, Ph.D." and later says, "Only thing worse than a lawyer is a doctor." Dr. Baumbauer is a New Ager, and if this film were truly the representative of New Age hokum, as some reviewers have suggested, she would be the film's arbiter. She isn't. She is charming and lovable, but she is not likely to convince the audience that the harmonic convergence is everything she thinks it is. Like Dr. Reynolds, audiences may have had enough of the talk about the healing power of water and harmonic convergence and might applaud at least a little when he can contain himself no longer. Thus starts one of the most delightful scenes in the film.

The threesome are sitting close together in the car, with Reynolds and Baumbauer in the front seats and Blue squatting with his head and shoulders between them. After taking in all three, the camera moves in to focus on each one as they cite the sources they believe in to describe their worlds.

Reynolds goes into a description of DNA, "the essential constituent of life" and ends with the citation, "Watson and Crick, *The Double Helix*, 1953." Renatta responds with "All healing comes from the divine within. Absolute faith makes fear and worry an impossibility. Edgar Casey, 1943." It is then Blue's turn, and he responds with a rap: "I think the rain'll never let up / I try to keep my head up / Still keep from gettin' red up / When it rains it pours / They got money for wars / But can't feed the poor. Tupa, 1994." This scene makes it impossible to see any of the three totally right—or totally wrong.

Renatta drops the two off in Flagstaff, where Blue hotwires a pink Cadillac convertible with huge fins parked in the lot of a church. It is an all-black church, and the sign on the wall says they are "Praying for the Sick in the Name of 'Jesus.'" As Blue and Reynolds talk in the lot, the church sings, "Let it go. Believe," which could be the whole movie's theme song. At this point, it would be easy to imagine the film slipping into a New Age, feel-good quest for the Native's spiritual power, and it most certainly gets to that edge. However, the doctor learns to believe, but in believing and trusting generally. He does not try to put on a Navajo spirituality.

Reynolds grows even more concerned about Blue, who is beginning to look really awful. He wants to take him to a hospital immediately. Blue responds, "Fuck you. The way you walk. The way you talk. The way you act. The way you carry yourself. You don't understand a fucking word I say." It's true. He doesn't. He replies, "How can I? Half of what you say sounds like it's in a foreign language." That's true, too, not because Blue is being irrational, obtuse, or even belligerent but because he is speaking from another culture—maybe two other cultures—and Reynolds is only beginning to understand. Blue tells him to go, but Reynolds won't go. Blue says, "What's your problem? I got you down as gone, so why don't you get the fuck gone?" Reynolds is angry, but he climbs back in the car and Blue speeds away while the church members sing, "Let's Work It Out."

Reynolds' conception of Navajo people is set aright when they finally reach the reservation. But first they hit a police roadblock. Reynolds sees some Navajo boys herding horses in a nearby arroyo and turns the stolen Cadillac in to follow them and get lost in their dust. The plan works, and the police don't see them go by. When they stop, Blue talks to one of the boys in Navajo, and then Reynolds tries to ask if they can continue with the herd until they're out of sight of the police, but he does so in Tonto-talk and crude sign language, assuming the Navajos are like those from the old western movies. The young man on the horse says, "What are you trying to say, man?"

They finally make it to Skyhorse's stone hogan at Shiprock. He isn't there, but his granddaughter (Talisa Soto) drives up in a four-wheel-drive truck. She is beautiful, packs a gun, and hoists a fifty-pound bag of dog food with ease. She tells them she heard about them on *Good Morning America*, and the doctor responds, "You have a television?" (Could this be the "wise and cheesy" "New Age" Native American Polly noted?) She sneers, "No. I get *Good Morning America* by smoke signal." Reynolds isn't a quick learner, but he's getting there.

They tell her they're there to see Webster Skyhorse, the medicine man. She says, "My grandfather may be a medicine man, but he's also been a lot of other things. Now he's playing hide-and-seek with the IRS. Good-bye cowboys." This single sentence upsets the idea of Indians "living off the taxpayer," and the word "cowboy" resonates with irony.

She walks away and Reynolds follows her. He tells her that her grandfather is the only person in Blue's short life that has meant anything to him, and that he's dying the hard way—of abdominal cancer. She stops and says, "Who are you, his Great White Savior? Federal boarding schools are full of half-breed Indian boys just like him. I work with them every day. They're my people. Mine. I've seen enough college-degree white people like you to last me a lifetime. So why don't you just leave?" This stops Reynolds short, and before he can respond, Blue slumps over in the car seat. When she sees that Blue is really dying, she decides to tell them how to get to her grandfather. But she adds a warning, "Dr. Reynolds, for you there's probably nothing up there, except a lot of rock and snow and grief—very deep grief. But to the Navajo nation it is a dwelling place for the spirits, the shape the earth takes to tell its stories. Don't go there unless you're prepared to listen."

In effect, the trip has been preparing Reynolds to do just that, to listen to his own heart, his own past, and allow himself to believe in something requiring no empirical evidence, without judgment and without posturing. As he begins to pull and carry Blue up the mountain, he hears in voice-over his brother Jimmy's voice. "Don't be afraid. Just do it. For me, Mikey. Mighty Mike."

Unfortunately, the scene in which they finally meet the medicine man is spoiled by silliness. Skyhorse appears over the summit of a hill and puts forth his hand, releasing a small bird—it is stereotypical mystical-magical shaman hokeyness. Hawks have been watching the progress, and if they are meant to represent the spirits, their juxtaposition with the other "birds," the police helicopters on the other side of the mountain, is an interesting one. However, one of the birds appears to be a poorly done special effect, which adds to the hokum of the scene.

The old man asks Reynolds a single question, "What do you really want?" It is a good question, and Reynolds answers truthfully. He wants to know if the sacred lake really exists and if it will really work. He doesn't get the kind of answer he would previously have needed, but it doesn't matter to him now because he has begun to believe in believing.

While not a great film, *The Sunchaser* is commendable in focusing on a contemporary urban Indian, in managing to tell a white man's story *and* a Native story without appropriation of identity, and in presenting the Navajo people, beliefs, and ceremonies with respect. It may not be the film Cimino has been waiting for, but it may end up as one of the most interesting films he ever makes.

Dead Man (1995)

Jim Jarmusch is not one to wait for anything, or to do anything in any way but the way he wants. He's an independent filmmaker, one of the very few who owns the negatives to all his films, which means that whatever we find in a Jarmusch film is of his making, not a studio's or a producer's. As Jonathan Rosenbaum explains, this sets him apart, even from the other "independents" in the United States.

> [Jarmusch] provides one model of American independent filmmaking, but not the one that most of the media are currently preoccupied with. Their model tends to gravitate around the Sundance Film Festival, where success in the independent sector is typically defined as landing a big-time distributor and/or a studio contract—the exposure, in short, that goes hand in glove with dependence on large institutional backing. And though it would be wrong to assume that Jarmusch isn't himself dependent on such forces to get his films into theaters (Miramax is distributing *Dead Man*), the salient difference between him and most other independents is that he's strong enough to afford the luxury of brooking no creative interference when it comes to making production and postproduction decisions.[71]

It is fortunate that Jarmusch can afford that luxury because it is almost inconceivable that *Dead Man* would have seen the light of day if anyone concerned with numbers had had anything to do with its making. As one reviewer noted, "Jim Jarmusch is about as Hollywood bankable as Jean-Paul Sartre. . . . Jarmusch is a reader's director. . . . *Dead Man* evokes Kafka and Conrad as well as Blake. . . . Jarmusch may be a dead man in Hollywood, but he's one of the few American directors who have made the cinema as personal as poetry or fiction."[72] Jarmusch wrote the script from scratch, directed it, and chose every artist involved in the film. The question is, what kind of movie has this renegade director made?

It is, on the one hand, a very realistic film. There is no smoothing over of violence, including the head squashing and cannibalism that even Jarmusch thinks might have been over the top. As Susanne Maier points out, "When the bullet hits human flesh it does so with an audible thud and leaves a gaping . . . wound."[73] On the other hand, it is a very complex and subtle film, poetic and beautiful, one that gets better each time you see it. Once is definitely not enough for this film.

It has been called a neo–western, a postmodern western, a parody of a western, even an acid western by its various reviewers, which is a clear indication that this film is not easy to pin down. It takes place in the mid to late 1800s; it is a "hero's journey" to the West; there are marshals, bounty hunters, a missionary, a prostitute turned good girl, a greedy capitalist, buffalo hunters, trappers, horses (four legged and iron), and of course there are Indians. Okay, so it's a western, but it's like no other western ever made, though Jarmusch says he wasn't really trying to deconstruct the genre. "The film begins with a convention, almost a cliché of a young man going out West to find his future. What happens to him early in the film collapses that convention and from then on, the film departs into a stranger story that is not a conventional Western. . . . The Western in America has always been a very American one and a way of processing history for Americans and stamping ideology onto the film for the audience in a way."[74]

Although he may not have tried to deconstruct the genre, Jarmusch goes a long way toward doing so. Gary Farmer, the Cayuga actor who plays Nobody, the Native co-lead in the film,[75] said in an interview, "They're waiting for it to try and sell them something . . . And it never does."[76] That's true. It isn't a didactic monologue on what should have been or could have been, but it is an interesting and very different look at the characters and scenes we have come to expect in the western genre.

A thorough description and analysis of this film would require a book of its own—it is that complex. There is the musical score improvised in rhythm to the film by Neil Young, an intricate weaving of metaphors, poetry conveyed through visuals (such as scenes/stanzas with line breaks/fades), artistic and negative depictions of the westering of technology and capitalism (a soulless metalworks owner, played by Robert Mitchum, runs a thoroughly despicable town called, appropriately, Machine), a tongue-in-cheek play with names and characters (such as punk rock godfather Iggy Pop as a trapper in drag),[77] and artistic considerations such as the truly remarkable black and white photography by Robby Müller.[78] It is mind boggling. Even concentrating solely on the depiction of the American Indian, Nobody, takes some doing.

One of the most positive things about *Dead Man* is that its creator consciously avoided making Native Americans into an all-purpose metaphor for the oppressed, or a typical noble or bloodthirsty savage. In an insightful interview with *Cineaste,* Jarmusch said,

In Hollywood Westerns even in the thirties and forties, history was mythologized to accommodate some kind of moral code. And what really affects me deeply is when you see it taken to the extent where Native Americans become mythical people. I think it's in *The Searchers* where John Ford had some Indians who were supposedly Comanche, but he cast Navajos who spoke Navajo. It's kind of like saying, "Yes, I know they are supposed to be French people, but I could only get Germans, and no one will know the difference." It's really close to apartheid in America. The people in power will do whatever they can to maintain that, and TV and movies are perfect ways to keep people stupid and brainwashed. In regards to *Dead Man*, I just wanted to make an Indian character who wasn't either A) the savage who must be eliminated, the force of nature that's blocking the way for industrial progress, or B) the noble innocent that knows all and is another cliché. I wanted him to be a complicated human being.[79]

And complicated he is. His name is actually Xebeche, He Who Talks Loud Saying Nothing (an in-joke for those familiar with James Taylor's "Talking Loud and Saying Nothing"), because he was captured as a small boy and transported in a cage to England. There he impressed his captors by his excellent imitation of their actions, which convinced them that he was intelligent enough to educate. He learned to read and write, and he developed a particular fondness for the poet William Blake. After escaping and returning to his people, he was shunned because his story was so unbelievable. He was already something of an outcast due to his mixed parentage—he is Blood and Blackfeet, two warring tribes, so apparently neither thought of his departure as much of a loss. Therefore, he prefers the name Nobody. Since this film is an odyssey, it seems appropriate that this character take the same name as Odysseus, who also found it was safer not to throw his name around in his adventures.

Nobody is therefore a very complex man even before the film begins. Jarmusch chose to make Nobody a mixed-blood because he "wanted to situate him as a Plains Indian, so [he] chose those two tribes that did intermix at certain points historically but also were at war with each other. So his parents in [his] mind were like Romeo and Juliet; there was even a reference to that in the script."[80]

That Nobody was taken as a young boy to be exhibited in a cage is also from Jarmusch's historical research, and the attitudes of the colonizers are very clear in a flashback to Nobody's childhood, where he sits in a cage with uncaged animals next to him. That he impresses the

English by mimicking them is also an interesting idea that implies that Native Americans were only considered human when they adopted the ways of the colonizers. This is certainly not news to anyone familiar with the enthusiastic efforts of the missionaries and educators to "kill the Indian and save the man."

There are also two extended jokes in the film that are important as well as entertaining. We are introduced to the first when Nobody meets the wounded young accountant from Cleveland who has just blundered his way through a shoot-out with the fiancée of the woman he was sleeping with. Nobody is shocked to hear that the man's name is William Blake. Some reviewers have indicated that Nobody really believes that this "stupid white man" with the "white man's metal" next to his heart is the original poet. A more likely explanation, given the personality that evolves for Nobody during the film, is that he *chooses* to believe. He tells Blake (Johnny Depp) that he (Blake) has been a poet, a painter, and now a killer of white men. His amusement at this makes it difficult to determine which of those three he finds most admirable.

That Nobody behaves as though Blake is the real McCoy provides some humor in the film, mostly because Nobody remembers much of the poet's work and says he is surprised that Blake doesn't. He recites Blake's poetry at pivotal points in the film. For instance, at their first meeting he says, "Every night and every morn / Some to misery are born. / Some are born to sweet delight / Some are born to endless night" (from *Augeries of Innocence*). Blake has been to misery born, and now he is dying. Nobody takes it upon himself to deliver the man to the "mirror of water," the bridge to the next level of life. Now whether this is due to his innate kindness, his respect for the poet, or his desire to produce evidence for his story about England we are never really sure—and it doesn't really matter.

An interviewer asked about the notion of "passing through the mirror" and its structural bases for the film. Jarmusch responded, "they do somehow connect with that abstract idea that Nobody has to pass Blake through this mirror of water and send him back to the spirit level of the world. But what was more fascinating to me is that these cultures coexisted only so briefly, and then the industrialized one eliminated the aboriginal culture. Those specific Northwest tribes existed for thousands of years and then they were wiped out in much less than a hundred years. They even used biological warfare, giving them infected blankets and all kinds of stuff—any way to get rid of them. And then they were gone. And it was such an incredibly rich culture."[81]

All the people of the Northwest tribes are, of course, *not* extinct as Jarmusch suggests, although the attempted extinction is factual, and in the case of a few tribes the annihilation is also factual. It is unfortunate that he presents *all* the Northwest tribes as extinct for the interviewer since he obviously knew differently—he used real Northwestern Native people in making this movie. Fortunately, however, the film shows those tribes very much alive. He continues,

> I don't really know of any fiction film where you see a Pacific Northwest culture. . . . They spent a lot of time developing their culture, their carving, their mythology, and their incredibly elaborate ceremonies with these gigantic figures that would transform from one thing into another, with all kinds of optical illusions and tricks. That's why the long house opens that way [the huge image of a thunderbird opens its "wings" to reveal a doorway] in *Dead Man*, when Nobody goes inside to talk to the elders of the tribe and eventually gets a sea canoe from them. It seems to open magically, but it's based on a real system of pulleys that these tribes used."[82]

As they travel, Blake asks questions and Nobody replies "the eagle never lost so much time as when he submitted to learn from the crow" (from Blake's *Proverbs of Hell*). Nobody and Blake eventually enter a trading post run by a loquacious and extremely racist missionary (Alfred Molina). The man sees Nobody and says, "The Lord Jesus Christ wash this earth with his holy light and purge his darkest places from heathens and philistines." Nobody replies, "The vision of Christ that thou doest see / Is my vision's greatest enemy" (from Blake's *The Everlasting Gospel*). As the *Cineaste* reviewer, in an unconscious bow to the stereotype, says, "The funny thing is, they sounded like Indian sayings in the film." Jarmusch agrees and says that was the intention. There are other quotes he chose that didn't make it into the film, including "'Expect poison from standing water.' 'What is now proved was once only imagined.' 'The crow wish'd every thing was black, the owl that every thing was white.'"[83] These are, indeed, what an audience might expect a noble savage to say, and it is wildly funny that they were actually written by one of the icons of romantic poetry, the very English Mr. Blake.

Jarmusch's use of Blake's poetry is inspired. Not only does it get the message across in immediate terms, but it also points out that the seemingly quaint sayings of the Natives might just be something more. Perhaps even poetic. It also depicts an American Indian man who not only knows poetry, something no one else in the film seems to have a clue about, but he uses it at very appropriate moments. No primitive savage here.

The second joke in the film is the constantly recurring question, "Do you have any tobacco?" This is a joke Jarmusch wrote in "for the indigenous American people." What an interesting concept, to privilege the Other audience in a film made by a white guy. More than that, he did his homework:

> [T]here were indigenous to North America some forty strains of tobacco that are far more powerful than anything we have now. I have a real respect for tobacco as a substance, and it just seems funny how the Western attitude is, "Wow, people are addicted to this, think of all the money you can make off it." For indigenous people here it's still a sacrament, it's what you bring to someone's house, it's what you smoke when you pray. Our cultural advisor, Cathy, is a member of the Native American Church and even uses peyote ceremonially.[84] We used to go up on these hillsides sometimes early in the morning before shooting, usually with just the native people in the cast and crew, and pray and smoke. She'd put tobacco in a ceremonial pipe and pass it around, and you'd wash yourself with the smoke. She prays to each direction, to the sky, to the earth, to the plants and all the animals and animal spirits. And what cracked me up is, as soon as the ceremony was over, we'd be walking back down the hill and she'd be lighting up a Marlboro.[85]

Each time Nobody asks Blake if he has some tobacco, Blake answers, "I don't smoke." As the film progresses, Blake gets more and more irritated by the question because he doesn't realize the significance of the question or the substance. Finally, as Blake comes to consciousness as he drifts off in the funereal sea canoe Nobody has lined with cedar boughs, he notices the tobacco twist in his hand. Jarmusch says he hopes "the last line of the film, 'But Nobody, I don't smoke,' will be a hilarious joke to them [Native peoples]: 'Oh man, this white man still doesn't get it.'"[86] It is funny, no doubt, but it's also easy to read that last line as a friendly joke between these two men from different cultures—that Blake finally does "get it" and is letting Nobody know he appreciates it.

The tobacco joke is not the only element in the film that is geared solely toward Natives. There are three American Indian languages spoken by Nobody in the film—Cree, Blackfoot, and Makah—and they are neither subtitled nor interpreted. They are Jarmusch's "little gift for those people who understand the language."[87] Some of the scenes with Native languages must be hilarious to this privileged audience. For instance, at the end of the three-day fast and vision quest that Nobody has produced for Blake without his consent, Blake comes upon Nobody and an unidentified, beautiful woman making love in the woods. He interrupts what Nobody terms "a very romantic moment." The woman (Michelle Thrush) drapes a buffalo robe around her naked body and stomps over to tell him off in Cree. She goes on for some time, ending with a spit at his feet before she huffs off. Blake's only response is, "She's upset." After she leaves, Nobody says, "She didn't mean to call you that." The audience, of course, would love to know what she called him, which is exactly the response Jarmusch had in mind.

The languages are authentic, not the usual Hollywood fabrication. Michelle Thrush, the woman who plays the Cree lover, is in fact Cree, and she helped Jarmusch write the dialogue and then translated it. The Makah language is evidently quite difficult to master, and Farmer had to read it phonetically from cue cards to get it right. The key point here is that there was a real effort to get it right.

Not everyone thinks Jarmusch's baby is pretty. *Dead Man* has been referred to as cinematic history's longest death scene, and *People Magazine*'s Tom Gliatto says it "goes on and on, one static, cute-weird scene after another. Robert Mitchum talks to a stuffed bear. Iggy Pop, in a filthy gingham frock, recounts the tale of Goldilocks. You soon give up taking in the pristine black-and-white photography of the bleak forest and listening to the dreamy buzz of Neil Young's electric guitar on the soundtrack. *Dead Man* is the equivalent of two hours in the floatation tank. It was one of the dumbest things I've seen in a while, but I left feeling refreshed. How about that? Hell and nirvana in one film."[88]

Perhaps the reason he left so refreshed was that he slept through the entire film, but this is the type of response the film gets from many viewers who expect the "normal" film that Hollywood has been cranking out for the last hundred years. A more insightful response came from Kent Jones in a review for *Cineaste*:

There is no mastery here among white men, as there is in most Westerns, no instinctive understanding of the land. There is only mute incomprehension or violently aggressive dominance—in Blake's case we see the progression from one to the other—and it's as though there are no alternatives available to dislocated intruders. This subtle insight is realized purely through action, and it gives the film a firm foundation on which its symbols and haunting associations with modern American experience can rest. . . . Not to be hyperbolic, but *Dead Man*, particularly in its final vertiginous moments, has the superreal physical impact of Murnau's flights into abstraction. . . . This may be the supreme cinephilic compliment, but it's also accurate.[89]

Whether one likes the film or not, there are a few undeniable facts about *Dead Man,* one of the most important of which is that Jarmusch's film shows a significant effort to depict a Native existence stripped of the stereotypes of the last hundred years of filmmaking. It is a very good start.

As the Century Turns

A new American Indian image has emerged in the last decade of the century. This one is the most dangerous and confusing of all to those who thought the Indian Problem settled except for a few worrisome details. The new Native American warrior comes armed with attorneys and economic clout, and one of the main battles getting under way is one of sovereignty.

A few tribes have attained economic prosperity through casinos and tourism, and the number of Indian lawyers increased more than tenfold between 1980 and 1998. The American Indian presence in Washington DC is stronger than ever before. As John Echohawk, executive director of the Native American Rights Fund said, "What we've seen is simply the civil rights movement for Native Americans. Tribal rights are finally being enforced because more and more tribes have the resources to have their own lawyers."[90]

Many Americans don't understand the concept of tribal sovereignty, including former Speaker of the House Newt Gingrich, who admitted he had trouble grasping the concept.[91] This failure is largely due to the fact that Americans have usually seen Indians as potentially dangerous in isolated instances but generally powerless. That educated American Indians of the late 1990s are serious about the declaration regarding tribal sovereignty found in Article 6 of the U.S. Constitution comes as quite a shock to them. "What it really boils down to is the right to make your own laws and be ruled by them," stated Kevin Gover, a Pawnee who is the new Assistant Secretary of the Interior for Indian Affairs.[92]

Tribes are beginning to function more like states and counties—

levying taxes, enforcing their own land use regulations, building codes and criminal statutes, and using money gained through the "new buffalo" (casinos) to lobby for Indian rights in Washington.[93] This is not well received in those states with large reservations within them, and it is certain that Congress and the Supreme Court will be facing many challenges from both sides in the coming years. The twenty-first century will be a very interesting time in the nation's Native American story. As a plaque in the National Museum of the American Indian in New York City says, "We are still here." Perhaps a good addendum to that plaque would be "as long as the grass grows and the rivers run."

The new image of Native Americans held by many Americans is also changing—but at a snail's pace because the noble and bloodthirsty images of the past are hard to disassemble. American Indians are seen now as potentially dangerous by non-Indians living near reservations (and the politicians they elect), as "those rich Indians" by many of the whites who flood casinos, and as ecological crusaders by those who have embraced the natural ecologist image. The good news here is that these new images, whether positive or negative, are at least contemporary, complicated, and differentiated. With luck, the new images in the films of the twenty-first century will also be contemporary—dealing with American Indians as real, complex people with ideas and cultures that have deep roots and flourishing new growth.

6

The American Indian Aesthetic

That's where we're at as Indian filmmakers. We want to start partici-
pating and developing an Indian aesthetic. And there is such a thing
as an Indian aesthetic, and it begins in the sacred. – Victor Masayesva
Jr., quoted in Steven Leuthold, "An Indigenous Aesthetic: Two Noted
Videographers"

American Indians have been, for the full run of film history, a sort of
weathervane of social and political currents. Richard Hill has noted that
the image of the Indian changes with each generation. In looking at
current print media, Hill delineated the following contemporary views
and uses of American Indians:

- The alternative press uses Indians to strike out against capitalism and
  racism, using their struggle for rights to "play to the radical left, the
  Yuppie center, and the disenchanted children of the wealthy right."
- The environmental press tries to debunk the "myth" of the natural
  conservationist, saying "Make no mistake. The tribes are on the
  move. They aim to lay claim to as much land—your land—as they
  can get, and the plan to commercialize our fish and game resources
  . . ." (As Hill notes, this sounds suspiciously like something the Indians might have said about the Pilgrims.)
- The New Age press has turned the Indian into the all-purpose symbol
  of spirituality.
- The conservative press wants to end the treaties, saying that Indians
  are too expensive to keep.
- In mainstream dailies, the stereotypes are everywhere. The Indian is
  disempowered, alcoholic, uneducated, and in poor health. "*Time*
  magazine called Indians 'adrift in their own country.'"[1]

These images in the press are very much like those we find in most film
and video presentations. The result is a very confused image of American Indians. If one chooses to be wildly optimistic, it is possible to

think that this is a good thing. Perhaps confusion is better than certainty when the certainty is based on fallacy.

At the end of the twentieth century, "sympathy" for American Indians, for different and sometimes odd reasons, exists generally, but mainstream Hollywood filmmakers who have attempted to portray that sympathy have failed in one or more ways to portray Native peoples realistically. Their failure can be partly explained by the cultural and communicative gap between filmmakers and the people they are depicting.[2] It must seem to filmmakers telling a story about Indians that they are damned if they do and damned if they don't. Tell a story about a mixed couple who cannot be together and live—it's racist. Tell the same story and let them live happily ever after—the love story becomes a deadly form of assimilation. Make the Indians good guys and you're producing the noble savage stereotype. Show the Indians being bloodthirsty and you are likely to be shot by your own friends in Hollywood.

Perhaps the problem is in telling a story *about* Indians. What about the stories Indians tell of themselves? Are they able to bring historical, cultural, or emotional accuracy about their lives and cultures into a medium constructed by the mainstream culture? Are the media of film and video really, as Elizabeth Weatherford states, "a logical extension of the oral and visual communications of traditional Native American culture?"[3] If so, can the stories Native Americans tell be accessible to the economically necessary mainstream audience while privileging the Other, Native voice?

The answer is yes—they can. However, it is only now becoming possible because only recently have Natives been found in all areas of professional filmmaking. Only recently has it become possible to assemble a team composed of Native Americans as screenwriters, directors, producers, and actors.

The Writers

In a panel discussion at the 1996 Native Americas Film Exposition in Santa Fe, New Mexico, film directors, producers, and actors agreed that the first order of business in developing a Native film industry is finding Native writers to write good scripts that depict American Indian experiences in meaningful ways. It is obvious that a good script is imperative for a good film (*Casablanca* [1942] notwithstanding), and this would seem to be the job description most easy to fill because there are *many* Native American authors writing exciting novels, stories, drama, and poetry. The number of good novels written by Natives has, in fact, increased from a handful in the 1960s to hundreds in the 1990s, and a few of those have been made into films, although the directors and producers for those films have until *very* recently been Euro-American.

In order to get a general idea of the ways in which films written by Native Americans differ from those written by others, we can examine four films made in the last three decades—*House Made of Dawn* (1972), *Harold of Orange* (1984), *Medicine River* (1994), and *Smoke Signals* (1998).

N. SCOTT MOMADAY

House Made of Dawn (1972)
In 1969 Kiowa author N. Scott Momaday won the Pulitzer Prize for his novel, *House Made of Dawn*. A member of the Pulitzer jury stated that the award recognized "the arrival on the American literary scene of a matured, sophisticated literary artist from the original Americans." As Choctaw/Cherokee author Louis Owens pointedly asked, "Could it be that at last an indigenous writer had emerged who could emulate and imitate the discourse of the cultural center—Euro-America—so well that he could be accepted, perhaps canonized?" He then describes *House Made of Dawn* as functioning beautifully as a modernist novel while simultaneously telling a very Native American story in very Native American ways: "With Momaday the American Indian novel shows its ability to appropriate the discourse of the privileged center and make it 'bear the burden' of an 'other' world-view. Momaday's novel represents more fully than any Native American novel before it the 'assertion of a different perspective.'"[4]

In 1972 Firebird Productions and director Richardson Morse attempted to produce a film of the novel, making it bear the burden of another type of discourse from another province of the privileged center. While the production received criticism for technical flaws, it also earned praise as one of the first films to depict a contemporary Indian experience. Its time period is just after World War II, which makes it very contemporary compared to the time period usually assigned to American Indian existence.

The film uses a complicated and sometimes confusing series of flashbacks in an effort to approximate Momaday's modernist style in the novel, which in the film is only partially successful. The flashbacks may also have been an attempt to approach the Indian vision of time as circular as opposed to linear; if so, it was a good idea that didn't work out as hoped. A Native audience might understand the impulse, but the rough jumps sometimes make the story difficult to follow for any viewer.

With the exception of John Saxon as Tosomah, the main characters in the film were played by Native American actors. Michael Hilger sees the acting of Larry Littlebird (Pueblo) as Abel, and Jay Varela (mixed-blood) as Ben, as the emotional center of the film. He noted, "The contrast between these characters reveals the dilemma of the modern Indian and the dialogue and acting provide a restrained but powerful impact."[5]

This "dilemma" is the question of whether an Indian can assimilate into the dominant society and remain an Indian. Momaday set his story at the beginning of the Termination era (1945–61), when U.S. government policy was to relocate American Indians, taking them from their tribal communities and placing them mostly in urban areas where they would learn to "fit in," another in a long line of attempts to solve the "Indian problem" by turning them into white people.

The relationship between Abel and Ben and the differences in their perspectives on "Indianness" are of importance to the novel as well as the film, but much of the novel's greatness is lost by making this the "emotional center" of the film. It is obvious that a filmmaker must make choices and can never show all elements of a novel, especially when that novel is functioning on at least two planes as *House Made of Dawn* is, but the omissions or lack of focus on Pueblo and Navajo attitudes regarding the correct way to approach evil and the power of words are disappointing to those who know the book.

The novel makes it very clear that evil is a part of the world that must be recognized but left alone. Abel is confronted by evil incarnate on three occasions in the novel: by an old woman he recognizes as a witch, by an albino, and by a crooked policeman in Los Angeles. In all three cases, Momaday uses snake imagery to convey the idea of evilness, an effective choice for a predominantly Christian audience. Though quite clear, this symbolism is difficult to convey on screen without resorting to some very heavy-handed audio or visual effects. The result will almost assuredly be, unfortunately, a misunderstanding one way or the other.

The second major problem in translating this novel into film is devising a way to get across a Native American attitude toward the power of words. The novel's most explicit example of word power is the sermon delivered by the Priest of the Sun of the Pan-Indian Church, John

Big Bluff Tosamah. Tosamah gives a long sermon in which he talks about the Christian Bible and the Power of the Word. He then shifts to a story about his grandmother, one which is also found in Momaday's autobiographical collection, *The Way to Rainy Mountain*. Tosamah is a "trickster and a fraud, a manipulator of language the import of which is undercut systematically by cynical superficiality that reduces his words at times to mere jingles or turns them against themselves."[6] The turning of words against themselves, a deconstruction of his own language, is a trickster characteristic a Native audience would pick up immediately, but a white audience is very likely to see the priest as either a simple con man or a blathering idiot. While it would be fine for the privileged Other to understand a depth of meaning not transparent to the general audience, giving that general audience a *mis*understanding is counter-productive, at best. Perhaps if the part had been played by a Native American actor such as Chief Dan George or Floyd Westerman, the message would have come through more clearly in the film version of *House Made of Dawn*, but this is speculation of a rather unuseful sort.

Overall, the film scores more points than demerits for two reasons: it was a serious attempt to depict contemporary Native American lives and issues in a form of discourse appropriated from the dominant culture, and the main characters of this film find meaning within themselves and their traditional culture. As Hilger states, "[Abel] is a complicated and heroic Indian whose significance does not really depend on comparison or contrast to white society, as is the case with the Indians in *Little Big Man* and other westerns. The filmmakers don't use [him] for some other purpose like instilling guilt; they empathize with [him] and show respect for the uniqueness of American Indian culture."[7]

In attempting to locate a film copy of *House Made of Dawn*, researchers generally have serious difficulty. It is simply not available from sources that apparently have no trouble obtaining films of twice its age and half its merit. It seems to have simply "vanished" from all but a few university video libraries.

GERALD VIZENOR

Harold of Orange (1984)

In *The Dialogic Imagination*, Mikhail Bakhtin wrote that "[l]aughter has the remarkable power of making an object come up close, of drawing it into a zone of crude contact where one can finger it familiarly on all sides, turn it upside down, inside out, peer at it from above and below, break open its external shell, look into its center, doubt it, take it apart, dismember it, lay it bare and expose it, examine it freely and experiment with it. Laughter demolishes fear and piety before an object, before a world, making of it an object of familiar contact and thus clearing the ground for an absolutely free investigation of it."[8] Had he been writing specifically about the laughter of a Native American trickster, he could not have come to a more precise description. The purpose of a trickster is to shake up the status quo with irreverent acts and words that cause us to look at ourselves again for the first time.

Gerald Vizenor's creation, *Harold of Orange*, is a thirty-minute baptism in the laughter-ridden whitewater of tricksterdom. Like most of Vizenor's impressive bank of fiction, critical theory, and autobiographical essays, *Harold of Orange* stars the tricksters, is the work of a trickster, and given celluloid life becomes a trickster. Much contemporary fiction by Native Americans involves a search for identity, but a trickster knows who he is, or at least he says he does.

At the beginning of *Harold of Orange*, before the opening credits, before the name of the production company (Film in the Cities), or before any sound, the tricksters' manifesto rolls up the screen.

> Harold and the Warriors of Orange are descendants of the great trickster who created the new earth after the flood.
>
> But the trickster was soon word driven from the land by the white man, who claimed the earth as his own and returned to the trickster only what he couldn't use.
>
> Now, Harold and the Warriors of Orange, tribal tricksters determined to reclaim their estate from the white man, are challenging his very foundations.

This is exactly what the audience sees the warriors do in the film. They attempt to "reclaim their estate" from one of capitalism's most powerful tools, the nonprofit, charitable "foundation," where—from a native American trickster's point of view—white money launders its conscience.

The first time we see Harold (Charlie Hill), it is in a long-distance shot as he drives down a country road toward the camera. Trickster is, as trickster always is, moving along. Original music by American Indian songwriter and singer Buffy Sainte-Marie sets the tone as the credits appear. It is music that combines English and Native words with a Native American sound.

Harold stops the car in front of the tribal coffeehouse, gets out and addresses the camera. Just about everything a trickster says is layered with meaning, and this address is no exception. He first describes the natural landscape, the reservation the Orange River runs through. The Warriors of Orange live on the best loop in the river, a "natural high rise" in the earth. That they live in a loop is interesting, in that the American Indian world is circular in time and space. That they live in a "natural high rise" sounds like the penthouse suite on the Orange—the trickster moves freely between worlds of mind.

Harold explains who the Warriors of Orange are. They are the "tricksters in the new school of social acupuncture, where a little pressure fills the pocketbook." They keep a clean coffeehouse, tend to their oranges, and speak of the mythic revolution of the reservation. He then invites us in for a "pinch" of coffee.

The oranges these warriors "tend" are those the foundation has funded previously. They are part of the mythic revolution because they have been the cause of funding and also because they are basically mythical. The warriors' oranges are miniature, and their one tree (in a pot) produces oranges about the size of a kumquat or small pigeon egg. Their new proposal for the foundation is the growing of pinchbeans for coffee and the establishment of coffeehouses on reservations "around the world." One of the warriors asks, "Who'd believe that?"

The answer is, "The same people who believed in the miniature oranges." They have no orchard, but Harold tells the man that their oranges are in tax-free bonds, the source of his allowance. Tricksters are not stupid, and they plan ahead—sometimes. They have purchased seven cases of organic oranges from the Southwest to take to the board meeting where they will pitch their pinchbean idea.

Harold has brought the costumes for the occasion, a necktie for each of them. He says, "Neckties are the pressure points in the school of social acupuncture." One warrior follows with a joke about neckties making the white men white by stopping the blood to their brains, and a mixed-blood retorts that the man is in no danger. The first replies that mixed-bloods are at a higher risk.

Though the scene plays out quickly, it is laden with issues. The wearing of neckties is a direct reference to what American Indian attorney, writer, and activist Vine Deloria refers to in his essay, "American Fantasy":

> During the OEO days when government agencies and private foundations were seeking Indian organizations to fund, we used to pick out

the handsomest of representatives. People give funds more readily if they are giving to a young man who looks like Tonto or a young woman who resembles Pocahontas. The technique worked perfectly; it was an appeal to imagination and not to the relevancy of the project under consideration. Only as the granting process became a well-beaten path did the Indian representatives begin to take themselves seriously and screw up what had been the perfect scam. Politics? Find an Indian with a nice haircut who could be the Indian Bobby Kennedy and you have the Democrats lusting after you; get an Indian princess who can do either the Lord's Prayer or the Twenty-third Psalm in sign language (or who can at least wave her arms in some sequential manner that looks like it might be sign language) and you gain admittance to any Republican meeting, convention (or even the Cotton Bowl), or caucus you want to attend. Church meetings—find either a young militant or a fundamentalist Indian minister (preferably a Baptist or Methodist) and you get whatever you want from the churches. The list, if you think about it, is endless and is limited only by the almost inexhaustible fantasies of the whites.[9]

Harold has determined that ties on Native necks will stimulate the giving impulse in the foundation's imagination. They each wear one, although none of them places it around the collar, just around his neck. One of the warriors wears a traditional bone choker with the necktie loosely hung around it—the perfect package.

Just before they leave the coffeehouse, after whooping it up like a "bunch of wild anglos," one warrior asks about the new woman on the foundation's board. Yes, she is a concern to Harold.

Fanny (Cathleen Fuller) is her name, and the first thing we hear from her is that her "real interest in Indians was stimulated in college." She is one of the many thousands of white people who have "studied" Indians. Later, we realize that she and Harold were close during their college years, and it is Harold that "stimulated" her interest. Harold the trickster is certainly not above using a white woman's interest in an "exotic" male to turn a profit. In fact, he still owes her a thousand dollars, which he borrowed to bury his grandmother for the fourth time that year. Later in the film she gives him an ultimatum, implying that if he wants the grant, he had better get the money back to her by the afternoon.

Corporate rape of American Indian land is also touched on in this film. An older board member, Andrew Burch (Alan Woodward) says,

"If you must know," even though it is a self-indulgent non sequitur in the conversation, "my father was in the timber business. We shared many adventures with some of the finest Native woodsmen."

Fanny is stunned by the announcement, which, aside from the stereotypical allusion, makes little sense. She responds with a sardonic, "Yes. I have studied corporate development of resources on the reservations." The use of reservation resources is a long-standing source of Indian-white problems.[10]

The idea of language is also tossed about as the president tells the other board members that Fanny studied Indian folklore. She corrects him, saying, "literature." Marion Quest (Barbara Davidson), the only other female board member, asks, "Oh, do Indians have a written language?" Fanny gets to say only that it is an oral tradition, before she is cut off again. For Gerald Vizenor, a writer who is indeed a "word warrior," the question of what constitutes "literature" is an important one, and the appearance of the question in this film is logical. A trickster always turns things upside down, however, so later when Harold privately asks if Fanny remembers the "oral tradition," he seems to be referring to something more interesting than any of the other board members might have thought.

A late arrival to the meeting is Ted, a delicate-looking man who made his fortune in tricks and games. He is anything but a trickster, however, except perhaps that he "tricks" himself. He proudly shows the other members his new product, a watch that clucks the William Tell Overture like a chicken. The Tonto and Lone Ranger theme is obvious enough, but he doesn't get the connection between his role in funding the Warriors of Orange and the music, much less the connection made by the fact that the theme is in a chicken's voice.

When Ted asks who the other board members have been talking about, Marion responds, "That little orange man." She doesn't use Harold's name, although it is later made clear that she knows it, but refers to him by his connection to the funding he receives for raising oranges. He is a man of color, although orange is an unusual choice even for a trickster. Most importantly, he is "that *little* orange man." On one level, she is, of course, talking about the miniature oranges, but he is also a little man from her perspective, someone to whom she is superior, someone who asks for what she and her cohorts are able to give, if they so choose.

There is nothing intentionally malevolent about Ted's product or Marion's statement; they don't *mean* to be insulting or degrading,

14. Robert Redford, Gerald Vizenor, and Charlie Hill at the Sundance Film Festival. Summer 1983.

which is the point. They are all, presumably, on the board because they feel the need to be helpful. The problem is in their psychic positioning. For a Native audience, the board is one more entity representing a long-established patriarchal, patronizing attitude.

Harold's last name is Sincer, and it fits him well. He is dedicated to being a trickster-warrior, and he works very hard at it. When the board members state his name, however, they do so with sincere looks on their own faces, underlining in a heavy-handed but very funny way that they are gullible people. Each fits precisely Deloria's description of a sincere white person. When Deloria asks, "Should Indians scam whites who are sincere?" he provides the answer Harold and his warriors have evidently come to: "Well, the answer is complex in an abstract sense but very simple in a practical, everyday context. The whites are sincere but they are only sincere about what they are interested in, not about Indians about whom they know very little. They get exceedingly angry if you try to tell them the truth and will only reject you and keep searching until they find the Indian of their fantasies. So if you have to deal with them to get the job done, that comes with the job."[11]

Since the warriors must pitch their pinchbean scam to this board, they decide to devise a presentation that will fit the fantasy, something a little different. The list they come up with includes a naming ceremony, to which Harold responds, "Not a bad idea"; a ghost dance, to which he responds, "Get serious"; some tipi-creeping, which makes everyone laugh; and a softball game, since they have all the equipment in the bus. The remainder of the film shows the Warriors of Orange going about their "presentation" in just those ways. Harold tells the board, "Once we climbed in church windows with heavy hearts and empty pockets. But now the guilt has changed and so have we. Once we took you to the orchards; now we'll take you to the pinchbean coffeehouses on the reservations. So follow me down the white road to the orange bus for the first red pinch."

As tricksters their role is to make others see themselves, and this is what they do for the discerning audience. The board remains clueless, except perhaps for Fanny, but that she knows Harold so well indicates that the "tipi-creeping" part of the plan has already been accomplished.

The warriors load the board members on the bus and cart them around the city for various parts of the presentation. While on the bus, they banter with the board members. Mr. Burch asks one warrior what he thinks about the Bering Strait migration theory and is quite unprepared for the response, "Which way?" It has obviously never occurred to him that the Native Americans might have been, as the warrior states, "here first." The older man is polite, and in a rather patronizing manner asks for more explication. All goes well until the trickster turns the conversation on its ear, stating that Jesus Christ was an Indian. This is going too far for even a liberal board member, and Burch clamps his thin, white lips together and whispers a parsimonious "Was he now? Who would have guessed?"

Later, Ted asks another warrior how many Indians were here when Columbus discovered America. The warrior, of course, says, "None," and explains that Indian is a misnomer. Ted patiently rephrases his question to refer to tribal peoples. The warrior then says that there were 49,723,196, and that included what is now Mexico. Ted is a trifle incensed, and the warrior gives a disgusted, eyes-to-heaven look before putting his Walkman earphones back on.

The president of the board, whose name is Kingman Newton (James Noah), an obvious play on head man and theorist, tells Harold that the board is impressed with the very knowledgeable warriors. Harold responds with "Warriors of Orange are trained in the art of social acupuncture. We imagine the world and then we cut our words from the centerfolds of history." Newton asks if that is a tribal tradition, indicating he hasn't a clue as to what Harold has just said, so Harold continues, "We're wild word hunters, tricksters on the run." Given a history of words on paper called treaties—perhaps the "centerfolds of history"— and the peripatetic nature of tricksters, this is not only a humorous response, it is truthful. Of course, Newton misses it and responds with a sanctimonious, "Well, we are impressed."

As Robert Stam has noted, "For the colonizer, to be human is to speak his language. In countless films, linguistic discrimination and colonialist 'tact' go hand in hand with condescending characterization and distorted social portraiture."[12] Harold and his crew impress the board members not because they say anything overwhelmingly brilliant but because they are articulate at all. They are impressed by the warriors' ability to converse like white men. From the audience's perspective, however, the warriors are actually running linguistic circles around the board members.

The first part of the presentation is the naming ceremony. In a parking lot they pull up to a stand selling Indian fry-bread. They pass around samples, which the board members look at suspiciously, asking, "Do we really have to eat this?" Then the ceremony begins. It consists of pulling Monopoly cards out of a cigar box. Newton doesn't know much, but he's pretty sure this isn't the way a ceremony is conducted. He steps up to Harold and whispers, "Are you serious?"

Harold leans back and whispers, "Who could be serious about anything in a parking lot?" He then draws Newton's new "Indian" name, Baltic, and starts a huckster routine, chanting, "Step right into an urban dream." He coerces Marion into stepping forward and continues, "The great urban shaman who directs the interstates has given me your name in a dream." The name turns out to be Connecticut. Any audience would see the ridiculous nature of this ceremony, and Native audiences would likely relate it to the recurring rash of "traditional Indian ceremonies" performed by shamans-by-mail, who are not tricksters but frauds.

The next stop is the university's anthropology department, where Harold makes a long, somewhat tedious speech describing the Ghost Dance. He says the full-bloods will soar above the ground, mixed-bloods will be buried as deeply as their white blood goes, and anthropologists will be buried upside down with their toes sticking up like mushrooms. In this way, even the Ghost Dance makes its way into the presentation, although it is one of the most blatantly didactic and therefore one of the least effective moments in the film.

At one point the skeptical Burch takes Newton aside and asks him about Harold. Newton, the theorist, replies, "He says he's a trickster."

Burch asks, "A confidence man?"

"No. Tricksters aren't insane. He's rather sincere, innocent even. He believes he can stop time and change the world."

Burch responds cynically, "With a foundation grant."

Newton continues the good-old-boy tenor of the discussion with, "Who could change the world *without* a foundation grant?"

Neither man seems to know what has been going on. Burch is closer to the truth when he assumes Harold is a con artist, although why Newton assumes that would necessarily mean he is insane is questionable. Harold is a trickster, and he does indeed think he can stop time, or at least make it into the circular time of a Native universe, and he is changing his world with a foundation grant, but not in the manner these men believe they can and will dictate. It is the trickster's talent to move with oily fluidity between elements, changing the social field in the process.

Back on the bus, Burch asks Harold about pinchbeans. He wants to know if they will ever see a live bush. Harold says, "The difference is in the telling." Like the trickster he is, Harold has some magic up the sleeve of his ribbon shirt. He draws a bush on a piece of paper, wads it up and pours it into Burch's hand in the form of pinchbeans. He then changes the beans into ground coffee, and when Burch asks, "How'd you do that?" Harold's response is, "Tribal secret."

The next stop is the softball game. As they get off the bus, the board members are wearing red shirts with the word *Indians* written in white. The warriors are wearing white shirts with the word *Anglos* written in red. They huddle for pre-game discussions, and Harold addresses the Anglo team, his fellow warriors. He tells them they must win this game in the name of God and send those Indians back to the reservation where they belong. Another warrior speaks up. "But if you should lose, don't count on a job with the BIA to get even." For an Indian audience who has experienced the "get back to your reservation" attitude, this is very funny. The BIA response is also humorous, but there is even more of an edge to this joke, since it acknowledges that the employees of the BIA have the power, even if not the inclination, to perform acts of personal revenge. While the Bureau of Indian Affairs is obviously run more humanely than depicted in *The Vanishing American*, this reference makes it clear that American Indians still do not feel they are in charge of their own existence.

Harold walks over to the other team while taking off his white shirt. Underneath is the red shirt of the Indian (white) team. He moves between the teams as a trickster must move between the worlds presented to him. When he addresses this team, he says, "Remember what the missionaries said our elders said—we're made up in dreams. It's the white man who must win. When he wins we're set free. He'll want to be just like us and we can leave him once and for all on the reservations he made for us." This strikes directly at what these board members are attempting to do, to appropriate an Indian existence by extending their money to the reservation. They, of course, miss the irony completely, and what follows is a hilarious game that neither side really wins.

The music playing during the game is Sainte-Marie's wonderful score, which combines a popular music beat and words with traditional Indian music. The result is not only enjoyable but very much in the trickster mode, moving quickly between worlds, appropriating and enjoying each.

The last stop is an art gallery displaying Indian heads in the form of portraits. The board congratulates the warriors on a wonderful, personal, ceremonial, "ever so memorable" presentation. Ted is still uncertain, however. He has a very "delicate" question. The warriors try to guess what it is, including a guess that he wants to meet a beautiful Indian woman. Ted stutters, "No. I mean yes, but only in a proper manner." When asked if it is about beads, Ted says they have enough beads. An old, dying Indian woman sold them to his wife in the hospital. This, too, is a very sensitive subject for Native Americans who are seeing their histories bought as artifacts and hung on living room walls.

No, Ted's question is about alcoholism. Like poverty, alcoholism is a genuine, life-destroying problem on reservations, one not even a trickster is likely to laugh about. When Ted congratulates the warriors on being so sober, as though it is a surprising thing indeed, they are momentarily stunned. Harold makes a quick recovery, though, and explains that it is due to the pinchbeans. They are "booze blockers." This wins Ted over completely—a quick fix is exactly the kind of thing the foundation wants to finance.

With the foundation grant obtained, Harold has only one more point of business. He has told Fanny she would have her thousand dollars back that afternoon. He has twice attempted to get the money from Newton, first as an advance and then offering to arrange a tour and hunt on reservation land. The advance is a legitimate approach, un-characteristic of a trickster, and Newton snaps the door shut on it im-mediately, saying, "We'll forget you asked." The royal plural pronoun puts the trickster in his place, and the next time he offers what the audi-ence knows will be another fleecing operation, something like a snipe hunt. Access to reservation land is something Newton would be tick-led to have, and so he falls for it but places the "hunt" in the future, so Harold must try again. The last time, he uses his grandmother's funeral once more. Fanny has already told us that he used this excuse four times in one year and that she was once one of his pigeons. Newton falls com-pletely for the traditional grandmother laid out on the kitchen table be-cause they had no money to bury her, and he writes a check. One could almost feel sorry for Newton at this point, except that he follows im-mediately with "May I attend the funeral?" Obviously, neither Harold nor Harold's grandmother are of tremendous interest to Newton, but the idea of attending a real, traditional Indian ceremony almost makes him drool. This is the type of cultural vampirism that Native audiences would recognize easily, and it makes it impossible to feel anything for Newton except disgust.

Back on the reservation, Harold and the Warriors of Orange invite the audience to come to the reservation coffeehouses for pinchbean cof-fee, and the credits roll.

For an American Indian audience, the film is an enjoyable romp through an issue a minute, told by a delightful bunch of tricksters. A non-Native audience might be hard pressed to understand much more than the board members they find themselves laughing at, but this is not a film that attempts to address both audiences—it privileges the Native audience in the way that Hollywood films have privileged the mainstream audiences from the beginning of film history.

In telling about the making of *Harold of Orange*, Gerald Vizenor said that when the film was newly finished he received an early morning call from the director, who was anxious about audience reaction. He was very upset and said to Vizenor, "You tricked me!" Well, of course—Vizenor is Harold's creator. But this time, Vizenor played it straight and suggested that the director's anxiety could be easily relieved by a couple of special showings. The director agreed, and the first showing was to an audience of Native Americans. They laughed uproariously. The second showing was to an audience of board members from var-ious not-for-profit institutions. They did not laugh. At all. When the director asked them why, they responded, "You didn't tell us it was a comedy."[13] Vizenor didn't say whether that relieved the director's anxiety or increased it, but it certainly answers the question of which audience is the "privileged" audience for *Harold of Orange*.

Because it is made for an Other audience, *Harold of Orange* is available only through obscure sources and an occasional university video library. It was not intended as a mainstream movie, and the result is, as are most films for Native Americans, a film that has received very limited exposure.

THOMAS KING

Medicine River (1994)

Medicine River, on the other hand, was made for general consumption. In fact, it is a movie made for the most general of all audiences, television viewers. This Canadian film takes a realistic approach to Native ideas, ideals, and issues in a manner that is accessible to non-Native audiences. Although the characters in the film come from a different background than the typical televiewer, have a different history to draw upon, and look toward different ideological horizons, the story is a universal one, understandable to any audience. The result is a film that privileges a Native audience but remains accessible to a mainstream American and Canadian audience as well.

Tom King's *Medicine River* is a delightful novel, and so is the film made from it, though the film is very different from the novel. Although the director (Stuart Margolin) is Euro-American, the actors who play Indian characters are Indian men and women, and King (Cherokee and Greek) wrote the screenplay, co-wrote the teleplay, and even acts as one of the minor characters, an imposing basketball player on the rival team. *Medicine River* privileges the Other audience, but it doesn't hit the stereotypes in a frontal assault the way *Harold of Orange* does, and that is intentional on King's part. As he said in an interview,

> You begin to chip away—not at the stereotypes because they're fixed in the imagination, but you begin to offer alternatives, different ways of reading, different ways of seeing the same drama. . . . Yes, we have the stereotypes and clichés. No, I can't do much about those particularly, nor do I want to beat my head against the wall trying to destroy those. There's a notion in this Judeo–Christian world that we seem to inhabit that good is the thing we want to have and evil is what we want to destroy, and so if you destroy enough evil, you get a place that's pretty good. I don't believe that. I'm more of the notion that

15. Thomas King with Graham Greene on the set of *Medicine River*. Photo by Greg Staats.

those things are in a balance of some sort, and the thing is to keep the balance. If you destroy too much evil, you wind up with just as screwed up a world as you had in the first place. You've fooled yourself. . . . All I'm interested in is saying, "Hey, you got that over there. Okay, enjoy it while you can, but how about looking at this over here?" Not as an alternative, just as maybe a continuation of this conversation.[14]

Continuing the conversation is a good description of what this film does. It speaks in a low, soft, very funny voice, but it is a voice that can't be easily ignored. It provides a "next step" in the conversation by showing Native Americans in roles that depict them as they are—as contemporary human beings. Although, like all other films that depict Native Americans in contemporary, realistic situations, it was never in danger of breaking any viewing records, *Medicine River* remains one of the most important films about and by Native Americans that has been made to date, and it is encouraging that it was so well received when it was aired on network television.

As in the novel, the film's protagonist is a man named Will (Graham Greene). In the novel, Will is first seen in his photography studio in Medicine River; the *film* begins, however, before the globe-trotting photojournalist Will returns to Medicine River, the place of his birth. Whereas the novel has the time and space to take "flash-back" trips through Will's childhood memories, the film's story line must be more direct. The film follows a Euro-American, linear time line, while the novel works with a circular, Native American chronology. The difference is necessary, but the result is that the film is less subtle and the focus slightly changed to become Will's search for identity, a focus that King didn't particularly want. "That was a problem in the movie for me," King remarked, "because I didn't want people to think that once native people left traditional areas or reserves that they would then not be able to return or have a problem returning that made life tough."[15] While this might bother King, a look at the film's content shows that much more occurs than a simple homecoming.

Will has no last name. He is simply Will, and his brother, whom we hear about regularly but never see, is simply James. When a more detailed introduction is necessary, he is referred to as Will, Rose Horse Capture's boy. Will and James have spent most of their childhoods in Calgary, where their mother worked at low-paying jobs to support them, receiving only occasional letters and promises from their white, rodeoing father. He is a cipher in the boys' lives, and his name is absent in both the film and the novel. His mother, however, was part of the community of Medicine River. She belonged to and with the people, and it is through her that Will is tied to Medicine River's tribal community. Since most Indian nations trace lineage through the matriarchal line, this is appropriate in a technical as well as an emotional way.

As the film begins, Will is sitting in a makeshift cell in the Malawi desert, which is a fairly decent excuse for not being around when his mother dies.[16] On his return home, he listens to a series of answering machine messages from James, which begin with "Mother is sick" and end with "The funeral is on Friday." His white girlfriend/boss/agent (Janet Laine Greene) drives him to the airport, and he flies to Medicine River.

He enters his mother's house and calls for James, but his brother isn't there. He picks up two photographs and sits in a chair to look at them. One is of his mother as a young girl in traditional dress. The other is of two boys, presumably Will and James. The scene cuts to the next morning, when Will is sound asleep in the chair.

He is still holding the photograph of the two boys, but in the frame's glass we see another face reflected. We are introduced in this appropriate way to Harlan Bigbear (Tom Jackson), a trickster, a reflection, a character easily recognized by an Indian audience. Always moving, always contradicting himself and reality, Harlan jokes and tricks others into self-knowledge. Like Coyote, Rabbit, or the other tricksters of Native American stories, Harlan has no compunctions about fooling people, about placing them in situations without their consent, or even about telling outright lies. Sometimes a trickster's schemes work; sometimes they don't; sometimes the trickster tricks himself—but the result is a centering, a healing through self-awareness. A trickster is not totally trustworthy, but he is always interesting.

How Harlan knows Will has arrived is unexplained. It could be that the rather informal "taxi" driver alerted him, or perhaps Harlan has been expecting him. Artfully sidestepping all questions, Harlan hands Will a bag that he insists he carry with him and then suggests Will take a shower and get dressed so they won't be late. Will assumes he means for the funeral.

As Harlan drives Will out to the reservation, he talks nonstop about the people of the community and their relation to one another and to Will. It is, in fact, a description of the community's family tree, which leaves Will somewhat stunned under the avalanche of names and ties. Harlan is drawing a human map, showing Will where he belongs in the communal landscape. Before they reach their destination, Harlan stops the car and the two men get out. Will asks, "Are we there?"

Harlan points to a mountain in the distance and says, "Ninastiko." After a short pause in which Will follows Harlan's eyes and the tilt of his chin to focus on the mountain, he continues, "In the old days, people used to say that as long as you can see the mountain, you knew you were home."

Will looks at the mountain and says the only polite thing he can think of. "It's nice."

Harlan grins and says, "And here you are." He has shown Will his place in the physical landscape. Harlan knows where Will is, but Will hasn't yet realized that he is home. Will is beginning to suspect that Harlan is a bit "different."

They reach the cemetery, and Will asks, "Where is everyone?" Harlan points to the far side of the grounds and says, "She's over there. The funeral was last week." While this may seem like a rather unfunny joke, it is actually the trickster in action, and Harlan's obvious sympathy lets the viewer see that Will has indeed gone far away from his community. He is out of touch and out of time, and Harlan is bringing him back step by step.

They arrive at the Friendship Center in Medicine River. Harlan seems to have planned to go there all along, but Will is still in a bit of a fog. As they enter the lobby, they walk into the middle of a conversation between Eddie Weaselhead (Michael C. Lawrenchuk), who is dressed in a ribbon shirt, Levi's, bone choker, and an unusual hairstyle that looks like those worn by Blackfeet Indians of a hundred years ago—standing straight up and about three inches long on top with a low ponytail in back—and Big John Yellowrabbit (Ben Cardinal), the center's three-piece-suited director. Big John fingers the material of his jacket and says to Bertha (Tina Louise Bomberry), the center's receptionist, "What do you think, Bertha? Italian silk and wool."

Eddie interrupts, "I know a guy who thinks being an Indian isn't good enough, so he goes out and buys those three-piece suits."

Big John touches Will's suit and says, "Nice suit. People come to respect you if you dress right." He looks at Eddie again and adds, "I know a guy who likes to dress up like a Hollywood Indian. Wears all that cheap Japanese jewelry you buy at airport gift shops."

Eddie responds, "The guy I know can't tell the difference between polyester and silk!" Later on, he says, "Of course you'd have to get the right kind of polyester ties to go with that polyester suit, the kind with them little ducks on it."

Big John replies, "Nothin' sadder than a pretend Indian," and Eddie says, "Only thing worse is an apple."

Though these exchanges are the weakest in the film, the ideas they examine are very familiar and very important to Native Americans. The issue of Indian identity is one of the major concerns in most novels by contemporary Native Americans, and this is certainly true in *Medi-*

cine River. In an interview with Jace Weaver in *Publisher's Weekly,* Tom King said, "One of the questions that's important to ask is, 'Who is an Indian? How do we get this idea of Indianness?'"[17] This question has implications for full-bloods and mixed-bloods, as well as for the moderns and traditionals like Big John and Eddie.

In the novel, these two friendly enemies have extended arguments, which Harlan attempts to smooth over with a bone game. It only works for a while, however, because the two represent opposite ends of the political spectrum. Big John is the modern, assimilated Indian who wears white clothing and apparently respects the values of white society. Eddie is trying to hold on to the traditional Indian culture as much as possible by doing his best to look like an Indian is presumed to look. Although there is no judgment passed or even implied in the film or the novel, both men seem to be somewhat lost and looking for themselves in all the wrong places. Big John is what Eddie calls an "apple," someone who is red on the outside but white on the inside. Eddie appears to have "bought" the idea that to be an Indian one must conform to how white culture, AKA Hollywood, expects an Indian to look.

Harlan asks Bertha if she's heard from James, and she responds, "James Who?" Harlan laughs and motions to Will, who is holding the bag Harlan has insisted he not forget. He says, "This is Will, James's brother."

Bertha replies, "The one who was too busy to come to his mother's funeral? That Will?" Bertha is not one to mince words. Harlan asks her to show Will the studio, and she gets up, saying, "Ain't no tour guide."

Will follows unwillingly, still in the dark about these people and why he's being led around. He follows Bertha into the next room and is impressed. It is an extremely well-equipped photography studio. Harlan then explains that he thought Will would want to "get in on the ground floor." The ground floor in this case requires taking photographs for a calendar featuring the elders' pictures, something his brother James had evidently agreed to do. Will declines, saying that he is not a portrait photographer, and he will not be around long, but Harlan the trickster never gives up. When Will is finally about to walk out Harlan does an "innocent and dumb" routine, asking what the camera parts are for, particularly the time delay. Will patiently explains, but he knows that Harlan is just trying to shame him into staying and taking the photographs so the Friendship Center can continue. Will is about to make an escape when Harlan plays his trump card. He pulls a photo out of a box and says, "James did take one picture before he left." Will examines it. It is of his mother, taken just before she died. He has been suckered and he knows it.

A hilarious scene follows in which Harlan and Big John try to describe their reasons for producing the calendar. It seems that they were able to get a grant from the government to make a photographic study of wildlife migration patterns in Southern Alberta, mostly moose and elk, but they actually wanted the grant money to buy a van to take the elders to traditional festivities. "Like hockey games and bingos," Harlan says with a grin. But the government gave them photographic equipment instead of money, so they borrowed on the cameras to buy the van. That's where the calendar comes in. They borrowed money from the Band Council to produce a calendar featuring the elders. "Small business loan," says Big John.

Will suggests, "To pay for the van?"

Harlan says, "Stay with the tour, Will. To buy the basketball uniforms so the team will have pride and win the tournament."

In a nutshell, they are going to use the cameras to do the calendar, sell the calendars to pay back the Band Council, and use the prize money from the tournament to pay back the loan on the cameras. The audience is, by that time, as lost in the whirlwind as Will is, but he agrees to take photographs for as long as he is around.

The scene works to provide humor and motivation for Will's commitment to do the photographs, and for the later basketball tournament, but it also has a subtext aimed at a community of people accustomed to dealing with layers of governmental red tape and piecing together stratagems for obtaining what they need. The optimism of Harlan and Big John in the face of enormous odds is funny and admirable at the same time. Humor, tenacity, and optimism, the survival tools of a "vanishing" people, will get this Native American community through, whatever it takes.

When they leave the Friendship Center, Will stops and asks what is in the bag Harlan has been reminding him to carry everywhere. Harlan replies that it belongs to Will, so he opens it. He pulls out a basketball uniform that matches the jersey Harlan is wearing over his own shirt. Harlan explains that they need a center. As they pull away, one of the men standing in front of the Friendship Center says, "He ain't no Clyde Whiteman," which becomes a refrain through the rest of the movie. Clyde (Byron Chief Moon), the audience comes to learn, is an excellent basketball player, and at this point Will is not. He is no Clyde Whiteman in other ways as well. Clyde is in jail because he doesn't always adhere to the rules, and Will does. Clyde knows who he is, and Will does not. Clyde is an Indian, and Will does not yet know that he truly is as well.

Although Will has no court shoes with him, he agrees to play ball. Harlan guesses his shoe size to be thirteen, and Will corrects him, "No. Ten. Ten and a half." Harlan says that's great, but when he brings shoes for Will, they are thirteens. Harlan tells him basketball shoes should be big "so you can use lots of socks—fewer blisters that way." Will asks if he has any socks, and Harlan says, "Nope." For a trickster, reality is malleable.

The shoes he loans Will are important to the film. They are red high-tops that one of the ballplayers says look like antiques. They, too, are out of space and time. The other ballplayers wear new Nikes—they are contemporary Native American men living in the 1990s. They are the Medicine River Warriors, not the warriors of Hollywood westerns.

When Will walks out onto the basketball court, he realizes that the game is not, as Harlan had implied, just a practice session but a real game against a rival team. Will flops out onto the court in his ancient, huge, and very red shoes to jump against the Mustangs' center, Lester (Tom King). The six-foot-six Lester has fumbled around the court, dropping the ball, convincing Will that he is a push-over. He is, in fact, an outrageously good player who wears Will to a frazzle. As they stand in midcourt for the first tip-off, Lester says, "Nice shoes." Will doesn't fit the shoes yet, and it is no coincidence that they are red.

After the game, Harlan introduces Louise Heavyman (Sheila Tousey). Harlan tells her that Will has been asking who she was during the whole game; of course he hadn't. After she leaves, he tells Will he's never seen Louise so taken with anyone; she shows no such interest at that point. However, the trickster seems to see what is under the surface and sees past the present, into a future reality. Will does eventually find Louise extremely attractive, and she feels the same for him, but there are complications. She is six months pregnant, unmarried, and intentionally so on both counts. She does not want a man to marry or even to live with, which is why the baby's father is no longer in the picture. She is an accountant with her own business, she is independent, and she likes it that way. She is also loving, sweet, and sexy. She is much like the other Indian women in the film, and very much unlike the stereotypical Indian "princesses" and "maidens" of Hollywood westerns. For an Indian audience, especially a female Indian audience, she is a welcome relief from the dependent, subservient—to the point of suicide in her lover's interest—Indian woman.

Will comes to love her and her baby girl, and a normal Hollywood love story would probably end with her agreeing that they should marry and live happily ever after. Louise doesn't want marriage. The film ends with each of them living on their own, but with each other in their hearts and in their minds. They are comfortable with the arrangement and with each other because, by the film's end, Will has found his own identity and is finally comfortable with himself.

The journey to self-discovery is a tough one though, and only the perseverance of the trickster Harlan and his demi-trickster helper, Bertha, makes it possible. Harlan feeds Will information gleaned from postcards from James in Vancouver, then San Francisco, and finally New Zealand, and as James moves further away from the community, Will moves closer. During the time he is waiting for James to come home, he takes the photographs for the calendar, getting to know the people and the place. In one poignant scene at the local horse races, Will takes photographs of a very old man, George, who seems somehow very young and who shares a story with him. George tells of when Will was little and had gone to a rodeo with him and Will's father. His father had gotten tossed into a pile of manure and had to drive home wearing "that shirt that was covered in horse shit." Will had insisted on sitting on his father's lap, steering the car, "pretending you was bringing us home." Now it is the community, especially Harlan, that is bringing Will home.

Another day, Harlan announces the good news, that he has found the assistant Will has been looking for. Will replies that he doesn't want an assistant. Harlan then introduces Clyde Whiteman. Will asks, "The 'Ain't no Clyde Whiteman' Clyde Whiteman?" It is, but Will still doesn't want an assistant. He asks Clyde to give him and Harlan a moment during which he tells Harlan that he does *not* want an assistant. Harlan says okay, but Clyde will have to go back to jail if he doesn't have a job. He also casually mentions that if Clyde is out of jail he can play center on the team. Will understands that if Clyde plays ball he won't have to, so he agrees that he does indeed need an assistant.

Clyde turns out to be a very good assistant with an ability, an eye, and opinions that he has no trouble voicing. Later in the film, Will comes into the studio to find it has been emptied. He assumes that Clyde has stolen the equipment, since Clyde was in jail for theft from a camera store. He and Harlan race off to Clyde's grandfather's place on the reservation because Harlan says he thinks he will be there.

It isn't a quick trip because Harlan, who says that nobody knows the res like he knows the res, constantly gets "lost." In effect, he is showing Will around, letting him get to know the territory. Eventually, of course, they do find Lionel James's house. Lionel (Jimmy Herman) is one of the two elders that are "musts" for the calendar, but they never come into town, so they are the only two still left to photograph. When they arrive at Lionel's, Clyde is indeed there and in no way upset about being found. He has set up the studio in Lionel's house and is getting ready to photograph his grandfather. Harlan is not surprised at all, and Will is irritated that he was kept in the dark. Harlan is, of course, all grins and laughter, so Will doesn't stay irritated long. In fact, Lionel is very hospitable and very entertaining as he barbecues on his gas grill, wearing an apron that says, "No reservations needed."

Harlan tells Lionel that Will wanted to see the reserve, which is, of course, news to Will. Lionel replies that "There's a lot to see. I've lived here all my life, and I still haven't seen everything." The implication is that the reserve is more than a physical place.

Lionel is a very famous Indian man because he travels all over the world telling stories. As he says, "Everybody wants to know about old, dying Indians." A Native audience would find that very funny but also very true. The combination of the "Wise Old Chief" and the "Vanishing American" ideas come together to produce the "old dying Indian" syndrome.

Lionel tells them one of his stories, which, in true storytelling form, has been adapted to the times to be the old story told in the new way, but still the same old story. The photography in this scene is spectacular, with the four men silhouetted as they walk up the spine of a hill, bent like four Kokopellis, with a magnificent deep salmon sunset in the background. Lionel says, "It was a night like this that Coyote got on a plane to visit the Prime Minister. 'We're glad to see you, said the Prime Minister. Maybe you can help us with the Indian problem.' 'Sure,' said Coyote. 'What's the problem?'" To a Euro-American audience this might be entertaining, but to the problematic Indians in question, it would be hilarious.

With Lionel's photograph taken, there is only one elder left. She is Martha Old Crow (Maggie Black Kettle), who only sees people when she wants to see them, and she has sent word that she will see Will. Harlan drives him out to her place, getting lost along the way, of course.

They stop, and Will says, "I assume we have to walk the rest of the way." Harlan nods, licks his finger, holds it up to the wind, grins and points to Will's right. They walk to the edge of a very steep, sandy cliff. In the distance, across a river in the bottom, lies Martha's place—a house with a tipi beside it. The Will who arrived in Medicine River two months earlier would have simply turned around, but now he and Harlan bail out and tumble down the embankment, with Harlan yelling, "Roll, Will. Roll." At the bottom, a shaken Will stumbles into the river. It only comes to their knees, which the ever-optimistic Harlan sees as lucky. They didn't have to swim.

Martha is waiting for them in a lovely pink sweater and an ivory dress that she has chosen because it matches the recliner she is sitting in, in the middle of a meadow. She is a beautiful woman of about eighty, with a glint in her eye and a contagious laugh. Harlan introduces Will as Rose Horse Capture's son, and Martha asks if he's the one who paints or the one who takes pictures—the one who Rose always said was coming home any day but who never did until now. She says she supposes they'll have to find someone to adopt him. She also asks if he's the one in love with Louise Heavyman. He stutters a bit and says, "I like Louise." She says, "Like is good enough," and then she gets a handmade rattle out of a box and hands it to him. "Here. This was yours. Give it to your daughter." He tells her that he has no daughter, and she says that will give him time to learn the song. She tries to teach him the traditional song, but he is no good at it. She covers her ears and says, "You hear that thump? That was some big old elk falling over dead." He tries again, and she says, "You keep on singing like that and you'll freeze the river." She looks at him seriously for a brief moment, and then they all begin laughing.

Martha is a well-respected elder of the community, with a sense of humor and a mountain of life within her. She is a far cry from the old woman left to freeze in *A Man Called Horse* or the thousands of old Indian women seen shuffling their way through countless other Hollywood films.

About the time Will is beginning to feel at home in Medicine River, having traded in his Toronto suits for jeans and a cowboy hat, his girlfriend/boss/agent from Toronto comes to visit. She alluringly offers him adventure in his work, money, and sex. Disappointed when he declines her sexual advances, she asks, "You are coming back, aren't you?" He replies that there is nothing in Medicine River for him, but it is obvious by this time that he doesn't believe his own words. She offers to stay with him again, saying, "You can even leave your boots on." When he says nothing, she leaves, and he immediately takes his boots off.

Right after this scene we see him putting together a crib for Louise, kissing and joking with her. Once again she tells him she is not interested in living with a man, which he accepts, but unhappily so.

He has come part of the way home, but he is still pulled by his other life. When "that blonde woman from Toronto," as Bertha refers to her, calls to offer him a choice assignment, "South Africa—the Mandela thing," he accepts. He is less than enthusiastic, but as he later tells Louise, he wants the assignment. What he hasn't counted on is Harlan announcing it to a roomful of people gathered to celebrate the finishing of the calendar photos. Louise leaves the room crying, but she is understanding and blames her reaction on hormones.

Clyde is less understanding. He says, "It was fun while it lasted, eh?" Then he says something in Blackfoot that Will doesn't understand. He has come to look up to Will, to think of him as an uncle (a very important position in most Native American cultures) as Harlan said he would before the two had even met. He is deeply disappointed that Will is running out on them. He is so upset, in fact, that he gets drunk and takes a swing at a police officer. He misses but hits a parking meter, injuring his hand so he can't play basketball and once again lands in jail.

Will finds out about Clyde the next night when he is getting ready for the big game. It is for the championship, and he expects to sit on the bench next to Harlan but is surprised when he must play. The opposing team is the Mustangs, and again he finds himself tipping off with Lester. Lester looks down and says, "Nice socks." Will is now wearing socks, as Harlan had suggested, which means that he is now able to wear the red shoes comfortably. He is beginning to fit all the way around. When Lester then challenges him with, "You ain't no Clyde Whiteman," Will explodes inwardly and begins to play like he has never played before. The sum of Coach Harlan's game plan is for everyone to "Play like Clyde. Do what Clyde would do," so it is by sheer courage and tenacity that the Warriors do, indeed, win. The coach also says, "You don't want to embarrass yourselves in front of your relations," and this is important. It is not the other team but the extended family that matters.

After the game, Harlan is supposed to take Will to the airport, and he enters the darkened gym to look for him. "There you are," Harlan says, and it sounds very much like the "Here you are" from the film's beginning. They have come full circle, and Will is no longer anxious to leave.

Harlan takes the wrong road, and Will is surprised to find himself in front of the hospital. It then occurs to him that it is because Louise is having the baby. He rushes in, and when the nurse assumes that he is Mr. Heavyman, he goes along with it, even when the other friends who arrive tease him mercilessly. He waits through the delivery, and when the nurse comes out to tell him his "wife" has had a baby girl and asks him what they plan to name her, he glances over her shoulder and, reading aloud a hospital sign, says "South Wing." The nurse asks if it's a traditional Indian name, and he stutters something about its being a joke. The other men laugh uproariously, but the nurse puts the name South Wing Heavyman on the bassinet. Louise's father likes it, so the baby's name is South Wing.

The scene is funny, and it also points to the fact that many people have no idea what Indian names are about, why, for instance, someone who is "obviously" an Indian and an elder of a community might be called Lionel James (played by an actor named Jimmy Herman), and another might have a "real" Indian name, like Old Crow. South Wing certainly does have that "real Indian" flavor, which a Native audience would find very funny.

The nurse takes Will into the nursery to hold South Wing, and as he is sitting there, Harlan steps in. The nurse starts to protest, but Harlan waves her off, saying, "Don't worry. I'm indigenous." He then looks at South Wing and says, "Hmmm. Rug bug," and reminds Will that it's time to go to the airport. Will gently tells him to get out.

Later, a new nurse will see Will looking through the glass at the baby and will ask him which one is his. He points to South Wing and says, "That one," and it's true. She is his relation because he has become part of the community again. They belong to one another.

Will's new sense of relatedness is underscored in the next scene, as Clyde is being let out of jail by a woman who tells him he is being released into his uncle's custody. He looks over the railing and sees Will wave to him. Will has accepted the responsibility of being Clyde's uncle, and to a Native American audience, that is a serious commitment.

The ever-present trickster is waiting for them when they come out of the courthouse, and he grins at Will. "Busy day."

In the final scene, the tribal community is having a picnic, and Harlan suggests it would be a good time to take a picture of all the elders together for the front of the calendar. Will says okay but first lies down on a blanket beside Louise and South Wing. He looks off to the mountain and says, "Ninastiko. Must be home." The elders ask to have the grandchildren in the picture, and Will says okay. The children want their parents in the picture, and Will says okay. The photograph will include everyone, so they all line up, the elders sitting in lawn chairs in the front and the rest standing behind them. Will starts to take the picture, but they insist that he use that "time delay thing," so he can be part of it. As the credits roll, Will runs back and forth, trying to get a shot with him in the spot they have saved for him, front and center. He has indeed come home to the space that was always there for him.

This film works as a mainstream movie because, in addition to its highly professional direction, photography, and script, it contains all the best-loved tropes—a love story, a lost boy returning home, bonding buddies, even a sports event. For a Native American audience it works in all these ways, but it also overturns old stereotypes of female subservience and the wise old chief, thaws out the time freeze, and underlines an essential difference in Native cultures—the "hero" in this film is not Will. The real protagonist in *Medicine River* is the tribal community. In Native American fashion, the individual is not the center of the story—it is the relationships between the members that are important. As Harlan says, "You don't want to embarrass yourselves in front of your relations."

The Directors and Producers

The ranks of Native American directors and producers are growing, with more and more professionals learning their trade in the mainstream industry before moving to production of Native American films. Sources such as the Native American Public Broadcasting Consortium, the Inuit Broadcasting Corporation, the Institute of American Indian Arts in Santa Fe, The Native Voices Public Television Workshop in Bozeman, Montana, American Indians in Film in Los Angeles, the Northern Native Broadcasting organization and Studio II in Canada, and others are helping Native Americans learn their craft and produce quality films, videos, and documentaries. There is still a great need for these institutions, but young filmmakers also have some excellent role models among directors and producers, including the three examples this study will address—Victor Masayesva, Aaron Carr, and George Burdeau; there are others, including many talented women.

Masayesva, Carr, and Burdeau have been chosen because their work

16. Director George Burdeau.

represents the work of Native American filmmakers in general, which has up to now been heavily weighted toward the documentary. All three of these director/producers are also involved in feature filmmaking, but the bulk of their work has been in documentary productions. The chapter ends with a discussion of *Smoke Signals*, which has been advertised as the first feature film written, directed, produced, and acted by Native Americans.

Masayesva, Burdeau, and Carr have been called romantics because their films and videos are about personal relationships and, particularly, about their relationship to the land. As Steven Luethold notes, "[t]here are two poles of thought on this issue. One regards Indian nature imagery as an outgrowth of the special relationship Native Americans have with the land. The other holds that pan-tribal similarities in Indian imagery of the land may reflect an assimilation of the larger society's own romanticist imagery of Indians."[18]

The first of these explanations is a good one. It is no cliché that Indians are close to the land. The spiritual center of American Indian cultures is the Earth and all that inhabits it. The land is also a matter of some emotional and intellectual concern, since American Indians have been fighting for, pushed off of, and herded onto land for the last five hundred years. It is important in every conceivable way. And for those in the dominant culture who have turned up their cultural noses at the types of romanticism popular in the nineteenth century, all things Native American—especially the spiritual attachment to and belief in the sacredness of nature—have become the popular scratch for the romantic itch. This itch is the primary reason we see films like *Last of the Dogmen* (1995) appearing.

VICTOR MASAYESVA JR.

Victor Masayesva Jr. (Hopi) is one of the most respected Native American filmmakers. His work incorporates stunning effects and artistic choices, and he frequently moves to history and cultural tradition for his subjects, infusing a Hopi presence into his films and videos. As Leuthold points out, "Masayesva's strength lies in his 'strong visuals' (*Big Crane* 1992). He excels in composition," probably due to his strong background in still photography.[19]

Pueblo author Leslie Marmon Silko admires Masayesva's *Itam Hakim Hopitt* (1980; originally in Hopi but later translated into English with a combination of dubbing and subtitling) and *Ritual Clowns* (1988). She says they "reveal that the subtle but persuasive power of communal consciousness, perfected over thousands of years at Hopi, is undiminished. In Victor Masayesva's hands, video is made to serve Hopi consciousness and to see with Hopi eyes."[20]

Seeing with Hopi eyes is exactly what Masayesva wants from his camera. His films and videos are influenced in very powerful ways by the Hopi culture, and the manner in which he constructs his work—both thematically and technically—produces a film that a non-Indian filmmaker would have difficulty imitating. Partly, his work differs from the mainstream because he believes strongly that a filmmaker has a responsibility to show—and a responsibility to know what ought *not* be shown. In a talk to the Producer's Forum at the Two Rivers Film and Video Festival, Masayesva expressed his ideas about what Native filmmaking should do.

> A critical issue: what's different about Native filmmakers? Why do we even insist on being the storytellers? It has to do with, I think, that we are in the best position to censor ourselves . . . and what information is to come out of our mouths.
>
> We, in our total beings, come out of a background where information is not a commodity that's available to all. Here we are in a clash with a Western culture where everything is available.
>
> Starting out with the land: they called it wilderness; it was available [though] people lived on it, [farmed] it for hundreds of years. And I think they'll find that same principle with information . . . that it's available, and that's not how we were raised.
>
> [We believe] that an adult . . . at least in traditional communities . . . [has] to be initiated into information.
>
> So this is a contention between the Western world which wants to get everything and tribal groups where you only get information as you grow older. I think it's a point that needs to be considered. We're talking about: what's the difference between a native filmmaker and a non-native filmmaker?
>
> A Native filmmaker has the censorship built into him, the accountability built into him. The White man doesn't have that. That's the single big distinction. Accountability as an individual, as a clan, as a tribal, as a family member.[21]

For Masayesva as for most American Indians, knowledge is truly power, and that power carries with it a special responsibility. When mainstream producers and directors pluck a part of Native tradition or belief to market to the general public, as in the movie *A Man Called Horse*, it goes far beyond general exploitation—it is an attack on the identity, pan-Indian or specifically tribal, of the people it misdescribes.

Masayesva has a point when he says that non-Native producers and directors feel they have a right to present the American Indian story. When told "No, you can't film that," these filmmakers become frustrated. They believe in creative freedom, in freedom of the press, and some also feel they could actually be of service to the people they are attempting to depict. Masayesva understands their frustration. He says,

> there's another point. There's a point of different value and different viewpoint. . . . *Right now, we need to start with stories from Native Americans* [emphasis mine]. There is such a thing as the sacred hoop which includes all the different races. And there is ceremony that [includes] everybody, not just skin color. But, we have a responsibility to ourselves first. We need to care for ourselves first. So I just would say that we have a different perspective. That's what we need to be doing now: [concentrate on] these issues and hold the line on people—White producers—who are bringin' their money around and breaking our ranks. We need to stand up to these people and say, "Listen, if you want to do these stories, then you've got to participate on an equitable level." That's even giving ground.[22]

All of this assumes, of course, that there is a common center of value in the various Indian cultures that reaches across tribal boundaries. Louis Owens has addressed this point as it pertains to Native authors, including Native screenwriters. "When a postmodern critic or writer insists there is no such thing as a shared truth or global adjective beyond the text, that is a direction that is antithetical to the movement of Native American Literature. . . . These texts move toward a coherent center of value and that center is found within Native American cultural traditions."[23] It is this coherent center that Masayesva's work surrounds and in some vital ways holds together.

Imagining Indians (1992)

Masayesva's 1992 tour de force documentary *Imagining Indians* is a cleverly constructed commentary on issues involved in the making of films about or including American Indians. It is technically well done, with creative and artistic editing, framing, and manipulation. More importantly, it addresses in very powerful ways the problems and responsibilities involved in presenting Indians and in having Indians represent themselves.

As a framework for the issues raised in the film, Masayesva presents scenes of a young Indian woman's visit to the dentist. Throughout the film, we see the progression of the white dentist's extraction of the woman's bloody tooth. At first glance this would seem an odd framing, but considering the way most people feel about a trip to the dentist, it makes sense that Masayesva would choose this experience to set the tone of the film.

As he wields his gas mask, needles, drills and pliers, the dentist also talks. He tells the patient that he is very interested in Indians. He's seen *Dances With Wolves* many times, and he really "identifies" with Costner. He can't wait to do a sweat with a medicine man, and he has a "real estate/travel thing going" with some New Agers. They're going to build a "Higher-Consciousness Resort" in Phoenix and fly people in for weekend "Indian spiritual seminars." He adds that it promises to be lucrative, too. This is an almost funny depiction of what must be the Indian's worst nightmare—a New Age dentist with a drill and a dream, a dream that involves an appropriation of Indian identity.

As the patient fades into a groggy fog, the camera shows us the dentist's wall from her point of view. It is covered with film posters of old movies like *Taza, Son of Cochise* (1954), starring Rock Hudson. As the dentist begins his work, the film fades into an interestingly edited interview with an extra from *Dances With Wolves*. The young man was upset by the lack of concern for the welfare of the Indian extras during the filming, and tells of watching a woman bring water to the dogs while the Indian extras remained parched and thirsty in the summer sun. He is followed by an old man who had been an extra in an old De Mille film starring Gary Cooper. Masayesva shows us the actual footage as the old man tells, in his own language as well as in English, of "wild Indians" riding horses as fast as they could down a river for the filming. There was a wire strung just under the water, and when the unsuspecting Indians reached it, their horses went down, and many Indians as well as their mounts were hurt. Animal protection agencies would never allow such a thing to happen to horses today, so, in conjunction with the interview by the *Dances With Wolves* extra, the viewer is left to wonder, who's protecting the Indians?

People who worked on or witnessed the filming of *Thunderheart* (1992) also had something to say. More upsetting than the inaccuracies, such as shape shifting being attributed to the Lakotas although it is not part of their belief system, was the appropriation of Lakota spirituality. One woman found the filmmakers' asking children to bring tobacco ties deplorable, and many others were disturbed by their desire to film sacred ceremonies. Then, as real photographs of the massacre at Wounded Knee fill the screen, we hear one man say, "I felt so low and I felt so bad watching them practice the ghost dance. . . They justify what they're doing. . . . I get so tired of hearing, 'It's just a movie.'"

Masayesva's film clearly makes the point that mainstream films commodify the Indian existence just as Indian "artifacts" and spirituality have always been commodified and sold to the highest bidder. In a particularly interesting section of the film, Masayesva lets us hear, straight from the horse's mouth so to speak, from three people who make their living selling the Indian. The first is a white auctioneer who points somewhat stridently to the eagle on an Apache basket, saying that it is "only a design element" and that the Indian people upset by the sale of a sacred symbol really didn't know what they were talking about. He apparently thought he knew better than the people for whom the symbol is sacred.

Without editorial comment, Masayesva then moves to a second trader in Indian artifacts with definite opinions about his vocation. In defending his occupation, he says,

> On the other hand, if they had no respect for the material they wouldn't have taken it to begin with. . . . The collecting of this material, whether it be by a public institution or by private persons is really a study of history, and once these items pass through the lens of history, they don't really belong to anybody specifically any more, except perhaps as defined by the final marketplace. . . . I think it's difficult to come up with any hypothesis that is going to see this material as rightfully taken out of the museums or out of the marketplace or out of the private collections and put back in the genie's bottle. . . because that bottle no longer exists; it's broken. . . The people that live today who are descended from the Crow or the Hopi or the Navajo or the Nez Perce certainly have a legitimate interest in that material, but it is not theirs any more. It has passed through the lens of history.[24]

Either this man is an excellent actor or he actually meant everything he said, and unfortunately, he's a trader not an actor. He has evidently been dealing with Indian "material" and, presumably, Indians for quite some time, so it is a bit astounding that he would actually believe these things. On the other hand, his diatribe sounds like a shopping list for white national mythology makers and incorporates many of the beliefs that have allowed filmmakers and others to usurp the Indian identity without regard to rights, understanding, or permissions. A closer look at his monologue shows the traces of tunnel vision and stereotyping so familiar to American Indian communities.

The items he trades are referred to as "material," which cleanses them of any ties to family or tribe and especially of sacredness. He refers to collectors as historians, once more making Indians the subjects of study and once more historical—that is to say, past tense. His idea of the "lens of history" brings to mind Alice's looking glass; going through evidently changes everything. This feat of rationalization is his *propter hoc* argument to show that the items no longer belong to the Indians. Would the Liberty Bell or the Constitution, both historical "materials," therefore belong to whomever could pay the most for them? Following this man's line of reasoning to its logical conclusion, the "final marketplace" would determine what belongs to whom, and it seems—along with its oracle, the lens of history—the most sacred idea in the trader's world.

Onto his pile of presumptions and assumptions, the trader adds indignation at the very thought that the material would be taken out of the museums, the marketplace, or private (and lucrative) collections. His reasoning is that the genie's bottle is broken—it no longer exists. The assumption is that the people who made the items no longer exist; they have vanished. He graciously allows the descendants of the people who created the inventory the right to bid on them along with everyone else, but he emphatically states that they can't "hypothesize" that they have an inherent right to them. Not after they've passed through the magic lens.

Masayesva then moves to a trader who bought a Hopi mask that "spoke" to him, which he fed cornmeal and attempted to repatriate after a number of years on display in his home. His attempt at repatriation is somewhat suspect since the mask has been held in evidence in the district attorney's office for years, but an even more bothersome aspect of this man's testimony is his usurpation of a spirituality he evidently knows little about.

Masayesva still makes no editorial comment on the monologues of the three sellers, but he makes a very clever move in "erasing" them by having them dissolve into the background as they finish speaking. It is almost wish fulfillment for an Indian audience, who would understand what the men said even though they seem oblivious to it themselves. These men in the business of buying and selling Indian artifacts are not so different from Hollywood filmmakers. Each is selling an exotic piece of history and moving the story along to the final marketplace.

After nicely depicting the commodification of Indians and making the connection between the sellers of artifacts and the sellers of film stereotypes, Masayesva moves to the consumer/audience. At the Indian

Market in Santa Fe he filmed people who were buying Indian jewelry, blankets, and artifacts such as Kachina dolls as fast as they could. One man spoke with awe about the power of the "primitive" arts, and two university professors from Texas told how they learned about Native Americans by going to auctions such as this. One taught courses in Native American Studies, sharing all he learned from these shopping excursions—a particularly disheartening thought. The other talked about a lack of wall space for any more objects, saying, "We've made lots of Indians happy."

Just when the viewer is beginning to see why Indians over the years could have stood dumbfounded in the face of such ridiculousness, Masayesva delivers a stunning punch. As a young Indian man is saying that it is "in vogue to have sacred objects on the wall," the camera follows an old, bent Indian woman as she walks slowly off alone, leaving the crowds of happy consumers in the background.

Masayesva then sharpens the connection between the commodification of objects and spirituality with the selling of the Indian stereotype in film. He moves from the huge wooden Indian in front of a tourist-trap trading post to interviews with two Native American actors. The first is a man who has been a well-respected actor for many years, Floyd Westerman. The most important part of his talk is the idea that the "center of Indian existence is spirituality," and the viewer naturally expects the second actor, Rodney Grant, to have the same sort of thing to say.

Grant is the actor who played Wind In His Hair in the film *Dances With Wolves*, Mangas in *Geronimo*, and the Crow tracker in *War Party*. Reacting to criticism of the type found in other parts of this study, he says,

> I get squashed because I'm Indian but I'm not pro-Indian. I'm a young actor but I'm not totally White assimilated in society. I got my foot in both circles. I've got to feed my family. . . . If I'm going to be an actor, then I've got to take the roles that are offered to me. I accept that. I accept that story being told from a white point of view because basically if a non-Indian hadn't told the story, then the story wouldn't have gotten made. I know that for a fact. We have Indian producers and directors who are up and coming and yet, how organized are they? Do they got twenty million dollars to invest in a movie? I mean if they do, then heck, I'm speaking out of place. We're getting noticed—we're getting praised for it, finally depicting a true

Native American story. Now let's stop rocking the boat. Get on the bandwagon here. Shit, I mean, this is what Indian people are all about; they always have to cut something, something that happens to have a little success about it.[25]

Grant's frustration at doing a good job and then hearing massive amounts of criticism for what he thinks of as a work of art is understandable. The film industry is an extremely competitive market for an actor, so on one level his statement that he must take the roles offered rings true. However, the inclusion of Grant's statements in this film would indicate that Masayesva would be more inclined to agree with people like Sonny Skyhawk, Chairman and CEO of the Amerind Entertainment Group and founder of American Indians in Film.

American Indians in Film is an organization dedicated to helping American Indian actors, directors, and other film professionals learn their craft and offering both financial (in the form of scholarships) and emotional support. It also acts, as Skyhawk says, "as an organization that advocates the accurate and truthful portrayal of our people. We do it by consulting, by becoming a resource to the film and television industry, so they can call us if they are doing Indian subject matter, and if we don't have the information, we will get it for them. [As they did with *Last of the Dogmen* (1995).] We try to help our own people learn the methodology of filmmaking and in many ways act as a monitor of some of these films, also, so that we can hopefully persuade these people to think about what they do before they do it."[26]

Skyhawk understands Grant's concern and acknowledges that if "I [Skyhawk] were to turn down a role because it was demeaning or showed me as a drunk Indian, there are two options. I would be replaced and the person that would get the job would be a non-Indian that looked Native or would be an Indian that obviously has no family unit to go back to on a reservation, no responsibility to anyone." However, he does not "see that as a viable excuse at all, because if you are good enough as an actor there will always be another role, but if the role you are doing is disrespectful—well, so much harm can come from that that to me it is just not worth it."[27]

Masayesva's film also makes the point that it is just not worth it. After another scene in the dentist's office, where we get a close look at more Indian movie bills, starring people with names like George O'Brien, Jeff Chandler, John Wayne, Clark Gable, Paul Newman, and so on, we find ourselves at Hopi, in tribal meetings where Robert Redford's filming of Tony Hillerman's *The Dark Wind* is being discussed. Apparently the film will be made, even though most Hopis are against it, and Masayesva lets us see the bottom line in a clipping from the Hopi newspaper. "Today we face a difficult kind of encroachment. Some call it progress, others call it economic development, while others call it employment. We call it cultural and religious genocide."[28]

By the time the credits roll on *Imagining Indians*, an attentive viewer is likely to be exhausted. The superb editing, music, and effects (including the sound of rainsticks) makes the film compelling and sometimes beautiful to watch, but the breadth and depth of Indian issues regarding filmmaking addressed in this film require careful attention and would wrench an emotional response from any audience.

A. A. (AARON) CARR

Aaron Carr is a Navajo/Laguna Pueblo producer, director, and writer of screenplays and novels. He began making his own films in middle school, producing clay animation shorts, and has gone on to direct documentaries such as *Laguna Woman*, episodes of *Colores*, and the Emmy award–winning *War Code: Navajo Code Talkers* (1996), which he produced with his filmmaker mother, Lena Carr.[29]

Carr believes that American Indian directors and producers are needed even more than writers. He says that these are the positions that can make the most difference.

> The writer actually doesn't have that much power in a film. It is the director who has the most power, and he has the vision. . . . He is the one who has the whole product in his mind, or he should, if he is a good director. . . . The script is only half the film because film is a visual medium, and the film deals a lot with translating the script into a vision, into images, and that's really the work of the director. . . . Yes, we need everything, you know, writers, directors, producers, cinematographers, but the most important part we need is Native American directors and producers . . . because if the director is Native American, he will shape [the script] to his own sensibility, whatever it deals with. He will put in details that are important to him, because a director has control of the script; he can re-write it at will, and he usually does. So I think it is more important that we get Native American directors, because then we can begin building an aesthetic.[30]

But directors don't get the chance without funding, and that is where American Indian filmmaking is at its weakest—in financing. Carr points out that

> we need our own support, like African American filmmakers. . . .
> When *Malcolm X* (1992) was being made, Oprah Winfrey and Bill
> Cosby put money in when Spike Lee couldn't get any more money.
> They were able to do that because they make millions of dollars any-
> way. We don't have people like that. . . . Right now there is no Na-
> tive American cinema; there are no Native American studios. With
> African American cinema there's lots of support and there are many
> artists and people who are already in the entertainment industry. I
> think that really helps them make films that are specifically for them,
> and that has not happened for Native Americans. . . . Until that
> changes, we are still pretty much at the mercy of the studio system.
> That's for the commercial films. For documentaries there is a strong
> voice, definitely a strong Native voice, and growing even more so,
> but that's not as visible as commercial films. It's important for us to
> get hold of and use [commercial film] for our own purposes.[31]

The Native American Public Broadcasting Consortium and other
Native funding sources are producing films and videos as fast as they
can, but their funds are limited as well. Not having "people like that"
therefore creates a dependence on major studios and production
houses, and with that comes a loss of control, even in the realm of documentary production. Carr said that in making *War Code: Navajo Code
Talkers*, one of the most difficult tasks was dealing with the National
Geographic team. He is careful to point out that the director and others
tried very hard to be sensitive, but still, Lena and Aaron Carr "had to
fight so much for the way it was. The National Geographic people kept
putting back the dates, and we lost a lot of the code-talkers that we were
going to interview. . . . [National Geographic] wanted to make it
more exciting; they wanted to bring up the idea of oppression, that
these men were forced into becoming fighters. In fact, they wanted to
join, because they knew their country was being attacked by this enemy; they wanted to defend their country."[32] These are the kinds of
"details" that are so important in portraying Native Americans in a realistic way, even when that means something less dramatic or timely.
Without an Indian in a position of power, the point might have been
raised that these men volunteered, but it might also have been ignored
for the sake of drama.

Aaron and Lena Carr have recently finished filming another documentary, KINAALDA: *Navajo Rite of Passage*. Lena Carr is the producer for the film, and Aaron Carr is associate producer and director of photography. The documentary follows a Navajo girl through the kinaalda ceremony, and the people in the film are relatives of the filmmakers. As Aaron Carr says, "This is family, so it has to be done right." It is also a private ceremony, which means they are walking a fine line, constantly making decisions about what should or should not be shown publicly. So the question is, why make such a film? Carr responds,

> So many films by Native American filmmakers present Native America's glorious past, despairing present, and bleak future with no middle ground for us to hold onto. I know when I watch these films, ostensibly about myself, I begin to feel a certain desperation: What place do I have on this earth, in this society, in this life? And this desperation often turns to rage. Who are these "artists" that are constructing such a hopeless place for our children, and for the rest of us? And this is no place for such alien pronouncements as the freedom of the artist. Native American stories, images, life is centered on the community, on the family, on the place. That is why we regard them as holy and why so many prayers and ceremonies are built upon their foundation. The selfish irregard that says we should present our communities as hotbeds of self-destruction, with such self-loathing, is the pinnacle of the genocide that has been visited upon us. *Kinaalda* is a film that celebrates the existence of Navajo tradition within a very contemporary, healthy Native American family.[33]

Carr also sees a great need for more Native women in the film industry. He notes that filmmaking in general has many more men in control than women, and that it is even more so in Native American filmmaking. He finds that strange since so many tribes are actually matriarchal—it would seem that there would be more women's voices being heard. He points out that women in Native societies are very strong voices, and their voices are different from those of the men. Although filmmakers like Lena Carr, Geraldine Keams, and Arlene Bowman are currently producing exceptional films, videos, and documentaries, Carr sees the Native filmmaking scene as unbalanced at the moment and hopes to see more women filmmakers joining the ranks of Native American writers, directors, and producers—women like Valerie Red-Horse, whose new film Carr praises.

As this book goes to press, Red-Horse's film has not been released, but according to John Sacksteder, a reviewer for Internet Movie Data-

base, the film, *Naturally Native* (1998), is about "[t]hree Native American sisters (Red-Horse, Bedard, and Guerrero) [who] decide to try to
sell a line of cosmetics they call *Naturally Native*, based on old tribal
remedies, only to have to fight an uphill battle with racist business people. The film is actually Red-Horse's comment on her fight with the
movie industry to get her films made and the film is the first to be totally financed by an Indian tribe, Connecticut's Mashantucket tribe."[34]
Carr agrees that the herbal lotion is a metaphor for Red-Horse's real
product—films—but he states that the plot is more complex than Sacksteder indicates. "Corporations won't help them because the women
belong to a tribe that has a casino, and of course should have oodles of
ill-gotten money. But they cannot go through their tribe for financing
because, since they were given up for adoption when they were small,
they have no proof that they belong to any tribe. And since the tribe to
which they know they belong has a casino, registration for enrollment
is frowned upon by some of the members, because so many simply
want the distribution checks. The sisters are lost until, in desperation,
they decide to visit the elders, who are ensconced in a multimillion-
dollar community palace. Of course, the elders recognize them and
their family, and their product, 'Naturally native,' is fully financed.
The film was made quickly and economically, but since it was shot
with care, and with Panavision camera (cinematography by Bruce L.
Finn), the film has the patina of Hollywood. Not bad for a bunch of Indians! And I think that it's wonderfully appropriate that the true first
film by Native Americans should be funded by a tribe and produced,
written, and directed by women."[35] Not only did Red-Horse write, direct, and produce (with Pam Auer, Dawn Jackson, and Yvonne Russo)
the film, she also plays one of the sisters. The other two sisters are
played by Kimberly Norris Guerrero and veteran filmmaker Irene
Bedard.

This is indeed a film made by women, and it is a walk through a forest of contemporary Native issues that concern those women, including the stereotypes of rich Indians, the issue of adoption outside the
tribe, assumed enrollment for profit, and the community "palace." It is
interesting that what saves the sisters is their reentry into the center of
the community, the elders at the heart of the community who recognize the women for who they are without the overlay of labels or suspicion. No wonder Carr finds the film so rewarding. "We are always
going on and on about our Mother Earth and her children, and this totally inspiring film comes from our own sisters."

GEORGE BURDEAU

George Burdeau is a filmmaker and videographer whose work emphasizes attention to individual cultural detail but with a deep understanding of a coherent center of value. He has been called "pan-Indian," and
he agrees that the adjective fits. He has lived for long periods of time
with the Navajos, Pueblos, and other peoples as well as his own Blackfoot nation, and he considers his "pan-Indian lifestyle a gift," because it
started him thinking of more "global" issues.[36] This is one of the reasons he could so successfully work with people from a variety of different tribes in making *Pueblo Peoples: First Contact* (1992) and *The Witness*
(1997), among others.

Another reason for his success is his personality. He is an extremely
energetic man who gets a great deal accomplished, though he never
seems to be in much of a hurry. He takes time to stop, listen, talk, and
help. He has been described as the eye of a hurricane because he exudes
a very calm enthusiasm that is contagious. The hurricane metaphor
makes perfect sense when one sees Burdeau orchestrating four hundred
cast and crew members (as he did in making *Witness*) with an energetic
serenity that is difficult to describe any other way.

Burdeau's filmmaking career began almost twenty-five years ago
with *The Real People* (1976), and his most widely known work is the pilot episode (*Pueblo Peoples: First Contact*) for the *Surviving Columbus*
(1992) documentary, which aired on Public Television on Columbus
Day in 1992. His latest production is *The Witness*, an IMAX film of the
massacre of the Pequot nation, but he says the production he is most
proud of is one of his first, *A Season of Grandmothers*. He laughs at the
roughness of the camera work and other skills he has long since mastered, but the intertwined talks with elder women in this film are very
special to him. He says, "those women taught me a lot about making a
film" because they showed him that "the real power of creativity lies in
people and their relationships with each other and the natural world." It
was then that he developed "another way of doing things,"[37] a way that
is radically different from the director-as-god formula of Hollywood.
On a Burdeau set, as much attention is paid to the people behind the
cameras as to what is going on in front of them. Besides being a very
human way of directing a film, it is also very practical if you believe as
Burdeau does that "everything is an extension, so what's in their hearts
and minds is as important as their technical considerations."[38]

He was introduced to filmmaking when cast as an extra on *Nobody
Loves a Drunken Indian* (1970, later renamed *Flap*). He immediately saw

the possibilities of the medium but was horrified by the film crew's treatment of the people they were filming, especially when they were disrespectful to the elders, and he was disturbed by the generally distorted representation of Indian people. He says that things have changed some over the past twenty-five years, but that it is time to "create a new paradigm for ourselves," to use the experience gained by working in the industry to come together and "build systems which will allow us to step out and try professionally while also keeping in touch with our spirituality."[39] He sees the need to change the way Native American stories are told and says the process needs to change as well. Of paramount importance is getting more American Indian people working as professionals in the industry, and the ones already working need to "provide opportunities for others."[40]

Part of his past experience has been as a teacher at the University of Washington and as a director of the American Indian Film Institute in Santa Fe—and as a film director and producer, he is still in the business of educating and enabling new talent to succeed in the industry. One of the most extraordinary aspects of Burdeau's approach to filmmaking is his attitude toward learning. It is a Native approach based on traditional ways of working together, creating a circle of community that shares a creative vision. We see an example of this attitude in the making of the *Surviving Columbus* episode. Half the people he hired for that production were students with little previous professional experience. With Burdeau always on hand to support, suggest, and—most importantly—to *allow*, those people were free to learn, try, and perfect. The result is a new crop of Native American professionals who have an enthusiastic, unrestricted ability to create films with a Native American aesthetic that are of top quality (*Pueblo Peoples: First Contact* won an Emmy).

Burdeau believes in making use of new technology, technology that provides the means to describe and build new kinds of Indian communities that transcend former boundaries.

> We as Indian people have a real opportunity because of the technology that is out there to utilize it for our own purposes: to create for ourselves a system by which we can once again effectively communicate, not only in our own individual communities, but also in our regional and national communities, and to the world at large. . . . We need to be able to communicate not only within our own communities but with each other, to provide some sort of unity in our ability

and our efforts to try and improve our quality of life, not only for ourselves but for future generations. . . . Technology in the world at large tends to just go in its own direction. It doesn't seem to have a specific plan as to how it's been utilized. I think we as Indian people have something to offer. . . . We can use it for our own use, but I think we have as part of our history a cultural perspective that I think can provide some responsibility in the use of new technology.[41]

Burdeau's use of new technology in the field of film and video is respected by Indian and non-Indian critics. His work is meticulous, attentive to detail, and demonstrates an unusual ability to blend humanity and nature. When asked what the most important elements in producing and directing a film might be, his response was the same as if the question had been about life in general: "Honesty, integrity, truth and balance."[42] He envisions a community of filmmakers of all tribal affiliations working together with an understanding that comes from community. As he says, "it isn't necessary to always agree, but we can always be supportive."[43]

Surviving Columbus: The Pueblo Peoples (1992)

In 1992 the Native American Public Broadcasting Consortium supported the filming of *Surviving Columbus: The Pueblo Peoples* as the first of the *Surviving Columbus* series aired on the quincentennial anniversary of Columbus's run-in with the Americas. George Burdeau was coexecutive producer for the film, and evidence of his hand can be seen in the beauty and grace of the landscape photography, the sensitivity and humor in the interviews, and the thorough but never rushed content.

The Pueblos were an excellent choice for this first in a series on Native Americans because their history is one of intrusions by three separate forces: the Spanish in the 1600s, the Mexicans in the 1800s, and the Euro-Americans in the 1840s. Because they were never "removed" en masse, their history is centered in one geographic area, and their resilience and determination to hold fast to their place against unbelievable odds and through unspeakable atrocities provide a good sense of the strength of Native American peoples in general.

The film begins in Los Angeles, during the riots of 1992. A television newscaster (Conroy Chino) is first shown covering the riots, then sitting in a new automobile, with the city skyline reflected in a curve of window. It is an interesting beginning that places Pueblo culture, as represented by this man, firmly within the twentieth century—alive and doing very well. Chino will be the recurring presence and narrator throughout the film as he travels by train and moves within his community, the Acoma Pueblo.

Talks with Chino's extended family are interspersed with reproductions of historical events and interviews with anthropologists and other experts. A refreshing twist is that all the people in this film, including the experts, are American Indian. They tell the history of the Pueblo people, beginning with the creation myths and up through the conquest by the Spaniards, the revolt that sent the Spanish back to Mexico, the second conquest by the Spanish, the intrusion of the Mexicans, and finally the inhumane treatment they received from the U.S. government from 1840 to the present.

This is a great deal to tell in one film, but the mix of historical reenactment, drawings from the time periods, interviews, and absolutely gorgeous landscape make the story come to life without being overwhelming. The technical expertise is apparent in the fades, slow-motion photography, and subtle sound effects, all of which make the film pretty to watch as well as interesting. In the section entitled "It Was a Bad Wind," for example, conquistadors are filmed in twilight, with the wind slowly whipping dust around them and whispering behind the voice-over. The result is beautiful but foreboding.

Whether family elders or anthropologists, the people in Burdeau's film are articulate and interesting. Occasionally he includes poetry by Simon Ortiz (Pueblo), showing the poet at work with a laptop computer. These are the types of people mainstream audiences have seldom had a chance to associate with the idea of Native Americans—successful contributors to a contemporary world. The film pulls no punches about the hardships endured by the Pueblos at the hands of invaders, but the bottom line here is that the people are still strong, still living on their land, and, first and last, members of their tribal communities. They have suffered, but they are not victims.

The film is also representative of the kinds of things Burdeau says he is interested in doing with the new technology available to filmmakers. The film is about one nation, the Pueblos, but the aesthetic he is striving to create or express, the communication he is striving to produce, is one that involves all Indian peoples.

The Witness (1997)
This 70mm IMAX film is only thirty minutes long, because it was made specifically to be shown in the new Mashantucket Pequot Museum on

the Pequot Reservation. Yet in that short time frame, the film answers hard questions about people whose lives were ended or forever changed in a matter of a few months in the year 1637: What must it have been like to lose not only your family but your whole culture in one generation? What must it have been like to see your nation reduced to a few wandering encampments of people whose lives are constantly in danger of ending violently or in slavery? What must it be like?

For numerous tribes in the Northeast, the personal history of the English invasion of their lands has been glossed over by the Thanksgiving celebration myth, the Pocahontas story, and even the side notes of historians, which mention that things went badly between the white people and the Indians after a while. *The Witness*, Burdeau's newest film, dramatizes this moment in the history of the Pequot people.

The narrative is an historically documented story with real characters and characters created with assistance from diaries of people of the time. It is a superior creative effort because the people who made it, both American Indians and whites, are gifted professionals who understood the importance of the story. As the narrator says, "It is through the story that we survive."

The Pequots funded the film because they wanted the story told well, and they knew that to tell it well meant a large budget. This puts *The Witness* in a world by itself—it is a true story of American Indians, directed and produced by an American Indian, but with a real budget. Burdeau says that he always thought Native American filmmakers were as talented and had stories to tell which were at least as good as the Hollywood mainstream filmmakers but that "limited budgets generally had a negative impact on production values."[44] (Since documentaries are generally less expensive to make than feature films, this also explains why they appear more often than feature films.) The generous funding allowed Burdeau and his co-director and co-producer, Keith Merrill, to hire a top-notch crew of two hundred and a cast of many hundreds, to recreate the costumes and sets with meticulous historical accuracy, and to choose excellent actors.

Among the many examples of technical expertise in the film is the remarkable cinematography. The beautiful landscape provides an unbeatable backdrop, and the subtle manipulation of film speed, camera angles, and framing set this film securely in the category of art.

The story begins with a Pequot elder walking through the forest with a young boy. The elder, Wampishi, is telling the boy that it is time he knew the story, and that he will tell it to him because he, Wampishi, is the Witness. The camera cuts from the two to another boy (Edward Spears) walking in the forest, with the illusion that the camera is still moving in the same forest in the same way, but this boy is actually the elder as a young man. In voice-over narration, the elder will tell the story. For this reason, the young Wampishi never says anything during the film, but it is his voice as an older man we hear throughout. This provides a nice blending of oral tradition and film art.

The story begins with Wampishi running to the Pequot River's edge to see the English ships arrive. The scene is beautiful, but the narrator says that although they had seen other English ships before, never had they carried so many men with so many guns. It is clear that this is not a settler operation. These are soldiers.

In a council meeting, Kiquoquam, who is like a father to Wampishi, is chosen over Uncas to speak with the English. The background history to this is part of what the audience will know coming to see the film, so it is not explained in the film. There was a real Uncas, and he was a very interesting man. He was a sachem (subchief) of the Pequots who had more than enough ambition. He was, in fact, banned from the tribe on five separate occasions. Burdeau speculates that he was probably a very good speaker, a "real politician," since he was able to get himself reinstated each time. In the end, he aligned himself with the British and mobilized the Mohegans and Narragansetts against the Pequots. The British only had one hundred and sixty men, and it was the thousand more that Uncas brought to the fight that turned the tide for the Pequots. He was not a "good guy," and the scene in the council meeting is designed to show that.

Uncas is disgusted when Sassacus chooses Kiquoquam to talk with the English, and he stomps out of the meeting after first grunting rather brutishly at his wife to follow. The real Uncas was married to Sassacus's sister, so the woman who plays the wife covers her face with her hand as though she is very distraught as they leave the room. Uncas gives Wampishi a hard look as he leaves.

That Uncas is a negative character is important to the history of the Pequots, and it is also important to this film. This is a story told from a Native point of view, absolutely, but it is also a balanced portrayal, not just a white versus Indian tale.

While telling an historically accurate story, *The Witness* also deconstructs stereotypes in other ways. For instance, when Kiquoquam and Wampishi go to the boat to talk with the English, the soldiers on board stand with their guns butt down on the deck. Whenever the captain says anything they like, they whoop and use their guns to bang on the deck, making a tremendous racket. It almost sounds like the kind of inarticulate noise of the Hollywood Indian. Then, when Kiquoquam explains that Captain Stone was killed because their sachem was murdered, this captain says, "They were Dutch, not English." Kiquoquam responds, "Dutch and English are both strange to Pequots. Pequots see them both the same." The captain gives a condescending smirk over his shoulder in response to this childish response, but audiences are not likely to miss the intended irony. The Dutch are not English, but neither are the Pequots Cheyennes.

The depiction of tribes at war with each other is also unusual. When the Pequots suggest that they set aside their differences with the Naragansetts in order to fight the invaders, the "Naragansett resolved to join the English. They remembered the long hostility with the Pequot." The inclusion of details like these helps to present the Northeast of this time as an area with a history—not a Garden of Eden populated by innocents.

War was part of life for these people, though certainly not the focus of their lives. They were warriors, and they were good at it. This film shows a people with the military intelligence to lead soldiers into an ambush (which lovely music makes chilling in the film), and their village is a well-designed, double-walled encampment. The two parallel walls are made of upright posts with an alley between them and an entrance easily blocked by brush. Only the formidable guns of the English allow them to break into the fortress.

The war with the English is a short one, mostly because the enemy has muskets and Uncas has brought the Mohegans and Naragansetts in to fight the Pequots as well. It begins when the English who, instead of waiting to hear the Pequot response to their request for the killer of Captain Stone, attack a village and kill thirteen people, including women and children. In return the Pequots attack a British settlement, and they take the women. As Wampishi says, "The captive girls were not harmed. They were traded for our captured people." (In a touching scene in the village, he later gives a bonnet dropped by one of the girls to his little sister.) This attitude is reinforced when Uncas tells Mason that "it would be pleasing to our people if you would spare the women and children. It is our way." Mason brushes him off with "of course," but as it turns out, this is *not* the way of this English army.

An attack on Mystic Fort is ordered by the court in Hartford. John

Mason was brought in to end the siege, and we see him walk by Uncas while talking to his men. He gives Uncas a look of loathing as he says, "We deceive ourselves to underestimate the enemy." He continues, stating that the "Pequot are a great people—we are but a handful by comparison. They are cruel and warlike." Because of their "outrageous violence against the English, who have never done them the least wrong, the court in Hartford has ordered that we engage the Pequot in offensive war." His last line before entering the building is, "Our cause being just."

Inside, he says, "The face of God is set against those who do evil. It is his will that we go forth to don the ground with their flesh." He asks the Reverend to say a prayer. "Oh Lord, show favor to us, your poor, distressed servants. Manifest one pledge of thy love that our hearts might be encouraged in this work of thine."

What "manifests" at that moment is Uncas, who bursts through the door and throws a sack full of Pequot heads on the table. Mason is surprised but manages a slight nod to the positive.

This scene is something of a short course in Euro-American colonizers and their attitudes, including their belief in the righteousness of their actions and their assumption of authority. The attack on the Pequot fortress is well within the English conception of right, although as Wampishi says, "Over six hundred of our people were killed at Mystic Fort. In the year that followed, many of our people were hunted down, killed or sold into slavery. Sassacus was murdered by the Mohawks and his head was given to the English."

The attack on the fort was so well filmed it is painful to watch. When shooting everyone begins to be costly for the English, they burn the fort. The rows of houses are torched with women and children trapped inside. We see Wampishi's mother run out of one of those houses. Her back is on fire as she runs, but still she carries the child to whom Wampishi had given the bonnet. An English soldier shoots her in the back, then walks over and fires again as she and the child lie on the ground.

As the story closes, we see Pequot men in heavy chains as a soldier reads the terms of the Hartford Treaty. "To establish peace among the remaining tribes, captive Pequot shall be given as slaves to the Narragansett, the Mohegans, and the English. They shall no more be called Pequot. Use of the name Pequot is herewith forbidden forever. Those who were once called Pequot shall never again be allowed to occupy the lands of their former homes." This speech is followed by a long shot of a beautiful river and waterfall, where the old Wampishi sits with the young boy of the film's beginning. He says, "You are Pequot. You are a child of the ancestors. You must honor them and preserve the land where our people lie buried. Now you are the keeper of the story. Listen. Remember. The story of our people must never die. You must keep the story. You must keep the land." And that is exactly what the Pequots of 1997 did in making this film.

Since scenes are filmed out of order, keeping the whole story in focus isn't always easy while the film is in production. Burdeau tells the story of one very significant "focusing," which occurred when the fort scene was being shot. The families of the crew and cast gathered to make offerings, prayers, and ceremonies for the safety of the people telling this story. After filming the scene of Wampishi's mother and sister, Burdeau says he looked over at his codirector, Keith Merrill, who broke down in tears. He said, "It just finally hit me what I was doing." Merrill is not an American Indian, but the story had become suddenly real for him. [45] As Wampishi says at the film's beginning, "You must listen with your ears and with your heart," and Merrill had suddenly heard with both.

The Witness is a fine film because it overturns stereotypes, it tells a historically accurate story, and it depicts a Native existence from a Native point of view, and that depiction is complete and balanced—no racism and no white guilt. It is unique in that it was well funded and that the funding came from Native Americans. It is also a breakthrough in that two filmmakers, one American Indian and one Euro-American, joined forces and worked as a team to create it. This short film would work nicely as a prototype for narrative films from mainstream Hollywood. Let's hope it does.

[Burdeau's next directing project is a feature film about Ishi, for which he is also writing the screenplay.]

Written, Directed, and Produced by American Indians

In January 1998, Chris Eyre's film, *Smoke Signals* (1998), based on Sherman Alexie's book *The Lone Ranger and Tonto Fistfight in Heaven*, premiered at the Sundance Festival in Park City, Utah. It received the Audience Award for Dramatic Films, the Filmmakers Trophy, a nomination for the Grand Jury Prize, and a special showing and reception hosted by Robert Redford.

Not bad, all in all.

Eyre and Alexie are listed as co-producers of the film, along with Roger Baerwolf and others at Shadow Catcher Entertainment, making

Smoke Signals the first feature film written, directed and (co)produced by Native Americans to achieve such popular success.

Eyre is a very talented director and Alexie is a very talented writer—there's no doubt about it. Even so, their success is a bit surprising, given the lack of funds most American Indian filmmakers face. So how do independent filmmakers like these find a way (money) to make a first-class film? In this case, the answer was the Sundance Institute. Developing the project at Sundance was "great" according to Eyre "because the workshop helps you articulate exactly what you want to do. The film is very magical, lyrical. Sherman's material gave me a chance to try certain things that didn't work, and I'm glad I tried them there. I go by my gut, you know, just by my instinct."[46] This is an incredible and expensive luxury, the freedom to make mistakes, a luxury few Native American filmmakers have had before now.

But making a film at the institute doesn't guarantee entry into the Sundance Festival, where the competition is tough and getting tougher. Since Sundance Institute took over the tiny U.S. Film Festival in 1985, it has grown into a what has been called a "snowbound Hollywood, mixing increasingly prominent actors, agents, and cell-phone hugging acquisition executives of distribution houses, eager to snap up a hot flick."[47] Only a few years ago, the festival was an end in itself, but the addition of those cell-phone huggers has led to what some critics see as a negative commercialization of an serious art festival, and one of the major perks of having a film in the festival is the possibility of generating a bidding war for distribution.

Smoke Signals was not part of that war—not because it wasn't wanted; after all, it received two of the most prestigious awards presented. There was no bidding because a distribution contract had been signed a month earlier with Miramax. This is a surprising development, but Alexie said, "It might have been possible to get more money by waiting until after Sundance . . . but we didn't want to go in as sellers. Early on we decided that if the movie was just OK we'd go to Sundance and try to sell it. But we knew pretty quickly that we wouldn't have to worry about that."[48]

Apparently, they were right. The reviews have been more than appreciative. For instance, Geoffrey Gilmore says, "[s]imply put, Chris Eyre's *Smoke Signals* is a superbly told, deeply moving portrait. . . . Funny, raging, poignant, and revealing, *Smoke Signals* is a story told from a very personal point of view. As specific as it is, its payoffs are powerfully universal. Adam Beach heads a wonderful cast which includes Evan Adams as Thomas, and Gary Farmer and Tantoo Cardinal as Victor's parents. It is not novel enough to say that this is the first dramatic film directed and written by Native Americans. This film is blessed with inspiration."[49]

Is that "inspiration" American Indian? Partly. Partly not. Although Alexie is politically very outspoken, he has always been candid about the mass audience for his work. He says, "I want everybody in the world to see this movie. I'm not interested in making movies that don't appeal to a lot of people. So in some ways Chris and I are in the unique position of having to make this be a very accessible film in order for this to happen. Perhaps now, based on the success of this film, Indian filmmakers can get a little more adventurous and still find an audience. But we simply don't have the luxury right now. This film has to be safer in a sense and we're going to get taken to the rug [in Indian country] because of it."[50] So the audience for this film is not a Native American audience but "everybody in the world." However, it is doubtful that Eyre or Alexie will be overly criticized for it. For one thing, American Indian audiences are used to that, and for another, it is a very funny story told in a way that is at least partially recognizable as "Indian." But in some important ways they probably should be "taken to the rug" for letting the opportunity to make a high-profile film with a truly American Indian aesthetic pass them by.

Michael Jones points out that for Eyre and Alexie, "the project's first objective was to distance the story from the typical politics that surround the American Indian—skeletons of alcoholism, injustice, loneliness. They were eager to show a different set of standards—darkly comic, magical, beautiful—still tragic but subtly viewed from the Indian first-person. They don't need Kevin Costner to suffer for them."[51] If that is the case, then the film failed to achieve its "first objective." The specters of alcoholism, injustice, and loneliness form the skeleton upon which this film hangs, and the fact that it is also very funny doesn't keep it from showing a Native present that is devoid of much hope for the future. In significant ways, it falls into the clichéd stereotypes of mainstream Hollywood films; its saving grace is that the Native Americans are shown as contemporary humans with contemporary problems, emotions, and reactions. Still, the film holds much of the tone of the stories from which it was made—clever, funny, and bleak. As Alexie writes in "The Only Traffic Signal on the Reservation Doesn't Flash Red Anymore," "It's hard to be optimistic on the reservation. When a glass sits on a table here, people don't wonder if it's half filled or

half empty. They just hope it's good beer. . . . And, just like everybody else, Indians need heroes to help them learn how to survive. But
what happens when our heroes don't even know how to pay their
bills?" Although most American Indians who have seen the film have
found something to like about it, particularly the humor and the occasional in-joke, the implied acceptance of defeat in the film is also rather
disturbing.

This film is a story that is partially the story of a storyteller telling
stories. As Alexie wrote in the original story, Thomas Builds-the-Fire
(well played in the film by Evan Adams) is a "storyteller that nobody
wanted to listen to. That's like being a dentist in a town where everybody has false teeth."[52] Listening to Thomas tell his stories would seem
profoundly uncinematic, especially since the camera sometimes stays
stock-still while he does so, but they are actually usually rather touching. Other times, the audience sees the stories he tells as well as the
scenes from his childhood in flashbacks. Alexie says they didn't want
"this awkward *Wayne's World* flashback stuff. . . . I saw an episode of
St. Elsewhere that used flashbacks—any time someone walked through
a door, they went back to the past. And then I saw *Lone Star*, with the
amazing pans and tilts that moved you from past to present. I thought,
That's it! The way time works in Indian culture is a lot more circular, so
that the past, the present, and the future are all the same thing."[53]

Eyre uses the flashbacks skillfully, presenting a story that unfolds in
reverse, a story of Victor's parents' lives, particularly his father's descent into alcoholism and the trauma this causes Victor and his mother.
As Victor and Thomas travel to Arizona to take care of Victor's father's
affairs, we learn what it was like for the boys on the reservation of their
childhood, and Victor rediscovers his father through flashbacks nar-
rated by his father's new friend. This rediscovery and Victor's emerging ability to forgive provide the focus of the film, and except for the
rather clunky, didactic inclusion of a poem about forgiving fathers at
the film's end, this works rather well.

Smoke Signals is also a road trip/buddy film of sorts. Like in *Powwow
Highway*, we have two Indian men traveling without much money.
Like Buddy, Victor is athletic, good-looking and assertive. Like Philbert, Thomas is more connected to their culture, but while Philbert
yearns to be a Cheyenne warrior, Thomas wants to keep alive by telling
stories. In the short story "This Is What It Means to Say Phoenix, Arizona," Thomas only asks for two things in return for giving Victor the
money he needs to get to Arizona: he wants to go along, and he asks,

"Just one time when I'm telling a story somewhere, why don't you stop and listen?"[54] It's a fair deal, so Victor agrees. In both films, the more "modern" man learns to appreciate, quietly and without fanfare, the ideas and feelings of the other, who represents a culture that should not be ignored—their culture.

Once (in the "Phoenix, Arizona" short story), Thomas Builds-the-Fire jumped off the roof of the tribal school and flapped his arms like a bird because he believed he could fly: "One of his dreams came true for just a second, just long enough to make it real." Making it real is what makes the success of *Smoke Signals* such an exciting development in Native American filmmaking. While it is not the only film ever made by Native Americans, as the hype surrounding the film would have us believe, it is the first to get such widespread publicity—and Miramax as its distributor. Maybe the film is a success because it was made at the right time, when conditions were finally favorable, or maybe it was because of the talent involved and the help of the Sundance Institute. Either way, it provides the "second" of reality necessary to make the existence of American Indian filmmakers "real" for the film industry and represents an Indian entry into the world of mainstream filmmaking that will, hopefully, be the first of many.

7

Coming Attractions?

An American Indian leader reported that his young son took his hand as they left a movie theater. He said, "Daddy, we pretty near won that one!" – Virginia I. Armstrong, ed., *I Have Spoken: American History Through the Voices of Indians*

It is perhaps putting too much of a burden on a profit-driven industry, as filmmaking most certainly is, to ask that it carry the responsibility of preserving culture. The reality of our world, however, is that movies and television are so pervasive that they can't help but affect our lives in significant social, emotional, and psychological ways. The film industry must therefore accept the responsibility of clearing away the cobwebs of misinformation it has strung throughout the last century, webs that have wrapped the American Indian in a cocoon of misunderstanding, derision, hatred, and nostalgic guilt. *Dead Man*, *The Witness*, and *Smoke Signals* are wonderful films, but deconstructing the stereotypes can't be done solely by independent filmmakers, American Indian or not.

If Native American and mainstream filmmakers can meet on common ground on a more regular basis, if more viewers begin to recognize the stereotypes and accept them less willingly, and if more Native American film professionals can consistently place themselves in the positions of power—as producers, directors, writers, and consultants—some changes will occur that will allow the American Indian and the film industry to win one together for a change. The result will be Native Americans presented respectfully, but with a respect that does not preclude laughter, tears, pleasure, or even subversion.[1]

Notes

Introduction

1. See M. M. Bakhtin, "The Problem of Speech Genres," in *Speech Genres and Other Late Essays*, ed. Caryl Emerson and Michael Holquist, trans. Vern W. McGee (Austin: Univ. of Texas Press, 1986), 60–102.

2. M. M. Bakhtin, "Discourse in the Novel," *The Dialogic Imagination: Four Essays*, ed. Michael Holquist, trans. Caryl Emerson and Michael Holquist (Austin: Univ. of Texas Press, 1992), 276.

3. T. E. Perkins, "Rethinking Stereotypes," *Ideology and Cultural Production*, ed. Michele Barrett, et. al. (New York: St. Martin's, 1979), 156.

4. Perkins, "Rethinking Stereotypes," 157.

1. Genesis of the Stereotypes

1. Robert Stam has pointed out, "Rather than the direct reflection of the real, or even a refraction of the real, artistic discourse constitutes a refraction of a refraction, that is, a mediated version of an already textualized and discursivized socio-ideological world." Robert Stam, *Subversive Pleasures: Bakhtin, Cultural Criticism, and Film* (Baltimore: Johns Hopkins Univ. Press, 1989), 252.

2. Some of the many captivity stories have been collected in the following volumes: Kathryn Zabelle Derounian-Stodola, ed., *Women's Indian Captivity Narratives* (New York: Penguin Classics, 1998); Colin G. Galloway, *North Country Captives: Selected Narratives of Indian Captivity from Vermont to New Hampshire* (Hanover NH: Univ. Press of New England, 1992); J. Paul, ed., *Captivity Tales* (New York: Arno, 1974); Frederick Drimmer, ed., *Captured by the Indians: 15 Firsthand Accounts, 1750–1870* (New York: Dover, 1985); Alden T. Vaughan and Edward W. Clark, eds., *Puritans Among the Indians: Accounts of Captivity and Redemption, 1676–1724* (Cambridge MA: Belknap, 1981). Other stories and critical works are listed in the following biliographies: Clara A. Smith, comp., *Narratives of Captivity Among the Indians of North America: A List of Books and Manuscripts on this Subject in the Edward E. Ayer Collection of the Newberry Library* (Chicago: Publications of the Newberry Library, 1912); Alden T. Vaughan, *Narratives of North American Indian Captivity: A Selected Bibliography* (New York: Garland, 1983).

3. Mary White Rowlandson, *A Narrative of the Captivity and Restoration of Mrs. Mary Rowlandson*, ed. Frederick Lewis Wels (Boston: Houghton Mifflin, 1930).

4. Gretchen Bataille and Charles L. P. Silet, "The Entertaining Anachronism: Indians in American Film," *Kaleidoscopic Lens: How Hollywood Views Ethnic Groups*, ed. Randall M. Miller (Englewood NJ: Jerome S. Ozer, 1980), 38.

5. See Martin Barker and Roger Sabin, *The Lasting of the Mohicans: History of an American Myth* (Jackson: Univ. Press of Mississippi, 1995), 21; Donald A. Ringe, *James Fenimore Cooper* (New York: Twayne, 1962), 44; D. H. Lawrence, "Fenimore Cooper's Leatherstocking Novels," *James Fenimore Cooper: A Collection of Critical Essays*, ed. Wayne Fields (Englewood Cliffs NJ: Prentice Hall, 1979), 37–52.

6. "Johnson and Graham's Lessee v. William McIntosh," *Documents of United States Indian Policy*, 2d ed., Francis Paul Prucha, ed. (Lincoln: University of Nebraska Press, 1990), 37.

7. Robert Montgomery Bird, *Nick of the Woods* (New Haven CT: College and University Press, 1967), preface; 1837 reprint based on the 1853 revised edition.

8. In his introduction to the Penguin 1986 edition of *Last of the Mohicans*, Richard Slotkin describes Cooper's "manly realist" view. "Despite his relatively humane portrayal of Indians, however, Cooper would have been horrified at his association with the 'she-males' and clerical philanthropists, and would have identified with the orientation (if not the specific policies) of those who spoke as 'manly realists.' That 'manly' view—unpalatable (Cooper feared) in his own time, but predominant by the 1870s and 80s—held that the differences between white and Indian culture were fixed in the race or 'blood,' and held further that war between differing races was inherent in racial character, inevitable, and central to the process of American national development," xii.

9. Raymond William Stedman, *Shadows of the Indian: Stereotypes in American Culture* (Norman: Univ. of Oklahoma Press, 1982), 87.

10. Virginia Wright Wexman, *Creating the Couple: Love, Marriage, and the Hollywood Performance* (Princeton: Princeton Univ. Press, 1993), 71.

11. Peter Wollen, *Signs and Meaning in the Cinema* (Bloomington: Indiana Univ. Press, 1969), 14.

12. "Senator Frelinghuysen on Indian Removal," *Documents of United States Indian Policy*, 49, 51.

13. "Cherokee Nation v. Georgia," *Documents of United States Indian Policy*, 59.

14. Arnold Krupat, *Ethnocriticism* (Berkeley: Univ. of California Press, 1992), 135.

15. Bird, *Nick of the Woods*, 1853 ed., n.p.

16. Curtis Dahl, *Robert Montgomery Bird* (New York: Twayne, 1963), 97.

17. Stedman, *Shadows of the Indian*, 68.

18. Bird, *Nick of the Woods*.

19. From "Deadly Eye," as quoted in Edmund Pearson, *Dime Novels; or, Following and Old Trail in Popular Literature* (New York: Little, Brown, 1929; reprint New York: Kennikat, 1968), 122.

20. "Report of the Board of Indian Commissioners," *Documents of United States Indian Policy*, 132–33.

21. Benedict Anderson, *Imagined Communities: Reflections on the Origin and Spread of Nationalism* (London: Verso, 1983), 1.

22. As quoted in Russel Nye, *The Unembarrassed Muse: The Popular Arts in America* (New York: Dial, 1970), 207.

23. Nye, *The Unembarrassed Muse*, 191–92.

24. Nye, *The Unembarrassed Muse*, 192.

25. John G. Neihardt, *Black Elk Speaks* (Lincoln: Univ. of Nebraska Press, 1988), 214–23.

26. Dee Brown's novel *Bury My Heart at Wounded Knee* (New York: Henry Holt, 1991) is an excellent source for more information on the massacre at Wounded Knee. For another perspective, see Neihardt, *Black Elk Speaks*, 105–30.

27. Ralph and Natasha Friar, *The Only Good Indian: The Hollywood Gospel* (New York: Drama Book Specialists, 1972), 64–67.

2. The Silent Scrim

1. "Program of the Lake Mohonk Conference, September 1884," *Documents of United States Indian Policy*, 163–64.

2. Frederick E. Hoxie, "The Curious Story of Reformers and American Indians," *Indians in American History*, 2d ed., ed. Frederick E. Hoxie and Peter Iverson (Wheeling IL: Harlan Davidson, 1998), 190.

3. Robert F. Berkhofer Jr., *The White Man's Indian* (New York: Vintage Books, 1979), 171. For Pratt's own words on the subject, see Richard Henry Pratt, *Battlefield and Classroom: Four Decades with the American Indian, 1867–1904* (New Haven: Yale Univ. Press), 1964.

4. "Use of English in Indian Schools," *Documents of United States Indian Policy*, 175–76.

5. Judith Mayne, *Cinema and Spectatorship* (New York: Routledge, 1993), 77.

6. Angela Aleiss, "Native Americans: The Surprising Silents," *Cineaste* 21, no.3 (summer 1995): 34–35.

7. Donald L. Kaufmann, "The Indian as Media Hand-me-down," *The Pretend Indians: Images of Native Americans in the Movies*, ed. Gretchen Bataille and Charles L. P. Silet (Ames: Iowa Univ. Press, 1980), 34.

8. I am indebted to much of the information about Cody's *Indian Wars* to Ralph and Natasha Friar's book, *The Only Good Indian*, 70–75.

9. Henry Blackman Sell and Victor Weybright, *Buffalo Bill and the Wild West* (New York: Oxford Univ. Press, 1955), n.p.

10. Enrique R. Lamadrid, "Ig/Noble Savages of New Mexico's Silent Cinema 1912–1914," *Border Crossings: Mexican and Chicano Cinema*, ed. Chon A. Noriega (Los Angeles: USC School of Cinema-Television, 1992), 17.

11. Richard Schickel, *D. W. Griffith: An American Life* (New York: Simon and Schuster, 1984), 139.

12. Lamadrid, "Ig/Noble Savages," 17.

13. Nicholas A. Vardac, "Realism and Romance: D. W. Griffith," *Imitations of Life*, ed. Marcia Landy (Detroit: Wayne State Univ. Press, 1991), 3.

14. David Wark Griffith, "Pictures vs. One Night Stands," *The Independent* (11 December 1916) in Richard Koszarski, ed., *Hollywood Directors: 1914–1940* (New York: Oxford Univ. Press, 1976), 37.

15. Alan Casty, "The Films of D. W. Griffith: A Style for the Times," *Imitations of Life*, 364.

16. Louis Reeves Harrison, "The Bison 101 Headliners," *The Moving Picture World*, 27 April 1912.

17. D. H. Lawrence, "Indians and the Environment," *New York Times Magazine*, sec. 4 (26 October 1924): 3.

18. Francis Paul Prucha, introduction to "Bursum Bill," *Documents of United States Indian Policy*, 215.

19. "Report of the Board of Indian Commissioners, *Documents of United States Indian Policy*, 132.

20. Alvin M. Josephy Jr., "Modern American and the Indian," *Indians in American History*, 254–55.

21. Josephy, "Modern American and the Indian."

22. Angela Aleiss, "The Vanishing American," *Journal of American Studies* 25, no. 3 (December 1991): 469–70.

23. Aleiss, "The Vanishing American," 470.

24. As quoted in Aleiss, "The Vanishing American," 472.

25. Aleiss, "The Vanishing American," 472.

26. Aleiss, "The Vanishing American," 472.

27. Peter Brooks, "The Melodramatic Imagination," *Imitations of Life*, 61.

28. Kevin Brownlow, *The War, the West and the Wilderness* (New York: Knopf, 1979), 329.

3. The Cowboy Talkies

1. Robert Stam, "Bakhtin, Polyphony and Ethnic/Racial Representation," *Unspeakable Images: Ethnicity and the American Cinema*, ed. Lester D. Friedman (Urbana: University of Illinois Press, 1991), 256–57.

2. John A. Price, "The Stereotyping of North American Indians in Motion Pictures," *Pretend Indians*, 80.

3. Stam, *Subversive Pleasures*, 62.

4. Fredrick Jackson Turner, *The Frontier in American History* (New York: Dover, 1996).

5. Wexman, *Love, Marriage, and the Hollywood Performance*, 90.

6. Alfonso Ortiz, "Indian/White Relations: A View from the Other Side of the 'Frontier,'" *Indians in American History*, 3.

7. "Meriam Report," *Documents of United States Indian Policy*, 220.

8. "Indian Commissioner Collier on the Wheeler-Howard Act," *Documents of United States Indian Policy*, 225.

9. Mary Ann Weston, *Native Americans in the News: Images of Indians in the Twentieth Century Press* (Westport CT: Greenwood, 1996), 56–57.

10. Quoted in Weston, *Native Americans in the News*, 65.

11. Wexman, *Love, Marriage, and the Hollywood Performance*, 71–76.

12. Louis Owens, "Into the Territory: The Invention of John Wayne," *Icarus* 10 (spring 1993): 98.

13. Bataille and Silet, *Pretend Indians*, 101.

14. Wexman, *Love, Marriage, and the Hollywood Performance*, 80.

15. For a more complete discussion of scientific racism, see Elazar Barkan, *The Retreat of Scientific Racism: Changing Concepts of Race in Britain and the United States Between the World Wars* (Cambridge: Cambridge Univ. Press, 1993).

16. Francis Parkman, "The Conspiracy of Pontiac (1851)," *Native American Literature*, ed. Donald McQuade, et. al. (New York: HarperCollins College, 1993), 224–25.

17. Charles Ramirez Berg, "The Indian Question," *Cinema of Solitudes: A Critical Study of Mexican Film, 1967–1983* (Austin: Univ. of Texas Press, 1992), 137.

18. Wexman, *Love, Marriage, and the Hollywood Performance*, 90.

19. Louis Owens, *Other Destinies* (Norman: Univ. of Oklahoma Press, 1992), 82.

20. Quoted in Friar, *The Only Good Indian*, 97.

21. Ortiz, "Indian/White Relations," 9.

22. James F. Denton, "The Red Man Plays Indian," *Colliers* 113 (18 March 1944): 18–19 ("[*sic*]" in original).

23. John A. Price, "The Stereotyping of North American Indians in Motion Pictures," *Pretend Indians*, 76.

24. Peter Wollen, "Cinema's Conquistadors," *Sight and Sound* 2, no. 7 (October 1992): xxiii.

25. Alice P. Sterner, "A Guide to the Discussion of the Technicolor Screen Version of *Northwest Passage*," *Photoplay Studies* 6, no. 9 (1940).

26. Sterner, "A Guide to . . . *Northwest Passage*."

27. Quoted in Weston, *Native Americans in the News*, 87.

28. Quoted in Weston, *Native Americans in the News*, 87.

29. *The Squaw Man*, directed by Cecil B. DeMille, was the first film by the fledgling partnership of Goldwyn (who later founded Metro Goldwyn Mayer) and Lasky (one of the founders of Paramount Pictures).

30. Stam, "Bakhtin, Polyphony, and Ethnic/Racial Representation," 254.

31. John C. Ewers, "The Static Images," *Look to the Mountaintop*, ed. Robert Iocopi (San Jose: Gousha, 1972), 107–9.

32. Joseph McBride and Michael Wilmington, "The Noble Outlaw," *Great Film Directors: A Critical Anthology*, ed. Leo Braudy and Morris Dickstein (New York: Oxford Univ. Press, 1978), 331.

33. John Ford, "Veteran Producer Muses," *Hollywood Directors, 1914–1940*, ed. Richard Koszarski (New York: Oxford Univ. Press, 1976), 202.

34. "House Concurrent Resolution 108," *Documents of United States Indian Policy*, 233.

35. "Senator Watkins on Termination Policy," *Documents of United States Indian Policy*, 239.

36. *Christian Science Monitor*, 19 April 1952, quoted in Weston, *Native Americans in the News*, 105.

37. There are many good essays, articles, and books on the United States' termination policy. For a good overview of the policy, see Moxie's *Indians in American History*. Many of the essays in the collection discuss termination.

38. Weston, *Native Americans in the News*, 116–17.

39. Richard M. Fried, *Nightmare in Red: The McCarthy Era in Perspective* (New York: Oxford Univ. Press, 1990), 5.

40. Historians hotly debate the causes of the Cold War, and fear of nuclear war is an accurate but partial explanation.

41. Ralph E. Friar and Natasha A., "White Man Speaks with Split Tongue, Forked Tongue, Tongue of Snake," *Pretend Indians*, 95.

42. Stam, "Bakhtin, Polyphony and Ethnic/Racial Representation," 263.

43. Stedman, *Shadows of the Indian*, 112.

44. "Marriage Between White Men and Indian Women," *Documents of United States Indian Policy*, 176.

45. Philip French, "The Indian in the Western Movie," *Pretend Indians*, 103.

46. Dan Georgakas, "They Have Not Spoken: American Indians in Film," *Film Quarterly* 25 (spring 1972): 32.

47. Stedman, *Shadows of the Indian*, 115.

4. Win Some and Lose Some

1. "A Program for Indian Citizens," *Documents of United States Indian Policy*, 242.

2. "Declaration of Indian Purpose," *Documents of United States Indian Policy*, 246.

3. James S. Olson and Raymond Wilson, *Native Americans in the Twentieth Century* (Provo ut: Brigham Young Univ. Press, 1984), 163–66.

4. Vine Deloria Jr., "Evolution of Federal Indian Policy Making," *American Indian Policy in the Twentieth Century* (Norman: Univ. of Oklahoma Press, 1985), 251.

5. V. F. Perkins, "Cheyenne Autumn," *Pretend Indians*, 153.

6. V. F. Perkins, Review of *Cheyenne Autumn*, *Movie* 12 (Spring 1965): 36–37.

7. "President Johnson, Special Message to Congress," *Documents of United States Indian Policy*, 248–49.

8. Francis Paul Prucha, note to "Civil Rights Act of 1968," *Documents of United States Indian Policy*, 249.

9. Oliver LaFarge, "The Indians Want a New Frontier," *New York Times Magazine*, 11 June 1961, 12.

10. Weston, *Native Americans in the News*, 137.

11. Peter Collier, "Salmon Fishing in America: The Indians vs. the State of Wash-

ington," *Ramparts* (April 1971): 29–31, 39–45. Quoted in Weston, *Native Americans in the News*, 137.

12. Susan Rice, "And Afterwards, Take Him to a Movie," *Pretend Indians*, 146.

13. Georgakas, "They Have Not Spoken," 141.

14. Pauline Kael, "Americana: 'Tell Them Willie Boy Was Here,'" *Pretend Indians*, 164.

15. Georgakas, "They Have Not Spoken," 141.

16. Friar, *The Only Good Indian*, 312.

17. Ward Churchill, *Fantasies of the Master Race: Literature, Cinema and the Colonization of American Indians*, ed. M. Annette Jaimes (Monroe ME: Common Courage, 1992), 237.

18. Georgakas, "They Have Not Spoken," 136.

19. Churchill, *Fantasies of the Master Race*, 238.

20. *Film Quarterly* (spring 1972): 28.

21. Georgakas, "They Have Not Spoken," 136.

22. John W. Turner, "*Little Big Man*: The Novel and the Film," *Pretend Indians*, 158.

23. Friar, *The Only Good Indian*, 256.

24. Friar, *The Only Good Indian*, 256.

25. Vine Deloria Jr., "The American Indian Image in North America," *Pretend Indians*, xii.

26. Georgakas, "They Have Not Spoken," 139.

27. Georgakas, "They Have Not Spoken," 139.

28. "Indian Education Act," *Documents of United States Indian Policy*, 263.

29. Deloria, "Evolution of Federal Indian Policy Making," 253.

30. Deloria, "Evolution of Federal Indian Policy Making," 254.

31. Weston, *Native Americans in the News*, 143.

32. Weston, *Native Americans in the News*, 142.

33. "Behind a Modern Day Uprising," *U.S. News and World Report*, 12 March 1973: 36. Quoted in Weston, *Native Americans in the News*, 144.

34. "Establishment of the American Indian Policy Review Commission," *Documents of United States Indian Policy*, 272.

35. Deloria, "Evolution of Federal Indian Policy Making," 254.

5. The Sympathetic 1980s and 1990s

1. C. Patrick Morris, "Termination by Accountants: The Reagan Indian Policy," in *Native Americans and Public Policy*, ed. Fremont J. Lyden and Lyman H. Lagters (Pittsburgh: Univ. of Pittsburgh Press, 1992), 63–69, as quoted in Weston, *Native Americans in the News*, 153.

2. "Indian Policy: Statement of Ronald Reagan," *Documents of United States Indian Policy*, 301.

3. Weston, *Native Americans in the News*, 153.

4. Most profits from such enterprises are used for community services, including

schools, scholarships, health facilities, and community and youth centers. A very small percentage of American Indians who have benefited from gaming have personally received large sums.

5. Stedman, *Shadows of the Indian*, 217.

6. John Walker, ed., *Halliwell's Film Guide*, (New York: Harper Perennial, 1995), 1158.

7. The reference to Winnebagos is another joke intended for an Indian audience. The naming of automobiles, clubs, and sports teams after Native peoples is a source of irritation to most Native Americans.

8. *Incident at Oglala* includes a good examination of the realities of life on the Pine Ridge Reservation in the mid-1970s.

9. Richard Hill, "The Non-Vanishing American Indian: Are the Modern Images Any Closer to the Truth?" *The Quill* 80, no. 4 (May 1992): 36.

10. Aims McGuinness has noted that the New Agers are looking to Indian ceremony and spirituality for answers to 1990s problems. "In Arizona the Forest Service and environmentalists are up in arms over the predations of the West's latest arrival, the New Age Movement. According to Colorado's *High Country News*, the Cococino National Forest has been deluged with visitors seeking 'energy vortexes' from which consciousness-raising earth energy emanates. . . . What the New Agers have in common with these Indians is something, I suppose, you need the aid of an energy vortex to discern." Aims McGuinness, "Unwild West," *The New Republic* 204, no. 19 (13 May 1991): 42.

11. Skitty says this with a grin on his face, playing off the natural-hunter-who-never-steps-on-twigs stereotype.

12. Roger Ebert, "Powwow Highway," *Chicago Sun Times*, 28 April 1989.

13. Ebert, "Powwow Highway."

14. Roger Worthington, "Ritual of Treaty-Rights Protests May Be Nearing Its Final Season," *Chicago Tribune*, 15 April 1990.

15. "400 Mourn Wounded Knee Dead," *Chicago Tribune*, 30 December 1990.

16. Wes Smith, "After 150 Years in Exile, The Kickapoo Nation May Be Returning to Illinois to Restore Its Ancestral Capital," *Chicago Tribune*, 5 March 1995.

17. Andrew Bagnato, "Battle Lines Forming for the Tomahawk Chop War," *Chicago Tribune*, 25 October 1991.

18. Wes Smith, "Michael Haney Stands Up to Those Who Would Trivialize the Heritage of American Indians," *Chicago Tribune*, 28 March 1993.

19. Michael Kilian, "In These Politically Correct Times, A Name Can Lead to a Real Brouhaha," *Chicago Tribune*, 27 February 1997.

20. Weston, *Native Americans in the News*, 159.

21. Associated Press dispatch, *New York Times*, 3 September 1994. Quoted in Weston, *Native Americans in the News*, 160.

22. Timothy Egan, "Senate Measures Would Deal Blow to Indian Rights," *The Washington Post*, 27 August 1997.

23. Egan, "Senate Measures."

24. Jerry Gray, "Senate Shelves Proposals to Restrict Indian Legal Protections," *The Washington Post*, 17 September 1997.

25. Annie C. Fullam, "Prayer Group in Patterson Follows Rituals of Indian Purifying," *The Washington Post*, 10 August 1997.

26. Louis Owens, "D'une disparition à l'autre." *Revue d'etudes Palestiniennes*, n.s. 3 (1995): 47.

27. Louis Owens, "D'une disparition à l'autre," 47.

28. Jace Weaver, "Ethnic Cleansing, Homestyle," *Wicazo Sa Review* 10, no. 91 (spring, 1994): 27.

29. Churchill, *Fantasies of the Master Race*, 238.

30. M. M. Bakhtin, "Epic and Novel," *The Dialogic Imagination*, 12.

31. Irving Rouse, *The Tainos: Rise and Decline of the People Who Greeted Columbus* (New Haven: Yale Univ. Press, 1992), 169.

32. Peter Wollen, "Cinema's Conquistadors," *Sight and Sound* 2, no. 7 (October 1992): 14.

33. Wollen, "Cinema's Conquistadors," 14.

34. Wollen, "Cinema's Conquistadors," 14.

35. For more information on the Exposition, see *World's Columbian Exposition* (Philadelphia: Home Library, 1893), written by a former governor of Illinois, William E. Cameron, in 1893. For a more recent approach, see Neil Harris's *Cultural Excursions: Marketing Appetites and Cultural Tastes in Modern America* (Chicago: Univ. of Chicago Press, 1990).

36. Tzvetan Todorov, *The Conquest of America: The Question of the Other*, trans. Richard Howard (New York: Harper Perennial, 1984), 8.

37. Todorov, *The Conquest of America*, 10.

38. Todorov, *The Conquest of America*, 22.

39. "Loggers Move In: Lubicons Vow Direct Action," *Ecomedia Toronto Bulletin 88*, "Lubicon Negotiation Logs," <<http://net.result.com/-samuel/lubicon/1990/MO-NOV10.txt>>, 14 December 1998.

40. Tony Hall, "Calgary Eye-Opener," *Commentary*, 24 July 1990, transcript by Aboriginal Rights Support Group: Committee Against Racism, "Lubicon Negotiation Logs," <<http://net.result.com/-samuel/lubicon/1990/MO-NOV24.txt>>, 14 December 1998.

41. Geoff Pevere, "Hostiles," *The Canadian Forum* 71 (November 1992): 37.

42. Brian D. Johnson, "Epic Struggles: Revealing the Rage When Natives Meet Whites," *Maclean's* 104, no. 40 (7 October 1991): 73.

43. Johnson, "Epic Struggles," 73.

44. Pevere, "Hostiles," 36.

45. Pevere, "Hostiles," 36.

46. Johnson, "Epic Struggles," 73.

47. Johnson, "Epic Struggles," 73.

48. Gavin Smith, "Mann Hunters," *Film Comment* 28, no. 6 (November-December 1992): 77.

49. Grenville Goodwin, *Myths and Tales of the White Mountain Apache* (Tucson: Univ. of Arizona Press, 1994), 2.

50. Much of this section is from a previously published article. See Jacquelyn Kilpatrick, "Disney's Politically Correct *Pocahontas*," *Cineaste* 21, no. 4, (January 1996): 36–38.

51. Betsy Sharkey, "Beyond Tepees and Totem Poles," *The New York Times*, 11 June 1995, Arts and Leisure.

52. Stam, "Bakhtin, Polyphony, and Ethnic/Racial Representation," 153.

53. Sarah Kershaw, "Coming to Classrooms: The Real Pocahontas Story," *New York Times*, 12 July 1995, Education.

54. Kershaw, "Coming to Classrooms."

55. Sharkey, "Beyond Tepees and Totem Poles," 22.

56. Cindy Perlman, "What's an Animated Girl to Do?" *San Jose Mercury News*, 25 June 1995.

57. Patricia Troy, "The Beauty and the Beastliness of Writing for Animation," *The Journal of the Writers' Guild* 8, no. 7, (July 1995): 16.

58. Perlman, "What's an Animated Girl to Do?"

59. Sharkey, "Beyond Tepees and Totem Poles," 22.

60. Pat Dowell, "Immaterial Girl," *In These Times* (10 July 1995): 28.

61. Karin Lipson, "Pocahontas: Just Whose History Is It?" *New York Newsday*, 20 June 1995.

62. Sarah Kershaw, "Coming to Classrooms."

63. Troy, "The Beauty and the Beastliness," 17.

64. Pocahontas is not the only story Disney has retold in its own way. For instance, there is an ancient Chinese tale of a young girl who disguises herself as a boy and goes to war to bring honor to her family. Disney has taken that legend and animated it, producing *Mulan* (1998). According to an article in *Parade Magazine*, 8 March 1998, "the studio found this idea unsavory and changed the tale. The Disney version has a be-true-to-yourself theme: Mulan is discovered to be a woman, gets thrown out of the army and becomes a hero in her own right. . . . China was disturbed when Disney released *Kundun*, about Tibet's Dalai Lama. Wonder how it will feel about having a legend rewritten" (22). Disney, as well as the other successful Hollywood studios, reacts to the buzzwords of the day, and in an age of diversity and multiculturalism, it is expected that it would make films about non-white people. What is deplorable about this is that Disney apparently also feels it has the right to make "modifications" to those ethnicities' stories in order to sell tickets.

65. Lipson, "Pocahontas: Just Whose History Is It?"

66. Sonny Skyhawk, personal interview, 11 September 1996.

67. F. X. Feeney, "Talking with Michael Cimino: Between Heaven and Hell," *People Weekly* 46, no. 20 (11 November 1996): 22.

68. Lisa Schwarzbaum, "Sunchaser," *Entertainment Weekly Movie Review*, avail-

able through the archives at <<http://cgi.pathfinder.com/ew/complete/search/
review/0,1727,1,00.html>>, 14 December 1998.

69. John Polly, "Sunchaser: What's it worth? Please. They should pay you to see
this one," "What's It Worth Film Vault," <<http://www.roughcut.com/whats/
alive/sunchaser.html>>, 14 December 1998.

70. According to *The Merck Manual of Diagnosis and Therapy*, rattlesnake bites are
often more frightening than harmful, since a snake does not inject venom 20 to 30
percent of the time, so the doctor could possibly get away with just a sore leg—
with or without the jump-start. According to Dr. Carl Lieb, associate professor of
biological sciences and curator of the herpetology lab at the University of Texas at
El Paso, the efficacy of the shock is questionable. He said that "[s]everal years ago a
group of medical missionaries [in South America] . . . began using electrical shock
to treat snakebite envenomation in individuals who appeared in their jungle clinic.
They claimed, and as far as I know, continue to claim, positive results . . . and they
received wide publicity for it. The physicians who specialize in the treatment of
snakebite . . . were, and continue to be, highly skeptical that this electroshock
treatment has any beneficial effect in cases of snakebite envenomation. There are
also other safety concerns, specifically that administration of electrical shocks from
something like a car battery might well cause ventricular fibrillation and subse-
quent heart failure." Dr. Lieb is "mystified as to what possible mechanism the electrical discharge could have on the snake venom itself, or on the sequence of local
and systemic events that are set in motion when a snake injects venom into a person." Carl Lieb, personal e-mail correspondence, 10 March 1998.

71. Jonathan Rosenbaum, "A Gun Up Your Ass: An Interview with Jim Jarmusch," *Cineaste* 22, no. 2 (1996): 21.

72. Christopher Cook, "Jim Jarmusch," *New Statesman* 125, no. 4291 (5 July
1996): 41.

73. Susanne Maier, "Stranger in a Strange Land: Jim Jarmusch's *Dead Man* and
the Technology of the American West/ern," *Node9*, no. 1 (March 1997), <<http://
node9.phil3.uni-freiburg.de/1997/Maier.html>>, 14 December 1998.

74. Maani Petgar, "Jim Jarmusch—*Dead Man*: A Neo-Western on Life and
Death?" *Feature*, <<http://www.denafilms.com/cinema/may96/jarmusch
.html>>, August 1996.

75. Gary Farmer is Cayuga, from the Six Nations Reserve in Oshwegan, Ontario, Canada.

76. Gemma Files, "Better Dead Than Dumb: Dying Poetic with Gary Farmer
and Jim Jarmusch," *Eye.Net*, <<http://www.eye.net/Cover/1996/cv0523
.html>>, August 1996.

77. Jarmusch says, "It was mostly to amuse myself. . . . Benmont Tench and
George Drakoulias from Tom Petty's Heartbreakers, I mention them. The killers
are named 'Cole Wilson' (Lance Henriksen) and 'Johnny "The Kid" Pickett,' so I
got Wilson Pickett in there," and the list goes on. Raj Bahadur, "Young Man Goes

West: Jim Jarmusch Talks About DEAD MAN," "Cleveland Scene Film," <<http://
www.clevescene.com/weekly/film.html>>, August 1996.

78. Unlike other westerns, *Dead Man* has only two panoramic shots, and one of
those is through the slats of a train window. The other is the last scene in the film,
when Blake's canoe is drifting off in the vastness of the ocean. There is no emptiness
to this frontier. The camera focus is generally kept close in, as befits a film that is at
least as much internal as external. Müller's photography, with its high contrast but
broad gray palette, adds significantly to the aesthetics of the film.

79. Rosenbaum, "A Gun Up Your Ass," 22.

80. Rosenbaum, "A Gun Up Your Ass," 25.

81. Rosenbaum, "A Gun Up Your Ass," 27.

82. Rosenbaum, "A Gun Up Your Ass," 28.

83. Rosenbaum, "A Gun Up Your Ass," 24.

84. At one point in the film Nobody performs a peyote ceremony. It was filmed
in its entirety, which would have been distasteful to Native audiences, but it was cut
drastically so that very little of the actually ceremony occurs on screen.

85. Rosenbaum, "A Gun Up Your Ass," 25.

86. Rosenbaum, "A Gun Up Your Ass," 24.

87. Rosenbaum, "A Gun Up Your Ass," 24.

88. Tom Gliatto, "*Dead Man*," *People Magazine* 45, no. 20 (20 May 1996): 19.

89. Kent Jones, "*Dead Man*," Film Reviews, *Cineaste*, vol. 22, no. 2, (1996): 46.

90. Timothy Egan, "New Prosperity Brings New Conflict to Indian Country,"
The Washington Post, 8 March 1998.

91. Timothy Egan, "Backlash Growing as Indians Make a Stand for Sovereignty," *The Washington Post*, 9 March 1998.

92. Egan, "Backlash Growing."

93. Egan, "New Prosperity."

6. The American Indian Aesthetic

1. Hill, "The Non-Vanishing American Indian," 38.

2. Even Robert Flaherty, whose excellent documentary *Nanook of the North* (Path
1922) is still hailed as one of the most sensitive portrayals of Native Americans, felt
it necessary to "reconstruct" the lives of his subjects. Carefully avoiding telegraph
lines and modern clothing, he produced what he envisioned as the prewhite world
of the Innuits. As such it is very valuable, but it still remains a reconstruction of a
white vision of a vanishing Native way of life. Seventy-eight years later, Kevin
Costner's *Dances With Wolves* presents the same picture, but on the plains and in
technicolor. (See Brownlow, 474.) *Dead Man* is at this point the only film made by a
non-Native writer and director that manages to avoid the majority of American Indian stereotypes.

3. Elizabeth Weatherford, "Starting Fire With Gunpowder," *Film Comment* 28,
no. 3 (May June 1992): 64.

4. Owens, *Other Destinies*, 90–92.

5. Hilger, *The American Indian in Film*, 142.

6. Owens, *Other Destinies*, 108.

7. Hilger, *The American Indian in Film*, 143.

8. Bakhtin, *The Dialogic Imagination*, 23–4.

9. Deloria, "American Fantasy," xv.

10. Good documentation of the use and misuse of tribal resources is the 1985 Academy Award–winning *Broken Rainbow* (1985).

11. Deloria, "American Fantasy," xv.

12. Stam, *Subversive Pleasures*, 80.

13. Gerald Vizenor, personal interview, 1 July 1996.

14. Thomas King, "Contemporary Native American Authors," interview segment of telecourse, Prof. Jacquelyn Kilpatrick, Governors State University, University Park IL, filmed June 1996.

15. King, "Contemporary Native American Authors."

16. This scene was added by the filmmakers. King wrote the dialogue but was not particularly pleased with the addition of this razzle-dazzle introduction to his story.

17. Jason Gallway, "Thomas King." *Smoke Rising: The Native North American Literary Companion*, ed. Janet Witalec (Detroit: Visible Ink, 1995), 277.

18. Leuthold, "An Indigenous Aesthetic," 50.

19. Leuthold, "An Indigenous Aesthetic," 44.

20. Leslie Marmon Silko, "Videomakers and Basketmakers," *Aperature* 119 (summer 1990): 73.

21. Leuthold, "An Indigenous Aesthetic," 48.

22. Leuthold, "An Indigenous Aesthetic," 48.

23. Owens, "Contemporary Native American Authors."

24. Victor Masayesva, *Imagining Indians*, 1992.

25. Masayesva, *Imagining Indians*, 1992.

26. Sonny Skyhawk, personal interview, 11 September 1996.

27. Skyhawk, interview.

28. Masayesva, *Imagining Indians*, 1992.

29. *Navajo Code Talkers* won the Emmy for Best Documentary in 1996.

30. Aaron Carr, personal interview, 21 September 1996.

31. Carr, interview.

32. Carr, interview.

33. Aaron Carr, personal correspondence, 23 November 1998.

34. Carr, correspondence.

35. Carr, correspondence.

36. George Burdeau, personal interview, 31 October 1996.

37. Burdeau, interview.

38. Burdeau, interview.

39. Burdeau, panel discussion, Native Americas Film Exposition in Santa Fe NM, August 1996.

40. Burdeau, interview.

41. Leuthold, "An Indigenous Aesthetic," 43.

42. Burdeau, interview.

43. Burdeau, interview.

44. Burdeau, personal interview, 18 July 1997.

45. Burdeau, interview, 18 July 1997.

46. Jones, "Alien Nation," 86.

47. "Sundance Keeps Its Quirky Touch," <<http://nandonet.com/newsroom/ntn/enter/012098/enter4_25962_noframes.html>>, 14 December 1998.

48. Ted Fry, "Killer Indians," "Film.Com," <<http://www.film.com/features/smoke-2htm>>, May 1998.

49. Geoffrey Gilmore, "Smoke Signals (Phoenix Arizona)," <<http://www.sundancechannel.com/festival98/filmguide/films/smokesig.tin>>, 14 December 1998.

50. Jones, "Alien Nation," 87.

51. Jones, "Alien Nation," 86.

52. Sherman Alexie, "This Is What It Means to Say Phoenix, Arizona," *The Lone Ranger and Tonto Fistfight in Heaven* (New York: The Atlantic Monthly, 1993), 61.

53. Jones, "Alien Nation," 87.

54. Sherman Alexie, "This Is What It Means to Say Phoenix, Arizona," *The Lone Ranger and Tonto Fistfight in Heaven*, (New York: The Atlantic Monthly, 1993), 75.

55. It looks like Alexie's dream has only begun. Next he will write the screenplay and also direct a film based on his novel *Indian Killer*. The film has already been optioned by Shadow Catcher Entertainment.

56. Alexie, "This Is What It Means," 71.

7. Coming Attractions?

1. See Stam, *Subversive Pleasures*, 239.

Filmography

Note: The following filmography includes only those films to which reference was made in the text. It is not a complete list of films including, by, or about Native Americans.

Year	Title	Director/Producer	Chapter
1908	*The Redman and the Child*	D. W. Griffith	2
1910	*White Fawn's Devotion*	James Young Deer	2
1912	*A Pueblo Legend*	D. W. Griffith	2
1912	*Massacre*	D. W. Griffith	2
1914	*The Battle at Elderbush Gulch*	D. W. Griffith	2
1914	*The Indian Wars*	William F. Cody	2
1925	*The Vanishing American*	George Seitz	2
1939	*Allegheny Uprising*	William Seiter	3
1939	*Scouts to the Rescue*	Ray Taylor	3
1939	*Stagecoach*	John Ford	3
1940	*Northwest Passage*	King Vidor	3
1942	*They Died With Their Boots On*	Raoul Walsh	3
1944	*Buffalo Bill*	William Wellman	3
1946	*Bad Bascomb*	Sylvan Simon	3
1950	*Broken Arrow*	Delmer Daves	3
1956	*The Searchers*	John Ford	3
1961	*Two Rode Together*	John Ford	3
1964	*Cheyenne Autumn*	John Ford	4
1966	*Stagecoach*	Gordon Douglas	4
1968	*Scalphunters*	Sydney Pollack	4
1969	*Tell Them Willie Boy Was Here*	Abraham Polonsky	4
1970	*A Man Called Horse*	Elliot Silverstein	4
1970	*Little Big Man*	Arthur Penn	4
1970	*Soldier Blue*	Ralph Nelson	4
1972	*House Made of Dawn*	Richardson Morse	6
1972	*Ulzana's Raid*	Robert Aldrich	4
1975	*One Flew Over the Cuckoo's Nest*	Milos Forman	4

Year	Title	Director/Producer	Chapter
1976	*Buffalo Bill and the Indians*	Robert Altman	4
1976	*The Real People*	George Burdeau	6
1980	*Itam Hakim Hopitt*	Victor Masayesva Jr.	6
1984	*Harold of Orange*	Richard Weise	6
1985	*Broken Rainbow*	Maria Florio and Victoria Mudd	5
1985	*The Emerald Forest*	John Boorman	5
1986	*Stagecoach*	Ted Post	5
1988	*Powwow Highway*	Jonathan Wacks	5
1988	*Ritual Clowns*	Victor Masayesva Jr.	6
1988	*War Party*	Franc Roddam	5
1989	*Renegades*	Jack Sholder	5
1990	*Dances with Wolves*	Kevin Costner	5
1990	*Lonesome Dove*	Simon Wincer	5
1992	*Incident at Oglala*	Michael Apted	5
1992	*Thunderheart*	Michael Apted	6
1992	*1492: Conquest of Paradise*	Ridley Scott	5
1992	*Imagining Indians*	Victor Masayesva Jr.	6
1992	*Laguna Woman*	A. A. (Aaron) Carr	6
1992	*Pueblo Peoples: First Contact*	George Burdeau	6
1992	*Black Robe*	Bruce Beresford	5
1992	*Surviving Columbus: The Pueblo Peoples*	George Burdeau	6
1993	*Clearcut*	Richard Bugajski	5
1993	*Geronimo*	Walter Hill	5
1993	*The Last of the Mohicans*	Michael Mann	5
1994	*Cheyenne Warrior*	Mark Griffiths	5
1994	*Medicine River*	Stuart Margolin	6
1995	*Pocahontas*	Eric Goldberg	5
1995	*The Last of the Dogmen*	Tab Murphy	5
1996	*War Code: Navajo Code Talkers*	Lena and Aaron Carr	6
1996	*Dead Man*	Jim Jarmusch	5
1996	*The Sunchaser*	Michael Cimino	5
1997	*The Witness*	George Burdeau	6
1998	*Smoke Signals*	Chris Eyre	6

Index